SECRET
PLACES

SECRET
PLACES

100 Undiscovered Travel Destinations around the World

EDITED BY JOCHEN MÜSSIG

SCHIFFER PUBLISHING

4880 Lower Valley Road • Atglen, PA 19310

TABLE OF CONTENTS

(*LEFT TO RIGHT*) TWO GUANACOS LOOK CURIOUSLY AT THE CAMERA IN TORRES DEL PAINE NATIONAL PARK, CHILE. A FRIENDLY WELCOME AT THE INTRICATELY CARVED DOOR OF THE SHEIK-BIN-ALI HOUSE IN MUHARRAQ, BAHRAIN. THE PYRAMID OF THE SUN IN TEOTIHUACÁN, MEXICO, IS ONE OF THE LARGEST PYRAMIDS IN THE WORLD. A HIKER PENSIVELY CONTEMPLATES THE DRANGARNIR SEA STACKS OFF THE FAROE ISLANDS. TIGER'S NEST MONASTERY CLINGS TO A STEEP WALL ABOVE PARO IN BHUTAN.

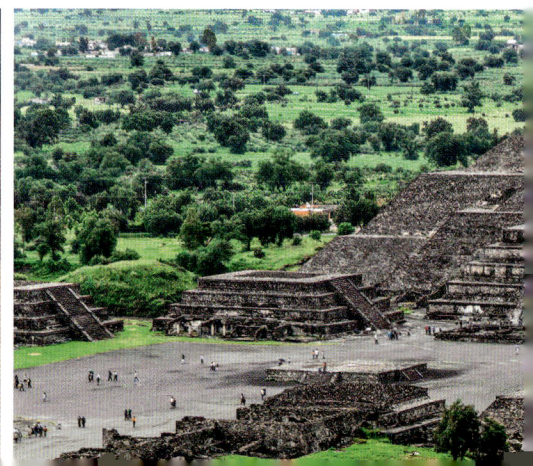

THE TORRES DEL PAINE, THE "TOWERS OF THE BLUE SKY," LOOM OVER SOUTHERN CHILEAN PATAGONIA.

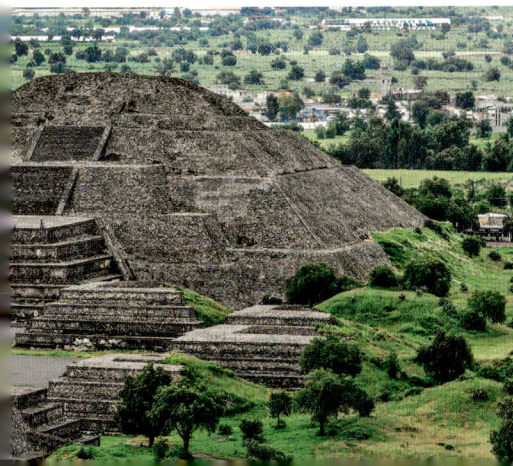

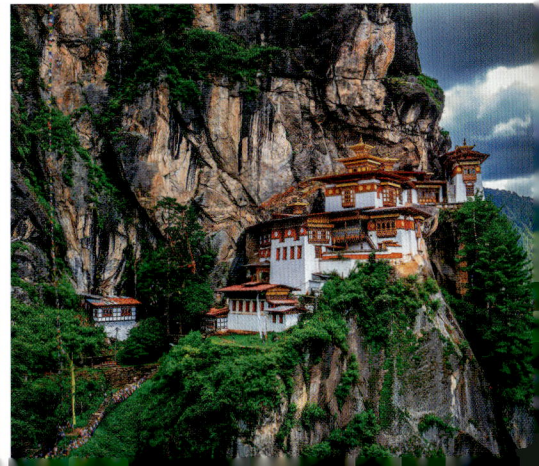

ASIA

(*LEFT TO RIGHT*) A WOMAN IN A SARI WALKS THROUGH A PORTICO IN PUSHKAR, INDIA. THE TO SUA OCEAN TRENCH ON THE SAMOA ISLAND OF UPOLU IS AN IDEAL NATURAL SWIMMING HOLE. THE SUN RISES OVER THE PEAKS OF OMAN'S HAJAR MOUNTAINS, SOME OF WHICH ARE 9,800 FEET (3,000 METERS) HIGH. KAILASA CAVE TEMPLE IS NEAR AURANGABAD IN THE INDIAN STATE OF MAHARASHTRA. FLAMINGOS FISH FOR FOOD IN LAGUNA COLORADA IN BOLIVIA.

MORNING MIST ENVELOPS THE PAGODAS IN THE HISTORICAL ROYAL CITY OF BAGAN.

OCEANIA

Beaufort Sea
Banks-I.
Alaska
Dawson
Anchorage
Watson Lake
Gulf of Alaska
Prince Rupert
CANADA
Victoria-I.
Hudson Bay
Ellesmere I.
Greenland
Spitzbe
Baffin Bay
Baffin I.
Labrador Sea
Labrador
Norwegian Sea
ICELAND
Reykjavík
NORWA
Bergen
Co
h
North Sea
London
IRELAND
FRANCE
Paris
Calgary
Vancouver
Seattle
44
Winnipeg
Lake Winnipeg
Lake Superior
43
Lake Huron
Lake Michigan
Quebec
Toronto
Boston
Halifax
New York
Washington, D.C.
Memphis
Atlanta
42
Chicago
San Francisco
45
46 47
Las Vegas
USA
Los Angeles
San Diego
48
MEXICO
Gulf of Mexico
Miami
CUBA
Greater Antilles
73 Kauai
Hawaii
Mexico City
49
50 51
Guatemala
Managua
53 52
56 55 54
60
Panama City
61
Gulf of Panama
COLOMBIA
62
Bogotá
Quito
63
PERU
Lima
Cuzco
64 65 66
La Paz
67
BOLIVIA
Caribbean Sea
Cartagena
Caracas
Lesser Antilles
57
58
VENEZUELA
59
Amazon River
BRAZIL
Brasilia
Rio de Janeiro
São Paulo
69
68
Andes Mountains
Santiago
Buenos Aires
URUGUAY
ARGENTINA
CHILE
Bahía Blanca
70
Comodoro Rivadavia
72
71
Falkland Islands
(Galapagos Islands)
(Ecuador)
PACIFIC
OCEAN
ATLANTIC OCEAN
Azores
Madeira
Canary Islands
Madrid
Lisbon
29
30
28
31
Rabat
MOROCCO
ALGERIA
32
S
a
MAURITANIA
MALI
Dakar
33
Freetown
Monrovia
Accra
Niger River
1
12
13
14
15
16
17
N
0   1500 km

Franz Josef Land

Alaska

Laptev Sea

Novaya
Zemlya

Kara Sea

Barents
Sea

Anadyr

6

Murmansk

Magadan

Kamchatka

FIN-
LAND

Stock-
holm

Helsinki

St. Petersburg

Perm

Khanty-Mansiysk

Krasnoyarsk

RUSSIA

Sea of Okhotsk

Aleutian Islands

7

Tallinn

93

Riga

Ob

Petropavlovsk

Moscow

Sakhalin

Vilnius

Astana

Irkutsk

Lake Baikal

Khabarovsk

Minsk

Warsaw

Kyiv

8

MONGOLIA

Hokkaido

Vienna

UKRAINE

Gobi Desert

Budapest

19

KAZAKHSTAN

Ürümqi

Beijing

Sea of
Japan

Honshu

JAPAN

Bucharest

20

Black Sea

Dunhuang

Jiuquan

Bohai
Sea

Seoul

Istanbul

Tashkent

CHINA

92

me

Athens

Baku

Samarkand

Yellow
Sea

Shanghai

21

22 23

TURKEY

74

Caspian
Sea

Dushanbe

Xi'an

Tehran

Kabul

24

AFGHA-
NISTAN

Himalayas

Mediterranean Sea

IRAQ

IRAN

Chengdu

Cairo

75

New Delhi

Kunming

Taipei

EGYPT

SAUDI
ARABIA

76

PAKISTAN

79 78

82

LIBYA

Hong Kong

Nile River

34

77

Arabian
Sea

INDIA

83

87

Riyadh

80

Vientiane

SUDAN

OMAN

Mumbai

84

86

Manila

YEMEN

Bay of
Bengal

Phnom
Penh

South
China
Sea

Khartoum

35

Sanaa

85

91

Addis Ababa

81

Bangkok

88

CHAD

ETHIOPIA

SOMALIA

Sri Lanka

Maldives

ndé

Mogadishu

89 SINGAPORE

D.R.
CONGO

Lake
Victoria

KENYA

Nairobi

Kalimantan

PACIFIC

OCEAN

Kinshasa

Lake
Tanganyika

Dar es Salaam

Sumatra

INDONESIA

New Guinea

Sulawesi

Solomon Islands

Luanda

TANZANIA

36

Samoa

94

NGOLA

Lake
Malawi

37

Jakarta

90

Tonga

95

Java

Antananarivo

Darwin

96

MIBIA

38

BOTS-
WANA

Madagascar

Broome

97

Cairns

NEW CALEDONIA

0

INDIAN

Alice Springs

ndhoek

41

Pretoria

98

AUSTRALIA

Brisbane

Johannesburg

99

Durban

SOUTH
AFRICA

Perth

OCEAN

Sidney

e Town

Adelaide

Canberra

Melbourne

Tasman Sea

Aukland

Tasmania

100

Wellington

NEW ZEALAND

Christchurch

SWEDEN

Baltic Sea

Wolga River

Mozambique Channel

Kongo River

S   i   b   e   r   i   a

U   r   a   l

Yenisey

Lena

Ob

THE CONES OF DOZENS OF VOLCANOES TOWER INTO THE SKY ON THE KAMCHATKA PENINSULA.

DISCOVERIES SOUGHT—AND FOUND

Nowadays people like to share, whether it is carsharing, smartphone photos, or social media. When it comes to vacation, however, the fun of sharing stops when the words "mass tourism" come into play.

Low-cost airlines have democratized traveling, simultaneously reducing it to the discount supermarket level. Everyone can, may, will. That's good! Yet, the more that destinations are overrun by hordes of strangers, the more resentment spreads— among both locals and tourists. And that is not good.

Kindred spirits? Yes! The masses? No! So it is time to pull out a phrase that also has suffered from overuse: "secret places," travel destinations far from the floods of tourists. Where you meet a few kindred spirits, but not the crowds. Where there is already a little tourist infrastructure, but no tourism industry yet. And so my colleagues and I set out to

find fantastic beaches and natural wonders, wonderful cities, and superb routes away from mainstream tourists and light-years away from overtourism. Our travels took us from the distant corners of Australia to Cyprus. We found pyramids that can compete with those of Giza; a worthy alternative to the Galápagos Islands; the most beautiful, rugged "chocolate" mountains (not for eating); fantastic beaches on the Indian Ocean; a lake at 12,467 feet (3,800 meters) above sea level; and the 101st Département of France, located a good 4,970 miles (8,000 kilometers) from Paris: an almost undiscovered island where there are more monkeys than people. Some of these destinations are more than secret places. They are the places you carry in your heart, such as a small, engaging country called Bhutan.

A LOOK AT THE WORLD MAP

The world has lost much of its exotic quality due to media overload. Travel has also become banal, thanks to all of those social media posts: "Me having coffee," "Me in the gallery," "Me at the pool." We, on the other hand, wanted to lose ourselves in our travel destinations, to find places that our sharpen our senses. It was important to approach our home turf and faraway spots with equal curiosity, to find places that are a bit hidden away but still offer an experience. Such research often begins with a good map. I still remember very well that the good old *Diercke World Atlas*, in its brown linen cover, was my favorite school book. Journeys with a finger on the map soon went beyond the Alps and the Mediterranean. At some point I ended up in Asia, Africa, America, Australia. As a Diercke student I hadn't seen anything of the world, but there was no limit to the power of my imagination. That is still the best prerequisite for making discoveries.

Following insider tips and exploring the world's "secret places" is particularly rewarding because so much potential can be found off the beaten path. And, the best thing is that this book by no means portrays all the "secret places"; there is so much more to discover on our beautiful earth.

NOVICES STROLL THROUGH A CLOISTER IN BAGAN, MYANMAR'S HISTORIC ROYAL CITY.

EUROPE
Rich Variety in a Small Space

THE ROCKY COAST OF DEVON EMERGES FROM THE
MORNING MIST NEAR THE VILLAGE OF HARTLAND.

1 SECLUDED IN THE ATLANTIC — THE FAROE ISLANDS

A GUEST OF THE DESCENDANTS OF THE VIKINGS

Today around 50,000 people live on the Faroe Islands, which lie in the Atlantic, 372 miles (600 kilometers) beyond Norway. In the ninth century, Vikings fleeing from King Harald Fairhair settled down here to devote themselves to sheep breeding undisturbed on the "sheep islands."

NEAR THE VILLAGE OF GASADALUR, THE MULAFOSSUR WATERFALL RUSHES OVER A HIGH CLIFF AND INTO THE DEPTHS (*ABOVE*). DRANGARNIR SEA STACKS RISE BETWEEN THE ISLANDS OF TINDHÓLMUR AND VÁGAR (*RIGHT*).

Today, fishing, fish breeding, and fish processing are the main sources of income for the Faroese, as the island inhabitants call themselves. Some 95 percent of their income comes from the fishing industry. Tourism is still underdeveloped but is becoming increasingly important. Through all of this, the Faroese have retained their traditional way of life, which involves much more than just continuing to speak their own language.

CENTURIES-OLD TRADITION

The life of the Faroese has not changed since the Vikings settled here, although technical progress, of course, has reached even these remote islands. Yet, to this day, fishing is done mostly by men, while women take care of the modest amount of agriculture, which focuses on sheep breeding and growing potatoes. They benefit from the fact that every year, thousands of eider ducks come to the islands to breed; the people have formed something of a symbiotic relationship with these birds over the centuries. Since the ninth century, the islanders have been preparing nesting sites for the ducks under stones or in small huts and have guarded the clutches of eggs during the breeding season to protect them from the ever-hungry

NORDIC HOME COOKING

Eating and drinking are the best ways to get to know a country and its people. The Faroe Islanders love traditional home cooking. They eat what the islands produce. Fish and seafood, seabirds, occasionally pilot whale meat, and above all mutton and beef are on the menu. Visitors won't recognize all of these dishes as delicacies at the first bite, but the Faroese are happy when a guest indulges in the local cuisine, such as the Faroese holiday dish of *fyltur lundi*: puffins stuffed with a dough made from wheat flour, sugar, margarine, and raisins and then cooked. *Livurpostei* is a popular lamb dish, a tasty lamb liver pâté with fresh meadow cress. Bon appétit!

MORE INFORMATION

For comprehensive information on the most important tourist information: www.visitfaroeislands.com

seagulls and skuas. In return, they take half the eggs. After the eggs hatch and when the ducklings have left the nest, the Faroese collect the fine down left behind in the nests; they wash it and sell it as a filling for blankets and warm clothing. Not least, because of the islanders' awareness of tradition and their sustainable economic system, the Faroe Islands was declared the best travel destination in the world in 2007 in the November edition of *National Geographic Traveler*—ahead of the Azores and Lofoten archipelagos.

RUGGED CLIFFS AND GREEN LAND

Volcanoes formed the archipelago's eighteen islands around sixty million years ago. The last vestige of volcanic activity is the Varmakelda hot spring on the island of Eysturoy. The Vikings thought that the spring had healing powers, and still today the islanders celebrate a "Varmakeldustevna" festival here every two years at the summer solstice. For millions of years, the waves of the North Atlantic have been crashing against the islands' steep coastlines of basalt rock, crisscrossed by layers of tuff rock. The soft tuff rock has been washed away, causing the basalt layers to collapse and creating the

craggy escarpments. The most spectacular cliff is 2,474-foot-high (754 meter) Cape Enniberg on the island of Viðoy, the highest vertical cliff in the world. The islands received their final polishing touches, in the truest sense of the word, from the mighty glaciers of the last Ice Age, which ended around 10,000 years ago. They leveled mountains and left behind the softly rolling terrain that is characteristic of the interior of the islands. The highest point is Slattaratindur Mountain on Eysturoy. In good weather, you can see all of the islands from its 2,887-foot-high (880 meter) summit. A visit to the islands is also an "insider tip" because there are no mosquitoes there, thanks to the constant winds. However, the winds also prevent trees from growing—but this in turn makes it possible to let your view roam unhindered over the green landscapes. For over a hundred years, there have been attempts to plant trees in protected locations, but this has been accomplished only with great effort and to a very limited extent in small parks. But even without trees, the vegetation is very diverse. Lush green grasslands cover the hills. Several hundred species of lichen and moss defy the harsh, constantly blowing winds on rocks and cliffs. In the spring, marsh marigolds, the national flower, create bright-yellow dots of color in damp hollows and along the shores of ponds, lakes, and riverbanks, while the Faroese lady's mantle, with its pale-yellow inflorescence, spreads out on damp meadows. In summer, white puffs of cotton grass glow on the moors.

ISLAND EXPLORING IN FAROESE

Whether on foot, by bike, by car, or on the back of the Faroe ponies, which have mastered five gaits, there are many ways to discover the interior of the Faroe Islands. Go by boat to explore along the coast, or get a bird's-eye view from a helicopter. The destinations are as diverse as the ways of traveling to them. The highest mountain and the highest cliff are just as much a part of it all as the "Blásastova" open-air museum in Gøtu. The museum brings together an entire Faroese village, including a farm, fishermen's huts, and an old church.

Another absolute must is a boat trip to the huge bird colonies on the islands of Sandoy and Skúvoy. There are hundreds of thousands of puffins, razorbills, guillemots, murres, and stormy petrels populating the cliffs. During the breeding season there is a constant bustle of coming and going. The gray seals take things easier. They often lie about, completely relaxed, on the rocks. By the way, they are the only native mammals on the beaches and cliffs. Sheep, cattle, cats, dogs, and rabbits as well as rats and mice arrived on the Faroe Islands with the human inhabitants. Anglers will find a fishing "El Dorado" here. In the lakes and rivers, brown trout, salmon, and Arctic char seem to be just waiting to be hooked; in the sea, cod, haddock, and, with luck, halibut are the prey of the passionate angler.

Water sports are also a possibility. Sandy beaches are found in only a few places on the volcanic Faroe Islands, such as at Sandagerðisvegur, where a small section that

lies south of the port of Torshavn is ideal for swimming. However, water temperatures don't rise above 52 degrees Fahrenheit (11 degrees Celsius), even in the warmest months. Anyone who dares to swim will be rewarded with clean, refreshing water. Divers will find fantastic underwater worlds in over thirty locations in the clear waters of the Atlantic.

EVEN LONELIER THAN THE CHURCH IN THE VILLAGE OF HÚSAR ON KALSOY (*LEFT*) IS THE LIGHTHOUSE ON MYKINES AND HIGH ABOVE THE ATLANTIC (*BELOW*).

2 NORWAY'S ANCIENT CULTURAL LANDSCAPE—THE VEGA ARCHIPELAGO

SYMBIOSIS OF PEOPLE AND EIDER DUCKS

Some 6,000 islands, islets, and skerries, plus a history of settlement that goes back 9,600 years—all this is why the Vega Archipelago is a UNESCO World Heritage Site. The few inhabitants of this northern island world, with its rocks, meadows, and moors, live from fishing and agriculture.

THE TINY FISHING VILLAGE OF NES IS A UNESCO WORLD HERITAGE SITE ON THE VEGA ARCHIPELAGO (*BELOW AND ABOVE RIGHT*). EIDER DUCKS EGGS ARE PROTECTED BY SMALL HUTS (*BELOW RIGHT*).

The first settlers arrived in the Vega Archipelago almost 10,000 years ago, when the glaciers of the last Ice Age had just retreated. Under the weight of the ice, large parts of the region had been pushed below the surface of the sea, to depths up to 197 feet (60 meters).

Of the more than 6,000 islands and rocks that exist today, at that time only three projected from the sea and could be occupied. Over time the land rose steadily and more and more islands were pushed above the ocean surface, offering space for newcomers. This geological process continues today; the islands are still "growing."

FLUFFY DOWN

Fishing, hunting, and livestock farming ensured a livelihood for the people—and the eider ducks that come to the islands every year to breed. By the ninth century, the islanders were carefully preparing nesting places for the ducks under stones or in small huts and protected them from nest robbers. In return, they would collect half of the eggs from the nests and then collect the fine down after the eggs hatched.

A unique cultural landscape and economic system emerged over many generations, but it came within an inch of being left to wither away. Between the 1960s and 1980s, small scattered settlements and individual farmsteads were abandoned as the government incentivized larger, central settlements. Today only four islands are permanently inhabited. As a result, the eider duck populations declined rapidly. No longer protected by humans from predators such as rats, foxes, and minks, many broods were lost.

Recognition as a UNESCO World Heritage Site in 2004 came just in time to revive the centuries-old farming traditions. The UNESCO certificate of recognition states the reasons: "As fishermen and farmers for 1,500 years, the people of the Vega Archipelago have preserved their sustainable way of life in the inhospitable seascape of the Arctic Circle for many generations, based on the use of eiderdown."

THE EIDER DUCK GUARDIANS

The Vegaøyan Verdensarv Foundation was set up to support landscape conservationists. Efforts to preserve this World Heritage Site are documented in the E-Huset Museum in the village of Nes on Vega. This eider duck museum is really worth seeing. Success was not long in coming. As a result of UNESCO recognition, many farms have been renovated, the "accommodations" for the eider ducks repaired, and the meadows that had lain fallow are extensively grazed again. Today farmers from Vega and the neighboring communities bring their cattle to graze on the islands in the World Heritage area. In the meantime, cattle, sheep, and goats are grazing on roughly sixty islands once again. These are mainly the islands north and west of Vega. The down is as popular today as it used to be, which is why the clutches of eggs are once again protected by the eider duck guardians. Thanks to this protection, the broods have increased enormously, and thousands of eider ducks are being registered again in the old villages. In the meantime, tourism has also arrived. Hiking, fishing, boat tours, and a visit to the eider duck villages are just some of the activities available.

EXCURSION INTO THE STONE AGE

Stone Age hunters and fishermen have left clear traces on Vega. A historical educational trail in the southeast leads through boggy terrain (rubber boots!) to what remains of the settlement in the Middagskarheia region. From the information board in Åkvika, you walk west toward Hammaren to the ruins of a 5,500-year-old house. You can admire a former natural harbor from the ridge of the Middagskarheia mountain range, because the sea level was more than 197 feet (60 meters) higher at the time the settlement existed. Further stops include the 9,600-year-old fishing settlement of Middagskarheia 1 and the settlement Middagskarheia 2, which is "only" 8,500 years old. Close to the starting point, there is a grave that, unfortunately, was looted, and some 5,500-year-old house ruins.

MORE INFORMATION

World Heritage Center and Vega Municipality:
www.verdensarvvega.no/en/home

3 THE MOUNTAINOUS NORTH—RONDANE AND DOVREFJELL NATIONAL PARKS

A NEIGHBORHOOD OF MUSK OXEN, REINDEER, AND BROWN BEARS

Rondane became Norway's first national park in 1962, followed by Dovrefjell-Sunndalsfjella in 2002 and Dovre National Park in 2003. The parks, covering a total of 1,650 square miles (2,656 square kilometers), beckon to visitors with their snow-capped peaks, rocky plateaus, valleys with clear lakes, and rich flora and fauna.

The national parks are part of the much more extensive Dovrefjell and Rondane mountain and plateau region. Dovrefjell forms the watershed between west and east; the 7,500-foot-high (2,286 meter) Snøhetta juts highest into the sky—the park includes the highest peaks in Norway after Jotunheimen. Thanks to its remote location, Dovrefjell has remained one of the few intact high-mountain ecosystems in northern Europe. Its flora and fauna are typical of this habitat. The most prominent and characteristic representatives of its animal world are reindeer, wolverines, and Arctic foxes. To the

southeast, Dovrefjell leads over to the Rondane Mountains. This is part of a high mountain range that extends from Dovrefjell almost down to the town of Lillehammer. In addition to 7,146-foot-high (2,178 meter) Rondslottet, there are another nine peaks that rise more than 6,500 feet (1,981 meters). Like all Scandinavian peaks, these mountains were formed by the Ice Age glaciers and by eroding meltwater after the glaciers thawed. The first traces of humans in Dovrefjell go back almost 9,000 years and come from Stone Age hunters who followed the reindeer here. They left reindeer corrals that are around 3,500 years old

UNIQUE NATURAL LANDSCAPES IN RONDANE NATIONAL PARK: LAKE BERGETJÖNNE NEAR MYSUSAETER (*ABOVE LEFT*) AND THE PROMINENT 6,621-FOOT-HIGH (2,018 METER) SUMMIT OF TROLLTINDEN (*BELOW LEFT*). MUSK OXEN HAVE BEEN REESTABLISHED IN DOVREFJELL NATIONAL PARK FOR A GOOD SEVENTY YEARS (*ABOVE*).

BOTANY IN KONGSVOLL

Kongsvoll, or Kongsvold, is an old post office on the Royal Route across Dovrefjell, which was used to make a pilgrimage to the grave of Olav II in Nidaros (now Trondheim). The Kongsvold Fjeldstue mountain inn (now Frich's Hotel & Spiseri Kongsvold) serves tasty, homestyle cooking. Fjellstue would be an inn like many others if the rooms were not also home to the Dovrefjell-Sunndalsfjella National Park's information center, and if it did not also feature a mountain botanical garden that provides a comprehensive overview of the plants that grow here. You can test your knowledge on a 1.2-mile (2 kilometer) loop hike on blooming Knutshø Mountain. The trail also leads past one of the historic reindeer corrals.

MORE INFORMATION

Kongsvold Fjeldstue, Dovrefjell, Oppdal; www.frich.no/kongsvold-fjeldstue-2

in the Rondane Mountains. These enclosures were built of stones or trees, with only one opening where they drove the animals in. The corrals were used well into the fourteenth century. Remnants can be found today at Grayhø and Bløyvangen.

HABITAT FOR SPECIALISTS

High mountains shield Dovrefjell and Rondane National Parks from the low-pressure areas approaching from the west; these clouds rain down on the western slopes of the mountains. To the east, the climate becomes increasingly continental, with cold, dry winters and relatively warm summers, although it is then that most of the precipitation falls. The average precipitation measured in Kongsvoll is 19.7 inches (500 millimeters). In winter, the thermometer drops to −33 degrees Fahrenheit (−36 degrees Celsius), and in summer it rises to 82 degrees Fahrenheit (28 degrees Celsius). In July, the average temperature is 50 degrees Fahrenheit (10 degrees Celsius). Little snow falls in winter, so no new glaciers formed here during the Little Ice Age. Most of the national parks extend above the treeline at 3,200 to 3,600 feet (1,000–1,100 meters). Anything that wants to survive here, whether plant or animal, has to be cold-resistant and able to live frugally.

Not many animals remain here year-round, but they do exist—above all the reindeer, which were widespread throughout Europe during the Ice Age and remained there long after the Ice Age ended.

Today there is only a small, scattered reindeer population south of the Arctic Circle, including in Rondane National Park. The estimates vary between 2,000 and 4,000 animals, which migrate seasonally. They not only stay in Rondane but also move to Dovrefjell-Sunndalsfjella National Park. Another relic of the Ice Age is the tundra vole, also known as the root vole. Once widespread in Europe, today it occurs only in the high mountain regions of Scandinavia and in a small remaining population in Mecklenburg–Western Pomerania. The next-closest populations are found in Siberia.

LONG-ESTABLISHED AND NEW RESIDENTS

Brown bears are not limited to small, residual populations, but they have become rare in Europe. Some of them are at home in Rondane National Park, from where they also regularly set out on hikes into neighboring Dovrefjell-Sunndalsfjella National Park. These omnivores feed primarily on plants but also like to enrich their diet with ground-nesting birds and their egg clutches, rabbits, lemmings, and tundra voles or carrion. The bears attack large mammals with which they share the same habitat, such as elk or roe deer, only if they are injured or weakened. They have no chance at all against the well-defended musk oxen from Greenland, which—although the name suggests it—are not related to cattle, but rather to goats, chamois, and mountain goats. The goatlike Asian gorals are their closest relatives. Musk oxen were common in Europe during the Ice Age but fell victim to changing environmental conditions and hunting. Shortly after the end of the Ice Age, they no longer existed in Europe. Musk oxen were first reintroduced into Dovrefjell in 1927, but the animals that were released did not survive World War II. The hoped-for success was achieved only after a new attempt in 1947. Today around eighty musk oxen are living in Dovrefjell. In 1971, a bull, two cows, and two calves migrated to Sweden and established an independent population there.

FEATHERED DIVERSITY IN DOVREFJELL

There is rich avian life not only in the national park itself, but also in the nature conservancy areas that surround Dovrefjell-Sunndalsfjella National Park like a buffer. The moors are resting areas for the high Nordic migratory birds on their way to the Arctic and breeding areas for cranes, red-necked phalaropes, whimbrels, Arctic loons, and bluethroats. A visit to Fokstymyra in the southern part of the park is a must for every bird lover. Golden eagles, northern harriers, and gyrfalcon circle above the plateaus, and even snowy owls have been seen hunting lemmings.

A MECCA FOR PLANT LOVERS

The Dovrefjell and the Rondane Mountains have been occupying botanists for more than 250 years, because the area is a good place to easily trace the immigration history of plants following the Ice Age. Some 420 plant species are found in Dovrefjell, including 170 of the 250 Scandinavian mountain plant species. They thrive on the calcareous rocks east of the

Drivdalen River. Some endemic species—species that live only in a particular region—also occur here. These include Dovre poppies, Dovre dandelions, and the Norwegian mugwort. Mountain avens, various saxifrage species, Arctic violets, and cloudberries cover the mountain areas with carpets of white, red, and purple in spring and summer.

THE COLORS OF THE NORTH—AT SUNSET OVER RONDANE NATIONAL PARK (*LEFT*) AND ALONG A MOSS-LINED STREAM (*BELOW*).

4 IN THE HOME OF THE GIANTS— JOTUNHEIMEN NATIONAL PARK

AMONG REINDEER, LYNX, AND PTARMIGANS

With its fantastic mountains, glaciers, lakes and rivers, and flora and fauna, Jotunheimen has inspired composers and poets and sends scientists into raptures. Since 1980, a national park has been protecting part of this mountain range where hunters and fishermen roamed thousands of years ago.

VIEW FROM THE BESSEGGEN MOUNTAIN RIDGE OVER LAKE GJENDE (*LEFT*); REINDEER ARE THE CHARACTERISTIC JOTUNHEIMEN ANIMALS (*ABOVE*).

According to Nordic legend, Jotunheimen is the home of the Jøten, the trolls assigned to these mountains by Odin and his brothers during their creation. This landscape has always fascinated and inspired people. Fridtjof Nansen was overwhelmed on his first visit to Jotunheimen: "Suddenly I was standing on the precipice and looked down to Lake Gjende. Far below, it stretched its bright-green-blue/emerald ribbon far away through the bottom of the chasm, between the mighty snowy mountains that rush toward it in wild succession. Mjølkedalstind and all the other sharp white spikes rise against the sunset in the west. It is as if all of Jotunheimen suddenly comes alive, opens its mighty gates to the soul, and draws it into its spell. I stopped involuntarily; it was as if I had to call out to the glacier world: Farewell!"

Jansen was by no means the only one captivated by Jotunheimen. Edvard Grieg was inspired by the old songs of the farmer's wife Kaja Gjendine Slålien, who lived beside Lake Gjende and used them in his music. It was the poet Aasmundson Olavson Vinje who, on May 1, 1862, used the name Jotunheimen—"Home of the Giants"—instead

SPENDING THE NIGHT AT ALMOST 6,500 FEET (1,000 METERS)

If you want to get to know Norway, you cannot avoid the DNT (Norwegian Trekking Association) hostels for hikers. In Jotunheimen the Gjendebu Turisthytte hostel is ideal. It was built in 1871, making it Norway's oldest tourist lodge. The hosts are there to take care of guests' physical well-being from the end of June to mid-September. The main building, with its 134 beds, is also open over Easter. Outside the season, you can use the DNT standard key to access the self-service part of the hostel. The Gjendebu Turisthytte can be reached via the E 16 and R 51 to Gjendesheim and from there by boat across Lake Gjende to Gjendebu.

MORE INFORMATION

Gjendebu Turisthytte,
telephone +47 47 61 15 33,
outside opening times +47 91 57 49 65;
https://gjendebu.dnt.no/en/

DNT (Norwegian Trekking Association):
https://english.dnt.no

of Jotunfjeldene, as the area had previously been called. During his hikes through Jotunheimen he wrote poems that are now Norwegian classics.

MOUNTAINS IN THE HEART OF NORWAY

The Jotunheimen massif extends over about 2,175 square miles (3,500 square kilometers) and is the highest part of the Skanden mountain range. The centerpiece is Jotunheimen National Park, established in 1980, which covers almost a third of the entire area in its 708 square miles (1,140 square kilometers). Another 186 square miles (300 square kilometers) in Utladalen valley have been designated as a protected landscape. Galdhøppigen and Glittertind, the two highest mountains in Scandinavia, rise up in the national park, and there are over 250 other peaks that reach more than 6,200 feet (1,900 meters); twenty of them are more than 7,500 feet (2,300 meters).

There are also some heavenly lakes in the national park, including Lake Gjende, admired by Nansen, which becomes turquoise green in late summer due to glacial sediments. Neighboring Bessvatnet Lake offers a wonderful contrast with its deep-blue water. In Jotunheimen, the denser forests of birch trees grow only around Lake Gjende and in Utladalen valley, where some pine trees have ventured.

The greater part of the park reaches above the treeline, which is at 3,900 feet (1,200 meters) here. Only mountain birches and individual conifers can survive under these extreme conditions; they cannot grow any higher up. Occasionally, larger perennials such as the northern wolf's bane or European goldenrod mix with the trees. A narrow belt of creeping dwarf Arctic willows and dwarf birches come after this last bastion of the forest. Together with small juniper bushes and blueberries, they are the last woody plants that can still be found here. The mountain tundra, the habitat for a multitude of herbs and flowers, begins even farther above. In summer, colorful carpets of Arctic violets, pyramidal saxifrage, moss campion, and purple gentian cover the *fjell* (Norwegian for mountain). Even higher up are the Alpine azaleas, mountain avens, and hermaphrodite mountain or black crowberry, which grow only on high mountains. The elevation record is held by the glacier buttercup, which climbs almost to the summit of the Glittertind. In the course of thousands of years, fens have developed in valleys that have no drainage. Here, in addition to the characteristic peat moss, Lapland lousewort and cloudberry grow.

IN THE REALM OF THE GOLDEN EAGLE

As meager as the living conditions in Jotunheimen are, many animals find sustenance here. Reindeer are the most characteristic mountain dwellers, and some wild herds still roam the western part of the national park. However, domesticated species have

displaced them from most of Jotunheimen. Hunting has also taken its toll. The other large herbivores, red deer and elk, can be found only in Utladalen today. The brown bear, which had its ancestral habitat here, has also disappeared along with the wild reindeer. With a little luck, however, you can still see lynxes, wolverines, and Alpine hares. You can occasionally see an Arctic fox chasing after a ptarmigan, which are still relatively common. But it is not just on the ground that there is something worth seeing. Rarely, you can see circling golden eagles, the kings of the *fjell*. Their smaller relatives are the buzzards, which are encountered much more often. European golden plovers and Eurasian dotterels are more likely to be heard than seen. Snow buntings, on the other hand, can be spotted at almost every turn in the higher elevations. During the breeding season, it is hard to overlook, or to fail to hear, the males in their showy, black-and-white plumage.

IN THE FOOTSTEPS OF HUNTERS AND TRADERS

Hunters and fishermen were already at home in Jotunheimen more than 5,000 years ago. Remains of settlements can be found at Lake Gjende and Russvatnet, and the remains of pits testify to early hunting of reindeer, the most important food source for the people. There was also a trade route through Jotunheimen—salt and fish, especially herring, were transported from the coast to eastern Norway along the Sognefjell road, and leather, butter, tar, and iron were transported back from there. People and pack horses carried the loads. Today the road is well developed; named the Sognefjell National Route, it runs through a fantastic landscape.

Tourists have been coming to the region since the nineteenth century. The DNT (Den Norske Turistforening; Norwegian Trekking Association), founded in 1886, also contributed to this by building hiking trails and overnight cabins throughout the country, including in Jotunheimen. However, the national park was not created until 1980.

NORWAY'S HIGHEST WATERFALL

Hardly an insider tip anymore, but because the trek there takes more than two hours, the Vettisfossen in Utladalen has been spared from mass tourism so far. With a drop of 902 feet (275 meters), it is Norway's highest waterfall and was placed under nature protection in 1924. In addition to Vettisfossen, there are two other large waterfalls, Hjelledalsfossen and Avdalsfossen, as well as a myriad of smaller waterfalls in Utladalen, Norway's deepest valley. Even today the valley has hardly been developed and remains in pristine condition. A visit to Vettisfossen is highly recommended. The easy hike is 3 or 4 miles (6 or 7 kilometers), initially on a gravel road, and later on a trail from Hjelle via Vetti.

AT THE RIDDERSPRANGET (KNIGHT'S JUMP), THE SJOA RIVER FLOWS THROUGH A NARROW RAVINE (*LEFT*); HIKERS IN JOTUNHEIMEN NATIONAL PARK MUST BE ABLE TO GO "OFF-ROAD" (*BELOW*).

5 DENMARK IN MINIATURE—SAMSØ

SLOWING DOWN WITH ISLAND ROMANCE

If you want to escape the hustle and bustle of everyday life, you don't have to travel to remote regions of the Amazon. You can switch off in Europe, especially on the Danish island of Samsø. The name invokes a pure idyll, but the visit is also worthwhile because of Sigrid and Louise.

DANISH IDYLL: HALF-TIMBERED HOUSES IN NORDBY ON SAMSØ (*ABOVE*); LOUISE VEDEL WITH FALCONS AT A DEMONSTRATION AT THE SAMSØ FALCON CENTER (*BELOW RIGHT*); HANNE STENSVIG IN HER SHOP (*ABOVE RIGHT*)

The island of Samsø is a small paradise in the middle of the Kattegat Strait; many people agree on that. Yet, in addition to idyllic landscapes and romantic villages, encounters with the unusually hospitable and cosmopolitan inhabitants add to the island's enchantment. Last but not least, Samsø is home to many artists, who give the island a special flair and offer "finds" on almost every corner.

SIGRID AND THE BOWLS

When you visit Martin in Haarmark with a prebooked group, you not only get to view his factory and taste some delicious cider,

you also discover another worthwhile destination in Nordby: the workshop of the respected stoneware designer Sigrid Hovmand. Her bowls, plates, vessels, and objects, whether large or small, are fashioned in a timeless, simple elegance. She likes to open her workshop to visitors who have booked in advance, and once she starts talking, there's no stopping her; you can sense her passion for handicrafts at the highest level. When she holds one of her bowls up to the light and examines it from all sides, the movement of her hands reminds you of the gentle waves on Samsø's beaches. These spacious beaches slope gently into the

water and are family-friendly while also offering romantic crannies.

Suddenly Sigrid's eyes start to shine; her smile shows pride in these beautiful and functional clay pieces. Her gallery has a creative, playful atmosphere that puts visitors in a good mood.

LOUISE AND THE FALCONS

You can also sense passion when visiting the falcon center in Samsø. There you get the opportunity to admire the flying skills of majestic eagles, fascinating owls, lightning-fast falcons, and clever hawks in an hour-long show. Falconer Louise, the owner of the falcon center, seems able to talk to the birds, even if they don't always listen to what she says. In the end, however, they do what Louise wants. After the flight demonstrations, you can take a closer look at these acrobats of the air.

You should never leave Samsø—which, by the way, produces all of the energy it uses and also produces a million pumpkins a year—without climbing Ballebjerg hill. This high point on the island offers a wonderful view of the island of Tunø. And you should definitely take a tour of Samsø in the vintage bus, a lovingly restored Chevrolet Six Fra built in 1943. For those who slow down this way, the island experience is one of pure enjoyment.

How do you get to the island? Very simple—either by the Samsø Rederi ferry from Hou to Saelvig, or from the other direction, by the Faergen shipping line from Kalundborg to Ballen. Both bring visitors to the island for day trips. Yet, there is so much to discover on Samsø that a longer stay is definitely worth it.

IN THE OLD GENERAL STORE

Retro is back in fashion, whether in clothing or furniture, cars, or other objects. Old styles are constantly being revived, then consigned to oblivion, only to rise again like a phoenix from the ashes. The "Købmands-gården" in Nordby can set your retro heart pounding. This old general store, dating back to 1844, sells food, sweets, and drinks from Grandmother's time, from jams and pastries to liqueurs and herbal teas, all gathered and made in-house, of course; here you can buy anything that bears the label "From the good old days." If you are lucky enough to be served by Hanne Stensvig, you will leave in a good mood for no extra charge.

MORE INFORMATION

www.visitsamsoe.dk/en/

Hotel Vadstrup 1771, Vadstrup 4 between Onsbjerg and Torup: www.vadstrup1771.dk

Falcon Center Samsø, Eskevej 4, https://falkecenter.dk/

6 HOT AND STEAMY—LAPLAND

SWEATING IN UNSPOILED NATURE

This region is a long way from Finland's capital, Helsinki, but that's also what makes it so appealing. In Finnish Lapland, almost everything revolves around special experiences in the outdoors and the sauna. A trip to Ylläs and Levi can easily turn into an unforgettable self-experiment.

IN LAPLAND YOU CAN FEED THE REINDEER IN PYHÄ LUOSTO NATIONAL PARK (*BELOW*) AND ADMIRE THE MAGICAL DANCE OF THE NORTHERN LIGHTS (*ABOVE RIGHT*).

Let's assume that you are going to northern Finland on May 1, and you are looking forward to unique adventures in nature, interesting encounters with other people, and some time to slow down. What comes to mind are pristine forests, crystal-clear lakes, mountains and valleys where bears and lynx roam, and wide plains with herds of reindeer trotting along sedately. You might also think of the Sami people, bear hunters, salmon fishermen, and husky-dog trainers. But isn't there something else? Of course—the Finnish sauna! And who invented it? Let's leave that, because there is no way to determine that decisively. This stony sweat bath is an ancient human cultural asset. It goes back as far as the Stone Age, sauna experts say—how could it be otherwise? The Finns have cultivated this tradition like no one else. At the same time, they are always coming up with new and creative ideas, including the pleasantly bizarre.

LOVE FOR LAPLAND ALSO COMES THROUGH THE STOMACH

In the far north, love for a country usually develops through delicious food and drink. This is true whether you try the bear meat at Esko Takkunen's Riihi restaurant near Levi, the lohikätto salmon and vegetable soup with rieska—Finnish flatbread—or tasty reindeer dishes. In Yläsjärvi, you should definitely visit the Pihvikeisari restaurant run by Jaana Sara, a gifted berry gatherer and cook. It offers Lapland specialties ranging from fish and meat to tasty salads, soups, and vegetarian dishes. Choosing is difficult. The nearby Sarakka Restaurant also belongs to Jaana and Tomi Sara and offers one more reason to come back, because it takes quite a while to try even half the menu.

MORE INFORMATION

www.lapland.fi/visit

Immelkartano, Tuomikuruntie 136, FI-99130 Levi; a log cabin for up to twenty people with a sauna.
www.immelkartano.fi

PLAINS, FORESTS, HIKING PARADISE

There are around five million Finns, two million saunas, and 200,000 lakes in Finland. And a well-known saying: "If schnapps, tar, and sauna don't help, then the disease is fatal." The country is also a paradise for hikers and canoeists, cross-country skiers, fly fishermen, and dogsled mushers. The north, in particular, has a magical aura. With an area of 58,409 square miles (94,000 square kilometers), Lapland makes up almost 30 percent of the total area of Finland, but only around 195,000 inhabitants live in its endless expanses. In fact, more reindeer call it home than people do.

BEAR HUNTER WITH BONES

Esko Takkunen's favorite places to roam with his dog are the forests around Levi, Kittilä, and Lake Immel. He hunted moose here with his father when he was a child, and as a young man he had a dream: to hunt down a bear. Since then, he has bagged two bears. The pelt of one hangs in his cozy restaurant, where his wife puts tasty, hearty dishes on the table. After the meal, Esko displays a frozen bear head and a special trophy: "A lot of men would like to have such a thing; what do you think it is?" Grinning, he holds up the little bear penis bone.

SAUNA BOAT WITH SELF-AWARENESS

Of course, Esko's boat-and-sauna man, Petri Vargala, is also a real rascal under the Lapland sun. Before the sauna boat takes off, you have to take a bath in the lake to purify your soul. Lake Immel is a sacred place for the Indigenous people of Lapland, the Sami, and according to legend, it is inhabited by dwarfs and trolls. So I obey and have a new experience: although I can handle the cold quite well, the icy water makes me scream, as if someone had laid me on a bed of nails a thousand times over. The subsequent trip across the lake in the comfortably warm sauna compensates for the shock of cold. For Finns, the sauna is an experience that is welcomed virtually anywhere. How else could they come up with the idea of installing a sauna gondola along with the other ski lifts on Ylläs Mountain? I wouldn't be surprised if Finnair will soon be offering a sauna on board the plane on medium- and long-haul flights.

7 KÄSMU AND THE COFFEEPOT— ESTONIA

QUIRKY MARITIME MUSEUM IN A NATIONAL PARK

In Estonia's Lahemaa National Park, handicrafts, a passion for collecting, and closeness to nature all play a major role. This can be seen, for example, in the small town of Käsmu, where a scientist has compiled a maritime collection of fascinating curiosities.

A BRIDGE LEADS ACROSS THE VIRU MOOR IN LAHEMAA NATIONAL PARK (*ABOVE*); HERE YOU WILL FIND PRISTINE LANDSCAPES (*BELOW RIGHT*) WHERE EVEN KINGFISHERS FEEL AT HOME (*ABOVE RIGHT*).

Aarne sits on a wooden bench on his veranda, like a German oak. Upright, with a face tanned by the sun, wind, and weather and watchful eyes that catch sight of every visitor even before they step into his front garden, Aarne Vaik turned seventy-six years young a few months ago but looks timeless. He has just supplied his food smoker with new wood, has turned the smoked fish, and is now devoting himself to the guests who want to visit his museum. That is perhaps a somewhat exaggerated term for it, because there is no entrance portal, no ticket counter, no museum plan, let alone a brochure of images. Aarne Vaik and his house, including the compound, are the

museum in Käsmu, in Estonia's Lahemaa National Park. And one that is particularly worth seeing.

AARNE FROM KÄSMU

Vaik means "resin" in English, but Aarne is by no means hard and brittle. Low key and friendly, he guides visitors through his rooms, which serve both as his apartment and as exhibition spaces. He knows how to tell a story about each piece, and in three languages. English, Estonian, German—everything fits together like the kaleidoscope of his exhibits. There is an old dugout canoe like the one formerly used by fishermen on Estonia's lakes, as well as everyday objects from a bygone era, collections of bottles and ceramics, old canned-fish cans, antique books, lexicons of seafaring, and a living room and bedroom of a captain's family maintained in its original condition, including postcards from the time of the Russian tsars. A faded photo album even revives the days of German kaiser Wilhelm. Käsmu is known as Estonia's "captain's village" and was the location of the country's largest captain's-training school. Aarne studied biology in Tartu in southern Estonia, specialized in ichthyology, the science of fish, and then worked at a fish farm for many years. Finally he was drawn back home to Käsmu Bay, to his property, where his ancestors have lived for over three hundred years. And he is satisfied; he collects, exchanges, and finds all those things that make life by the sea and in the country unique. Gathered around his smoker by the bay, you can also try freshly smoked fish and Estonian vodka—if you make a reservation beforehand—and listen to Aarne's stories about the national park, the lake, and the fishermen, as if time has stood still.

LAHEMAA NATIONAL PARK

The feeling that time has stood still also applies to the entire Lahemaa National Park, which lies east of Tallinn. It was founded in 1971 to protect the region's richly varied natural and cultural heritage. Today it covers 72,500 hectares, around a third of which is below the ocean surface. The pretty Vihula manor house, the large Sagadi estate that today houses the state forest administration, the popular vacation resort of Võsu on the coast, and small villages such as Altja and Palmse give the cultural landscape its character. The "Kaffeekanne" (coffeepot) cafe-restaurant in Palmse, which is run by a German family, also adds to the region's charm. Beyond all this, its forests, rich in many species, as well as its rocks and boulders, lakes and bogs, and rivers and waterfalls, together with elk, beaver, bear, and lynx, and of course its numerous bays, make Lahemaa the "bay country," a true paradise.

FROM FISHERMEN TO ART

The northernmost headland of Estonia, the wild and romantic Purekkari Peninsula, and the neighboring village of Viinistu are also worth a visit. If you are thinking of Finistère in France and Land's End in England, you won't be so far wrong. In the pretty village of Viinistu, a cultural complex emerges, like a spaceship from distant worlds, which has made a name for itself far beyond the country's borders. No wonder, since it belongs to none other than Jaan Manitski, the former manager of the pop group ABBA and former Estonian foreign minister. He has transformed an old fish smokehouse into a remarkable museum for Estonian artists, with a hotel, restaurant, and modern chapel with a view of the sea, which also hosts theater performances and concerts. www.viinistu.ee/en

MORE INFORMATION

www.visitestonia.com

Vihula Manor Country Club,
Vihula, Lääne-Virumaa, 45402 Estonia:

www.vihulamanor.com

Lahemaa Kohvikann:
www.kohvikann.com

SINGLE FILE TO THE CORNCRAKE— LOWER SILESIA

8

DISCOVERIES IN THE LAND OF PALACES

Poland is famous for its geese walking in single file; less well known are its architectural riches: there are more than three hundred palaces and fortresses in the Jelenia Góra Valley alone in Lower Silesia (Jelenia Góra was called the Hirschberger Tal, or Deer Mountain Valley, in former German times). The region along the edges of the Śnieżka (Snow Peak) and the Giant Mountains awaits visitors with many places to discover.

UNKNOWN BEAUTIES IN THE JELENIA GÓRA VALLEY: PALACE WOJANÓW (*LEFT*) AND PAKOSZÓW MANOR (*ABOVE*) ON DISPLAY IN THEIR OLD SPLENDOR.

" I'm a White Kołudzka. I beg your pardon— don't you know me? I think not. No, not a beauty queen, although there is a certain grace in my appearance and movements. I would also cut a fine figure on the red carpet. No, I'm not a pop starlet either. Still, my singing can be heard, even if some think I am honking. Is it slowly sinking in? All right, you still have one more try, so go ahead, but please remember: if you are wrong this time, you will be stuck with a vegetarian lunch menu, or even vegan if I have anything to say about it. One more thing: the 'phone a friend' lifeline is not allowed, nor is googling.

"Last week I encountered a couple of visitors from, well, a country where a certain roast bird is popular at Christmastime. Pardon me, but they were real idiots. In fact, they should have heard of me, because in previous centuries my ancestors were driven on foot in flocks to Berlin. They were on the road for a week, only to be sold there in the markets. I am happy to guide our guests through the Lower Silesian Voivodeship (Polish

RETREAT AT PAKOSZÓW MANOR

Who hasn't experienced it? There are moments when all of us feel the effects of stress and burnout syndrome in these fast-paced times. It's good to know about places of retreat where the soul can get some rest. The exclusive Pakoszów Manor hotel is such a refuge. Ingrid and Hagen Hartmann were physicians in Saarland for decades before they acquired their former family property in the Jelenia Góra Valley in Lower Silesia. They have transformed this once-dilapidated baroque palace into the region's first five-star hotel. Now they are returning to their roots and are organizing concerts and exhibitions as well as wellness weeks for guests.

MORE INFORMATION

www.palac-pakoszow.pl/en

administrative region), which I call the Silesian Kingdom of Heaven. That's because roast pork and beef top the specialty menu there rather than poultry, as in my home in Kuyavian-Pomerania."

KARPNIKI CASTLE—A GEM

The palaces in the Jelenia Góra Valley on the edge of the Giant Mountains offer more than a romantic setting. They are also good starting points for nature and hiking adventures in the region around Jelenia Góra, providing overnight accommodations, candlelight dinners, and wellness facilities. I have taken visitors to the tranquil village of Karpniki and its castle. The centuries-old fish ponds are the defining element of this small town at the foot of the Rudawy Janowickie (Landeshut Ridge). Among them are the two ponds in the historic landscaped Karpniki Castle park. Visitors can relax while fishing, and the

pond landscape invites long walks. The carp in the Karpniki ponds were once reserved for the local aristocracy and their guests. These included Prince Wilhelm of Prussia, who acquired the palace and park in 1822 as a summer residence. With their tranquil reflections and natural banks, the ponds lend the landscape an idyllic character.

The first of the twenty-two ponds in the village were dug in the fifteenth century, when the castle and village belonged to the important Lower Silesian noble family of Schaffgotsch. Most of them were dug later by the Cistercian monks from Krzeszów monastery, some 18.6 miles (30 kilometers) away. The order, known for its fish farming, had taken over the area in the second half of the eighteenth century. Between 2010 and 2014, Jacek Masior, an entrepreneur with a weakness for antique furniture, faithfully restored the two castle ponds and reconstructed the park. Different species of fish were again

established in the pond at the castle entrance. In addition to carp, they include perch, tench, crucian carp, and roach.

IN BUKOWIEC PALACE PARK

After a long nap, our group visited Bukowiec and its magnificent park. Visitors can experience the full beauty of the landscape—originally created by human hands—on a hike to the neighboring palaces in the Jelenia Góra Valley. It is only 2.5 miles (4 kilometers) to the palace-park complex in Bukowiec and about 3.7 miles (6 kilometers) to the neighboring Lomnica and Wojanów palaces. The hilly landscape, crisscrossed by woods and brooks, offers hiking trails of different lengths.

IN THE REALM OF THE CORNCRAKE

My guests then trotted after me on the famous, approximately 3.7-mile-long (6 kilometer) "Königsweg"("King's Way"). It leads first through the pond landscape and then on through the picturesque Jelenia Góra Valley to Mysłakowice. This country road was the quickest connecting route for Prussian King Friedrich Wilhelm III from his summer residence to his brother's castle in Karpniki.

Some of the ponds are now privately owned and are still used for fish farming. Many parts of this well-watered area of around 210 hectares (519 acres) have developed into an extremely valuable biotope. It not only serves as a nesting place for many species of water birds, but also as a retreat for such rare species as the gray woodpecker or the corncrake.

CULINARY DREAM

Oh, yes, Lower Silesia is known for its cuisine. You cannot leave this beautiful voivodeship without tasting one of the famous Silesian dishes. In that setting you may discover what a White Koludzka is: the beauty queen among geese, which can sing gracefully, occasionally strays into the Jelenia Góra Valley in Lower Silesia.

GEESE IN CLASSIC SINGLE FILE: WHITE KOLUDZKA (*LEFT*); KARPNIKI CASTLE (*BELOW*) WELCOMES GUESTS, AS DOES HOTELIER WACŁAW DZIDA IN THE BAROQUE STANISZÓW PALACE (*BOTTOM*).

9 ON THE "CROOKED MEADOW"— ČESKÝ KRUMLOV

IN THE GHOST TOWN

In Český Krumlov, the Vltava River forms two loops, and the first loop almost surrounds the entire historic Old Town. It is a UNESCO World Heritage Site, and the entire Old Town is a protected landmark. The 13,000-inhabitant Bohemian town of Krumlov has a lot to offer.

ČESKÝ KRUMLOV'S OLD TOWN LIES DIRECTLY ON THE VLTAVA RIVER (*ABOVE*), WHICH CAN BE EXPLORED BY BOAT (*ABOVE RIGHT*). AUTOMOBILE DRIVERS ARE ALSO STYLE-CONSCIOUS HERE (*BELOW RIGHT*).

In the Baroque Castle Theater, the last one of its kind in the world, the unique, original stage machinery is still fully functional. There are hundreds of stage sets stored below the Castle Theater, in the second-largest castle in the Czech Republic (after the one in Prague). The view of finely restored facades in the Český Krumlov Old Town makes you feel like you are a player in a period drama, surrounded by the Vltava River. You just have to imagine that the signboards, the boutiques and fast-food outlets, and the modern clothes people are wearing just aren't there. Germany's

Rothenburg ob der Tauber almost looks like a modern city compared to Český Krumlov.

WORLD HERITAGE STATUS—AND CONSEQUENCES

The historic city center has been a UNESCO World Heritage Site since 1992. The result is that, except for about four hundred people, no one lives in the Old Town anymore; there is no supermarket, butcher, or baker. There used to be ten times as many people living in the city center. But rents rose along with the historic renovations that attract tourists. Now, only hotels, restaurants, and high-end shops can afford the prime locations. They include Market Square with the Virgin Mary column in the center, and the countless alleyways from which to view the castle and the striking Na Plášti (cloak bridge). Resembling an aqueduct from afar, it was built in 1767 as a three-story connecting corridor between the residential area and the theater. After all, ladies could not possibly be exposed to wind and weather on evening walks. The cobbled alleys, towers and corners, hatchways and stairs, and delicate plaster structures reveal how previous generations built, thought, and lived: it was both practical and beautiful.

KRUMME AU—CROOKED MEADOW

The Krumme Au (German for "crooked meadow;" Krumlov comes from the German "Krumau") on the Vltava River has been inhabited since the Stone Age. The first fortress was erected there in the thirteenth century, and its city charter was not long in coming. War has never destroyed the center of Český Krumlov, and not even the Communists committed the sin of building prefabricated apartment buildings there. Only the ravages of time have gnawed at it, and the political turning point may have come at the right moment to save a great deal. The city's unique authenticity was preserved, and its historic-landmark preservation status is well earned. A good three hundred houses, almost 90 percent of the Old Town, were restored in just a few years. It is hardly surprising that such a city is also associated with scary legends, not least that of Eleonora Amalie von Schwarzenberg. She was a member of the House of Lobkowicz who, through marriage, became princess of Schwarzenberg and Český Krumlov. She is buried under a heavy stone in the St. Vitus Church, which dates from the fourteenth century, while all the other Schwarzenbergs have their final resting place in Vienna. Baroque society and even ordinary people in Český Krumlov were suspicious of her. She drank wolf's milk and therefore was considered to be a vampire. Hence the heavy stone, intended to keep her from rising from the grave at night.

A THICKET OF BEER TAPS

It was the Bohemians who invented beer! No, it was the Bavarians! Strictly speaking, it was probably the Sumerians. This is the name of the people who may have brewed their first beer by chance, sometime in the fourth century BCE, living between the Euphrates and Tigris Rivers in what is now Iraq. At any rate, the Czechs are the undisputed world champions of beer, drinking 42 gallons (160 liters) a year per person. Germany ranks number four in beer consumption, at 110 liters. If the Bavarians were to be split off, the Free State of Bavaria would come in second at 29 gallons (140 liters). You can learn all this and much more on a tour of the world-famous Budweiser brewery, 15 miles (24 kilometers) from Český Krumlov. Of course, you will also be entertained with one beer or another.

MORE INFORMATION

In this region 109 miles (175 kilometers) south of Prague, you should spend a few more days in the beautiful Bohemian Forest; for example, at Lake Lipno: www.lipensko.cz/en/explore-territories

PŘÍJEM
OPRAVY
STRUNNÝCH
HUDEBNÍCH
NÁSTROJŮ
STŘEDA
17.30-20.00

THE GREATEST IMPACT

Český Krumlov is generally considered a ghost town. In the Old Town, allegedly there is also a ghost living in every house. If everything is going well, there is no sign of the ghost. However, if the inhabitants are experiencing domestic strife, the doors and windows open and close constantly; the ghost is showing its annoyance.

Moldavite stones are big business here. These stones (actually glass) were created by the impact of a meteorite fifteen million years ago, and they are the only gemstones in the world created by the impact of a celestial body on Earth. Jewelers' prices start at about $165. Visitors with a deeper interest in these precious stones will enjoy themselves in the small museum at Panska 19.

In addition to historic buildings, the Vltava, with its river bend, is a symbol of this pearl in the Bohemian Forest. Around two million tourists make the pilgrimage to this small city every year, which today has 13,000 inhabitants.

LIKE A SNAKE

The Vltava, the mother of all Bohemian rivers, can still be seen untamed in Krumlov. It seems to almost crush the Old Town like a snake. The view is particularly impressive from the Na Plášti bridge—just one of the many picturesque views that Český Krumlov has to offer.

TWO YOUNG WOMEN AT THE MEDIEVAL FESTIVAL (*ABOVE LEFT*); A SHOP FOR OLD INSTRUMENTS IN THE OLD TOWN (*BELOW LEFT*); LIVE MUSIC IN THE TRADITIONAL KRUMLOVSKY MLYN INN (*ABOVE*).

10 ROMANESQUE AND ROMANTIC—QUEDLINBURG

THE LOST TREASURE

Bumpy cobblestones, winding streets, a cathedral, and lost treasure: Quedlinburg offers a journey back to the Middle Ages. Its historic center, Schlossberg and Collegiate Church, makes it a UNESCO World Heritage Site, and 2019 marked the 1,100th anniversary of the royal election of Heinrich I as King of East Francia.

IN THE SEVENTEENTH CENTURY, QUEDLINBURG'S TOWN HALL WAS REBUILT IN RENAISSANCE STYLE (*BELOW*); THE DEFENSIVE SCHRECKENSTURM (TOWER OF TERROR) ON THE OLD TOWN WALL (*BELOW RIGHT*); TYPICAL HALF-TIMBERED HOUSES IN OLD TOWN (*ABOVE RIGHT*).

The story of lost treasure from the cathedral started when a US Army first lieutenant took twelve precious items home with him amid the chaos following World War II—and nobody knew about it. In 1990, when the soldier's heirs went to sell the objects, the pieces were traced to the Quedlinburg cathedral and were returned after lengthy negotiations. Six million marks were paid as a finder's fee. And so Germany's most valuable treasures, along with those of Aachen and Halberstadt, were restored in 1993.

HEINRICH I'S CORONATION CITY

Some 1,200 half-timbered linked houses from six centuries line the streets of Quedlinburg, comprising the most extensive protected landmark area in Germany, and were added to the UNESCO World Heritage list in 1994. But they are living history. A large number of the city's almost 30,000 inhabitants live in the historic buildings; others were turned into shops or cafés.

The landmark Romanesque Collegiate Church of St. Servatius, also known as the Schlosskirche auf dem Schlossberg (Castle

Back to the Middle Ages and off to the tower. In Quedlinburg, the Schreckensturm or tower of terror, dating from the sixteenth century, is a unique dwelling. You can live there as a tourist, high up and behind walls 6.5 feet (2 meters) thick. The vacation apartments have modern furnishings and offer a bedroom, bathroom, and kitchen, and the tower room with a breathtaking view of medieval Quedlinburg. The tower of terror, also known as Schreckensdüvel, was part of the city fortifications in the Middle Ages and is a historic landmark. Five floors and 131 feet (40 meters) high, its terrible name comes from its use in earlier days as a prison and a torture chamber. Information on renting it can be obtained from the city administration.

MORE INFORMATION

Quedlinburg is on the eastern edge of the Harz Mountains and can be reached by train and by car via the Straße der Romantik, or Romanesque Road. The season runs from April to October.

Church on Castle Hill), rises on a sandstone rock above the city. In 919, Heinrich, Duke of Saxony, was elected the first German king in what was then Quitilingaburg, and so 2019 marked the 1,100th anniversary of Heinrich I's election as king.

Around 1100, work began on the three-aisled church, one of the most important examples of High Romanesque architecture in Germany. The crypt contains Romanesque mural paintings and the sarcophagus of King Heinrich I. Two chambers hold some of the most precious church treasures from the Middle Ages. They include, among other things, several reliquaries made of gold, precious stones, and ivory; the Quedlinburg Evangeliary; and the staff of Sevatius.

The Quedlinburger Schlossberg—and with it St. Servatius, the abbey building, and many half-timbered houses—stands on clay. The castle has faced structural issues over the centuries because of the soft sandstone on which it is built and constant development around it.

800-YEAR-OLD NEW TOWN

A further highlight is the house where German poet Friedrich Gottlieb Klopstock

was born, and the attached museum. The poet and advocate of the French Revolution is considered the father of the German concept of the nation-state. Another special feature is the oldest half-timbered house in Germany. The building at the passage from Neustädter Kirchhof Street to the convent dates from the early fourteenth century. And the address, Neustädter Kirchhof (New Town Churchyard) 7, gives away its history. In addition to the Old Town, there is also a "new town" that is worth seeing, built around 1200 outside the walls of the Old Town. The residents came from surrounding villages seeking refuge in the fortified city from political turmoil and economic difficulties. The peasant farmers became "Ackerbürger"—citizens who continued to cultivate their fields from their new place of residence. Then and now, the city center is the Nikolaikirche (Church of St. Nicholas). Quedlinburg gets far fewer visitors than Weimar or even Dresden, yet you will not be completely alone in the summer season. This pearl of Saxony-Anhalt gets 150,000 overnight guests a year.

A ROMANTIC HIGHLIGHT: THE SCHIESSENTÜMPEL WATERFALL (*ABOVE*); VIANDEN CASTLE IS ONE OF THE LARGEST PRESERVED CASTLES WEST OF THE RHINE RIVER (*BELOW RIGHT*); ECHTERNACH MONASTERY WAS FOUNDED BY ST. WILLIBRORD (*ABOVE RIGHT*).

11 WONDERFUL HIKING TRAILS— THE MÜLLERTHAL

TAKE A HOP INTO THE DUCHY

Those looking for rest, relaxation, and active recreation will find it not far away from the capital of Luxembourg, in the Müllerthal region, a refuge that offers wide variety along beautiful hiking trails. In addition, you can discover the culture and history of the duchy in the palaces and fortresses in the town of Echternach.

The Grand Duchy of Luxembourg has one of the densest and most attractive networks of hiking trails in Europe. The routes lead through breathtaking landscapes, with valleys, forests, rock formations, rivers, and waterfalls. The Müllerthal Trail, awarded the designation of "Leading Quality Trails—Best of Europe," 70 miles (112 kilometers) long, is the most popular hiking trail in the Müllerthal region—Luxembourg's Little Switzerland. Via three loops, it goes through bizarre rock formations and past castles and palaces and offers magnificent panoramic views.

THE OLDEST CITY IN LUXEMBOURG

The charming center of the Echternach region is located on the Sauer River and was settled very early on: a Roman villa stood here in the first century. The second founding of the city goes back to the year 698. At that time, the monk Willibrord settled in Echternach and founded a Benedictine abbey here.

In the eleventh century it experienced a golden era and rose to be one of the most influential abbeys in all of northern Europe. The market square, narrow alleyways, and remains of the former city wall are evidence of an important past. Today Echternach is well known for its hopping procession, which always takes place on Whit Tuesday in honor of St. Willibrord. Since 2010 it has been on the UNESCO Intangible Cultural Heritage list.

BEAUFORT CASTLE

The medieval Beaufort Castle was built in three different periods between 1150 and 1650. By the eighteenth century it had been uninhabited for a long time; the castle ruins were opened to visitors at the beginning of the twentieth century. Visitors are particularly impressed by the torture chamber. The Renaissance castle, built in 1649, was always lived in by a succession of owner families, and it has been open to visitors since 2012. During tours, visitors can see the living rooms, the dining room, the gardens, and the distillery, where samples are available.

BERDORF AND A WATERFALL

The community of Waldbillig is located on a 820-foot-high (250 meter) hill and includes the villages of Waldbillig, Haller, and Christnach as well as Müllerthal, which has given the entire region its name. The remains of the legendary Heringerburg Castle can be seen not far away, and water rushes over the Schiessentümpel waterfall, certainly the most photographed motif in the entire region. Haller is a small flower village located at the beginning of the romantic Hallerbach valley; the birthplace of the most famous Luxembourg writer, Michel Rodange, stands in Waldbillig; and Christnach is the Duchy's model village because of its well-preserved village architecture. On Route 2 of the Müllerthal Trail, the Heringer Millen brasserie lures you to take a rest after hiking around 3 miles (5 kilometers). Via Consdorf the trail leads back to Berdorf, a day hike that couldn't be more beautiful. With the castles and palaces restored to their former beauty, you can see the cultural heritage of this beautiful landscape. To the north lies Vianden Castle, one of the most important historical fortifications in Europe. The castles of Beaufort in the Müllerthal region, Clervaux Castle, and the stately homes in the "Valley of the Seven Castles" in Guttland are all testimony to Luxembourg's glorious history.

WHAT BINDS HUMANITY TOGETHER

Clervaux Castle offers a remarkable exhibition, with models of Luxembourg's castles and a museum that commemorates the Battle of the Bulge in the Ardennes during 1944–45. It has another special highlight: photographs by artist Edward Steichen in the permanent *The Family of Man* exhibition, part of UNESCO's World Heritage. The exhibition was shown for the first time in the Museum of Modern Art in New York, and in 2013, after a complete restoration, it was moved to the Castle of Clervaux. Steichen was born in Bivange, Luxembourg, in 1879, immigrated to the United States in 1880, and became a painter, director, curator, gardener, and director of the photography department at MoMA. In 1964, he donated these works to the Luxembourg government, which honored his famous images of the world's people and cultures. www.steichencollections-cna.lu

MORE INFORMATION

www.visitluxembourg.com

Brasserie Heringer Millen,
1 rue des Moulins, L-6245 Müllerthal, telephone +352-26784717: www.heringermillen.lu

12 IN THE WICKLOW MOUNTAINS—GLENDALOUGH

IN THE FOOTSTEPS OF SAINT KEVIN

County Wicklow offers sandy beaches, wooded valleys, lakes, and a solitary mountain landscape for hikers in Wicklow Mountains National Park. The Valley of the Two Lakes, with the Glendalough monastic settlement, is an especially good place to trace the history of Saint Kevin.

THE ROUND TOWER (*BELOW*) **ON THE GROUNDS OF THE MONASTERY WITH CELTIC GRAVE CROSSES** (*BELOW RIGHT*) **IS A LANDMARK OF GLENDALOUGH AND, LIKE THE SMALL ST. KEVIN'S CHURCH, DATES FROM THE ELEVENTH CENTURY** (*ABOVE RIGHT*).

The times when Ireland was covered by forests of oak, beech, birch, and pine are long gone. To process charcoal for ships and barrels, the Irish forests were cut down until almost nothing was left. Today's reforestation is limited mainly to a fast-growing monoculture of conifers for timber, and these trees appear here and there like dabs on the landscape. This is why any contiguous wooded regions that have survived through the centuries have a special charm in Ireland. This is certainly true of the mountains and valleys in the Wicklow Mountains south of Dublin, which in their remoteness and silence are more reminiscent of the west coast of Ireland than the more vibrant east coast.

MEDITATIVE SILENCE

County Wicklow is also known as the Garden of Ireland because of its natural beauty. But there is more to be discovered here than magical gardens; the mountainous and hilly landscape of the Wicklow Mountains, formed around four hundred million years ago, also

THE GARDEN OF IRELAND

From the beginning of May to the end of September, the Wicklow Garden Festival transforms the region into a blooming summer dream. Some forty gardens are spruced for this occasion. A particularly attractive layout awaits guests at Mount Usher Gardens in Ashford. The 9-hectare (22 acre) garden and park along the Vartry River, laid out by Edward Walpole starting in 1875, is an excellent example of a Robinsonade in true Robinson Crusoe style: romantic, close to nature, overgrown. This style has nothing to do with the formal botanical gardens that had been fashionable until then. Nevertheless, you can find over 5,000 types of exotic trees, shrubs, and flowers here, all of which are ecologically grown and preserved in accordance with this philosophy.

MORE INFORMATION

Wicklow Tourist Office:
www.visitwicklow.ie, www.glendalough.ie

Mount Usher Gardens:
www.mountushergardens.ie

exudes charm. Valleys deeply carved during the Ice Age, such as Glendalough in the east and the gently rolling depressions in the west, form a harmonious scenery of meadows and forests, a region often enjoyed by hikers on extended trips along the Wicklow Trail. Ireland's oldest long-distance footpath connects Rathfarnham with Clonegall along 82 miles (132 kilometers). The Wicklow Mountains' sedimentary rock contain a high proportion of lead, iron, and zinc, and the region was mined until the last century. Isolated slag heaps and abandoned tunnels are silent witnesses of this bygone era. The area was settled as early as the Neolithic Era; the early Christians also valued the solitude of the mountains and the seclusion of the valleys. The visitor center at Wicklow Mountains National Park, which opened in 1991 and covers around 20,000 hectares (50,000 acres), is busier in the summer months. Rare and endangered bird and mammal species feel just as at home on the heaths, forests, and moors as the hiker who seeks meditative silence in the hilly Irish landscape.

KEVIN IN GLENDALOUGH

This silence, also found in the Valley of the Two Lakes in Glendalough, is likely what also inspired St. Kevin in the sixth century to settle down in harmony with nature, to live as a hermit, and later to found a monastic community. Today it is quiet only in winter, when fewer visitors flock to one of the most popular destinations on the entire Irish island. The former hermitage became a significant intellectual center in the early Middle Ages, where up to 3,000 monks and scholars pursued their studies. The cathedral, the round tower, the priest's house, and Kevin's Kitchen, another round tower that also served as a church, are preserved and are open to visitors. The sagas and legends of Kevin are as diverse as the Wicklow Mountains landscape. The saint is said to have been so closely connected with the animals that doe in the surrounding forests gave him their milk so that he could nurture a king's son; a bird laid its egg in his hands outstretched in prayer; and otters returned his prayer book, which had fallen into the lake, to him unharmed. However, the shy hermit was far less gentle with Princess Kathleen, who had her eye on him. He fled from her into a cave, but she tracked him down. Tired of being pursued, he threw her into the lake, where she drowned.

13 IN THE GREAT STONE CIRCLE — AVEBURY

A TESTAMENT TO THE BELL BEAKER CULTURE

In Avebury, England's Wiltshire has a prehistoric site to which—in addition to Stonehenge—no other site bears comparison. There is an entire village to be found inside the largest megalithic stone circle in the British Isles. The flow of visitors does nothing to detract from its charm.

THE MONOLITHS OF THE STONE CIRCLE BLEND INTO THE LANDSCAPE (*ABOVE AND BELOW RIGHT*); THE SUMMER SOLSTICE IS MUCH CELEBRATED IN AVEBURY (*ABOVE RIGHT*).

People with a special interest in prehistoric sites are occasionally assigned to the margins. But Avebury's ancient mysticism attracts even the most casual traveler. The unity of landscape, village, and stone circles is so clearly visible and palpable that some visitors are rendered almost speechless. As in Old Sarum in Salisbury, no grand gesture is needed to communicate the importance of this place. Avebury speaks for itself.

LIVELY ICONIC SITE

It doesn't hurt to have some knowledge as you move around in the village and between the earthen walls, but even the unprepared hiker senses the weight of the past. This aura is partly what has made Avebury a UNESCO World Heritage Site. A big draw for New Age fans, it is located some 15.5 miles (25 kilometers) north of Stonehenge and just under 6.2 miles (10 kilometers) west of Marlborough. With a diameter of a good 980 feet (300 meters), it is likely the largest stone circle in Europe. The complex comprises individual sarsen stones that form three rings, surrounded by earthen walls and trenches.

Since the boulders are relatively far apart, you can move around freely in this place of worship; families seated on a picnic blanket are not a rare sight. This gives the scene a lively and charming character.

PICNICKING WITH THE BELL BEAKER FOLK

There is a crossroads in the middle of the small village of Avebury; it runs in all four directions and is set in the middle of the stone circle. Actually, the circle is no longer complete, because well into the nineteenth century, people have helped themselves to the sandstone blocks that were lying around, using them to build their houses. But it is precisely this "incompleteness" that makes the scene so attractive. The result is that the stone circle is linked to its immediate surroundings and is not as isolated as Stonehenge is. Avebury was built between 2500 and 2000 BCE. The rock monoliths, weighing up to 20 tons, were transported from the Marlborough Downs, likely by members of the Bell Beaker people, as this Bronze Age culture is known in English. Stonehenge is also counted among the relics of this Stone Age culture. The Bell Beaker culture lasted until around 1800 BCE and then

disappeared into the mists of history. But before you get lost in Avebury, take a look at the imposing Elizabethan Avebury Manor and its beautiful gardens.

STEAM AND SMOKE

If you are interested in the great tradition of English steam locomotives, take a detour to Swindon, to the Steam Museum of the Great Western Railway. The history of the steam engine railroad is presented with impressive examples on the site of a former railroad factory. Once the largest railroad works in the world, its heyday was in the 1930s. At that time, over 12,000 people were employed here and built three locomotives a week. In 1986, the factory closed for good. The present-day museum displays not only historic locomotives but also the architecture of the Great Western Railway, as well as the life and the working world of the people, at the place where this legendary railroad history began. Then, following tradition, you turn toward the western part of southern England on the old Bath Road, which begins in London.

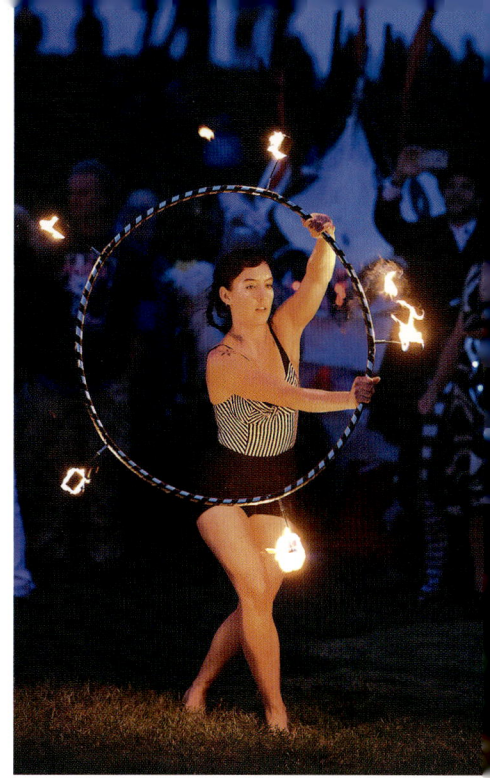

EXPERIENCING CONTEMPORARY HISTORY

The TV series *The Manor Reborn*, filmed in 2011, vividly showed how a historical manor house can be brought back to life. Nine rooms of Avebury Manor and parts of the gardens were redecorated and designed in five styles: Tudor, Queen Anne, Georgian, and Victorian styles, and twentieth century. All of this, of course, was done under the competent expertise of the National Trust and respected professionals, who used authentic furnishings. Best of all, visitors don't encounter any barriers: for example, one can sit at the Georgian dinner table and feel like a king. www.nationaltrust.org.uk/avebury

MORE INFORMATION

Avebury: www.english-heritage.org.uk/visit/places/avebury

Museum of the Great Western Railway: www.steam-museum.org.uk

Wiltshire: www.visitwiltshire.co.uk

14

MOORS, SEA, AND A BRIDGE— DEVON

WHERE ENGLAND IS STILL ENGLAND

Many places in Devon give the impression that they come from another world. Charming hamlets with names such as Hexworthy feature houses with slate facades, slightly askew thatched roofs, and a calm that speaks to seclusion and tranquility.

The real England lies in the countryside, as the British say. It means that things are very conservative and very British, leisurely and contemplative, certainly old-fashioned, and definitely well behaved. The world is still as it should be in England's rural areas. Or so it seems. Handwritten signs in front of the farms advertise eggs from free-range chickens, new harvest potatoes, and juicy apples.

Energetic horses play in their paddocks; sheep and cows graze happily on lush green pastures. And people prefer to wear clothes displaying Britain's notorious bad taste:

bright-green tracksuit tops made of glitzy polyester with old-fashioned gray pants and brown sandals. They take no notice. People live their lives and keep largely to themselves, just as it always was. A few youngsters occasionally fall out of character, looking like they have just come back from shopping along Oxford Street in London. They sport tattoos and piercings and are casually dressed. But on school days, these sassy girls and cheeky boys turn into proper children dressed in their uniforms: girls in skirts and white blouses, boys in a tie and white shirt.

THESE CURIOUS SHEEP IN DARTMOOR (*ABOVE*) ARE A BIT LESS WILD AND ROMANTIC THAN THE SUNSET OVER BIGBURY BAY (*LEFT*).

DISCOVER THE GREAT SEAFARING TRADITION

It shows its presence in every coastal town in Devon: this is home to a society that made history in seafaring. As a transshipment point for wool, Barnstaple was once one of the kingdom's most important ports. Plymouth continues to play a major role in the important circle of the country's leading ports. And Sir Francis Drake, born in Tavistock in 1540, was one of them, the men from Devon—and one of the great personalities of a great seafaring power. Drake was initially a privateer, then an explorer and the first English man to circumnavigate the globe. In doing so, he discovered the southernmost point of South America, Cape Horn. And he defeated the Spanish Armada, which earned him the rank of vice admiral. Queen Elizabeth I even knighted him in 1581.

MORE INFORMATION

Devon lies west of Cornwall, a 3.5-hour drive east of London.

www.visitdevon.co.uk

BUILDINGS OF A VERY SPECIAL KIND

It is a gray Friday morning. Fog hangs over what is perhaps the most eccentric building in Devon—although it is not immediately recognizable as such; A la Ronde, a sixteen-sided round house owned by the National Trust, is just outside the city of Exmouth. Two world-traveling women brought many ideas for living back with them, especially from Italy, resulting in this witty house in the round. This design allowed them to follow the sun, moving from room to room. The house is a museum on one side and the realization of a crazy dream on the other. The southwest of England is not exactly blessed with cultural highlights, but A la Ronde is definitely one of them. The most interesting prehistoric rock formation in Dartmoor is reminiscent of the world-famous Stonehenge. It lies between Holne and Hexworthy—an impressive relic of early settlements in a beautiful landscape. Single-lane paths meander over the moor, one of the loneliest nature reserves in Europe.

Exmoor, in the north, is the counterpart to Dartmoor. However, only a small area is part of Devon; most of it belongs to the eastern neighboring county of Somerset. The cliffs along the coast are among the highest in England. And the population of the so-called Exmoor ponies, which look like a cross between a horse and a donkey, is one of the few significant differences from Dartmoor.

SIMON & GARFUNKEL'S BRIDGE

Devon does indeed include cities such as Exeter, Torquay, and Plymouth, and their economic strength is a key part of life. But the rough landscape remains its characteristic feature; it has always wrested a little more from people than elsewhere, which has led to individualism and a deep-seated sense of home. Only two major roads cross Dartmoor, an inhospitable, foggy, cool, and humid region, which is shown as a circular shape on the map. The roads meet at Two Bridges. These small bridges span the West Dart River, which flows south to Dartmouth, where it flows into the

English Channel. Another bridge not far from Dartmoor is much more famous—the Bridge over Troubled Water. Everyone knows the elegant song by Simon & Garfunkel, but few realize that this bridge inspired the lyrics. The five-arch stone bridge is in the small town of Bickleigh, a few miles north of Exeter. Visitors arriving in Bickleigh want to see the little bridge and possibly feel the inspiration that the pop stars experienced here. There are always a few people wearing headphones in the thatched terrace café on the river, and if you ask them what they are listening to, they'll smile sheepishly and confess that they are playing Simon & Garfunkel's old ballad. What "Scarborough Fair"—another song by the duo—is for eastern England, "Bridge over Troubled Water" is for the west—an anthem to be proud of. Ironically, the River Exe is sluggish and as smooth as a mirror. Only the ridge under the bridge makes the water rougher.

SWIMMING AT 50 DEGREES FAHRENHEIT

In the summer, the English go swimming in the sea at 50 degrees Fahrenheit (15 degrees Celsius) and wear shorts when the weather warms to 54 degrees Fahrenheit (12 degrees Celsius) in the sun. Devon's first address for swimming is Torquay. One of the most famous seaside resorts in Great Britain, it has everything that defines a seaside resort— including tough Brits who don't let the chilly temperatures stop them from the joy of swimming. One hotel stands next to another, each one more beautifully renovated. There is a lively bustle along the promenade, amid the palm trees, in the cheerful stores, and on the inviting terraces above the colonnades.

The boulevard along the Torquay seafront is framed by steep red cliffs, where cozy little houses nestle into lush greenery. With its white gables, glazed conservatories, pretty roof terraces, and a wonderful pavilion with a cast-iron roof, the shopping roundabout is, so to speak, the tourist center of Torquay. There are also galleries of

deck chairs where seaside resort guests can enjoy sunbathing—in spring and autumn with a blanket. Starting from 50 degrees Fahrenheit (15 degrees Celsius), however, definitely without.

PLYMOUTH'S OLD PORT, SUTTON HARBOR, IS NOW A FISHING PORT AND MARINA (*OPPOSITE PAGE*). SEA THRIFTS ARE IN BLOOM ALONG THE CLIFFS OF HARTLAND QUAY IN NORTH DEVON (*BELOW*).

15 CHEERS FOR THE SUNNY ISLAND—JERSEY

SLOWING DOWN WITH ISLAND ROMANCE

From fine beaches to beautiful hikes and colorful festivals, Jersey has a lot to offer. And although the largest of the Channel Islands is easily accessible in the summer months, thanks to good ferry and flight connections, it is still largely spared from tourist masses.

THE LIGHTHOUSE JUST OFFSHORE IS THE LANDMARK OF CORBIERE BAY SOUTHWEST OF JERSEY (*ABOVE AND ABOVE RIGHT*); ST. AUBIN IS ONE OF THE ISLAND'S LARGEST PORTS (*BELOW RIGHT*).

The Channel Island of Jersey is enjoying growing popularity as a vacation destination, but this sun-drenched island, just 14 miles from mainland France in the English Channel, is seldom crowded. Good ferry connections and several direct flights from various German cities facilitate planning for such an "obvious" and extremely attractive vacation destination, which has a lot in store for hikers and nature lovers, water sports enthusiasts, and festival lovers.

HIKING FESTIVAL WITH TRADITION

Whether on coastal trails or in the island interior, hiking on Jersey in the autumn is a well-kept old tradition. During the popular Autumn Walking Week, which always takes place in mid-September, young and old head out to enjoy the autumn landscape on the Channel Island. There are plenty of free, guided, themed hikes. The highlights include sightseeing in castles or former gun emplacement platforms from World War II, a visit to the attractive lighthouse, and at low tide a tour to a former defense tower in the middle of the sea, or to the oyster beds off Jersey's east coast. There is a lot to marvel at, and the knowledgable guides are happy to pass on their knowledge of the island's history, diverse fauna and flora, bizarre legends, and special features.

Another popular tour is the Around the Island Walk, which covers five parts of the island and provides a good opportunity to test your hiking fitness without getting stressed: there are no mountains to be conquered, and the hilly landscape and well-marked coastal paths make hiking fun. The beautiful cliff trails take you along the north coast and across wide sandy beaches such as St. Ouen's Bay in the west, St. Aubin's Bay in the south, and Grouville Bay in the east. Everyone can walk at their own pace. In around five days, you will have completely circled Jersey—and on the way learned to know some of the most beautiful beaches in the Northern Hemisphere, such as Plemont Bay.

COLORFUL SKIES OVER JERSEY

Every September, the International Air Display Show is held. This unique air show is one of the largest in Europe. International flight veterans with spruced-up old propeller machines, military and civil planes, helicopters, and small private planes offer breathtaking acrobatic performances above St. Aubin's Bay. Many of the participating planes make a side trip to the island during the legendary Battle of Britain commemoration. The grand finale is the flyover by the Red Arrows team, which draws its colored lines in the sky over Jersey. Was there something else? Oh yes, the insider tips. We won't reveal them completely, but let's just say that anyone who has gone swimming in Plemont Bay, had tea at Paul Baxter's, and satisfied their hunger at the Hungry Man in Rozel Bay sleeps very well in the shadow of the lighthouse in the Highlands Hotel, which is ideal for hikers and water sports enthusiasts. Psst, don't tell anyone.

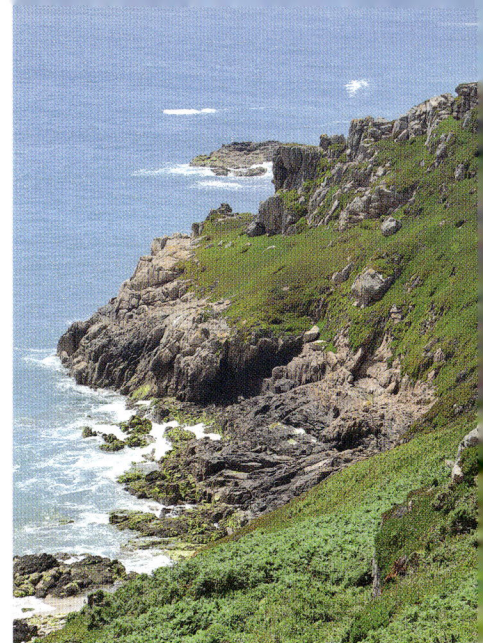

THE MOST BEAUTIFUL FLOWERS ON THE ISLAND

Every year on the second Thursday in August, Jersey literally blooms: this is when the spectacular Summer Flower Carnival is traditionally held on the south coast. The grand procession of floats, decorated with flowers and accompanied by musicians and dance groups, jugglers, and a colorful crowd, moves across Victoria Avenue from St. Helier. You shouldn't miss this very special island flower festival and its impressive atmosphere. The Jersey Battle of Flowers parade has been celebrated since 1902 and has grown to become the largest flower spectacle of its kind in Europe. Which of the local communities ultimately wins the competition is of secondary importance. What counts is the exuberant, colorful, and peaceful atmosphere. www.battleofflowers.com

MORE INFORMATION

www.jersey.com

The Highlands Hotel, La Corbiere, St. Brelade, Jersey
https://highlands-hotel-st-brelade.booked.net

16 THE BEAUTIFUL UNKNOWN—PICARDY

HORSES, SAILORS, ART, AND CATHEDRALS

Few people know about Picardy—but once you get to know this tranquil region, you'll be happy and surprised: unspoiled nature, lots of space, plenty of opportunities to take a deep breath, and just as many ways to give life a free rein.

THE CHÂTEAU DE CHANTILLY, WHICH DATES FROM THE SIXTEENTH CENTURY, HAS A FAMOUS COLLECTION OF PAINTINGS AND A STUD FARM (*BELOW*). LIFE IS QUIETER FOR THE PIPE SMOKER AT THE FÊTE DES BAIGNEURS (SWIMMERS' FESTIVAL) IN MERS-LES-BAINS (*BELOW RIGHT*) THAN IT IS FOR THE KITE SURFER IN CAYEUX-SUR-MER (*ABOVE RIGHT*).

It is the big day in Chantilly: the horse races! The Prix de Diane Longines is being held. This means an elegant wardrobe, a wide-brimmed hat, and a convertible are in order. The gentlemen strut with coattails waving, Mesdames in high heels to get the best view—and to be seen. And the "flics," as the policemen are called in France, busily direct the traffic. Chantilly is a pocket-sized ascot—not in terms of size and significance, but in terms of name recognition. Typical Picardy: this is an elegant country delight that hardly anyone knows about it, where the hats are the eye-catchers and the women are the stars. Nobody cares about the horses that are running for all they're worth.

MEDIEVAL CAPITAL CITY

Amiens is another example: in the capital city of Picardy, the largest medieval cathedral in the world rises to the heavens. The Cathédrale Notre-Dame is a UNESCO World Heritage Site twice over: as a prime example of Gothic architecture and as a station on the Camino de Santiago, or Way of St. James pilgrimage route. At 138 feet (42 meters), the vault of the nave is twice as high as that

JULES VERNE AND ALEXANDRE DUMAS

Jules Verne liked to retire to the fairy-tale castle Les Tourelles in the Picardy village of Le Crotoy. It was here that he conceptualized his novels, such as *Around the World in Eighty Days*, in a confined space but with a wide view over the sea. He was looking for relief from the chaos of Paris and was fascinated by the air and the flair of the Atlantic Ocean. Later the poet even moved here permanently, to what was then Rue Lefèvre, now Rue Jules Verne. Les Tourelles is now a hotel with bright-red paintwork and thirty-five rooms; rates start at eighty Euros a night. Picardy also produced another literary world star: Alexandre Dumas. The brilliant author of *Three Musketeers* and the *Count of Monte Cristo* was born in the village of Villers-Cotterêts.

of the world-famous Notre-Dame Cathedral in Paris. Heads are tilted backward. Eyes look upward: 656,000 cubic feet (200,000 cubic meters) should be explored first. And there are 7,000 figures made of stone (on the outer facade) and wood (inside) to discover. More discoveries await in the Musée Condé in the moated Château de Chantilly. After the Louvre in Paris, it is the most important collection of paintings in France. Among other pieces, *The Three Graces* and two other paintings by Raphael hang here. In contrast to experiencing the *Mona Lisa* and the Louvre in general, here you'll be able to appreciate the artwork without the crowds. At most, there is a crowd in Marcanterre ornithological park. Established on a refuge for migratory birds, 340 of the 600 bird species in France can be seen here.

SWIFT AS AN ARROW OVER THE SAND

Very close by is 15.5 miles (25 kilometers) of beach—a natural treasure providing aromatic sea air, foaming surf, and dunes as far as the eye can see. And along with it there is sand-sailing along the beach. This three-wheeled vehicle steered by foot, a sail, and a rope as a "gas pedal" is explained in five minutes, learned in ten minutes, and provides hours of fun. If the weather doesn't cooperate, the Aquaclub also offers watery pleasures under roof.

At low tide, you can cross the Somme Bay in three hours. What appears to be flat turns out to be a landscape of small hills and valleys. You have to repeatedly cross the runoff channels. Climbing down, wading through the water, back up to the plateau—and all that in rubber boots. But the provisions can be left at home, because they are growing in the sandy soil in the form of salicornia, a type of algae that tastes like pickles and is just as crunchy. In the evening, duck or lamb from the Somme Bay salt marshes is on the menu, followed by raspberries with crème Chantilly, rich whipped cream flavored with vanilla.

If you prefer a more comfortable ride around the bay, choose the steam locomotive of Marcellin. The journey starts in Saint Valery, the medieval type of a small Gallic village. Those invincible Gauls, Asterix and Obelix (for fans: there is also a Parc d'Astérix in Plailly!), were never allowed to clatter their way through Saint Valery, thanks to their creator, Albert Uderzo. But Joan of Arc did stop here—by force, on December 20, 1430, as a prisoner on her way to Rouen.

MORE INFORMATION

Picardy is located in northwestern France; it can be easily reached from Paris and western Germany and is not overcrowded, even in summer.
https://us.france.fr/en/northern-france

17 HISTORY OF BURGUNDY

A KALEIDOSCOPE OF EUROPEAN ORIGINS

For wine lovers, the name Burgundy melts on the tongue like a complex finish of one of the great wines from the Côte-d'Or region. It has been producing fantastic wines for over 2,000 years. In Burgundy you can discover wonderful sacred buildings, castles, and a fine culture of pleasure.

VINEYARDS NEAR FUISSÉ (*ABOVE*). A DREAM FOR WINE LOVERS: THE CELLAR OF THE DOMAINE DROUHIN LAROZE ON THE ROUTE DES GRANDS CRUS (WINE ROUTE) AND THE VINEYARDS OF THE HAUTES CÔTES DE BEAUNE, CÔTE-D'OR (*BELOW RIGHT*). THE SUBLIME HALL OF THE ABBAYE DE FONTENAY IN MARMAGNE (*ABOVE RIGHT*).

Burgundy has an almost mystical sound, and not only when it comes to wines. Even if you weren't always paying attention in history class, you have probably heard of the Dukes of Burgundy at some point. And the legendary castles, fortresses, churches, and monasteries of the Middle Ages appear to have known only one home: Burgundy. Just as the character of a great wine depends on many factors, the character of a region, its landscape, and its people, is rooted in the cultural, geographical, and social achievements and changes of the past centuries. There is hardly a region in present-day Europe where it is possible to see this course of history in such an impressive way—and above all where it is so visible in everyday life. There is a special atmosphere in the air here, a harmony of strength and serenity, a quiet glow that does not need to strive for attention because it knows that, sooner or later, everyone will succumb to its vibe.

Infatuation? Of course, but anyone who travels through southern Burgundy on a sunny late-summer day, roams the hilly landscape, experiences the small villages with their Romanesque churches, and shares a red wine with the farmers sitting on the bench in front of the inn inevitably wonders: Why move on? Well, you would miss a lot, because

VINEYARD SNAILS (ESCARGOTS) ARE A BURGUNDY DELICACY (*BELOW*). IN GUÉDELON, A CASTLE IS BEING BUILT USING MEDIEVAL CONSTRUCTION TECHNIQUES AS AN ARCHEO-LOGICAL EXPERIMENT (*ABOVE RIGHT*); THE PALACE OF THE DUKES AND ESTATES OF BURGUNDY IN DIJON WAS BUILT IN THE FOURTEENTH CENTURY (*BELOW RIGHT*).

here at the intersection of the most-important trade routes of the Middle Ages, you can see what decisively shaped Christian Western culture, where we come from, and in what direction Europe should develop. Thus, over time, an "ABC" emerges of sacred, castle, and palace architecture that could simply not be any more beautiful.

A FOR AUTUN

At the start of the Burgundy kaleidoscope is Autun, population 14,000. The city, which is surrounded by extensive mixed forests, is considered the gateway to the southern Morvan region. It was founded by Emperor Augustus as Augustodunum in 10 BCE, after the stubborn Gauls were finally defeated, and was located on the important Via Agrippa long-distance trade route. More than twenty towers are preserved from the ancient city wall; the clocks seem to run on a slightly different time in the winding alleyways of the pictur-esque Old Town and along the Arroux River. In addition to a Roman amphitheater, the main attraction is the Cathedral of Saint Lazarus. The Romanesque basilica towers over the city like a watchman from a bygone era. The tympanum on the west portal was created in the twelfth century by the Burgundian master Gislebertus and shows the Last Judgment; in the interior, the figurative representations on the column capitals astonish visitors.

B FOR BEAUNE

The city of Beaune is the economic center of viticulture in Burgundy. In addition to the Hospices de Beaune Wine Auction for charity, which provides a reliable economic barome-ter for the region, and the pretty Old Town with its markets and festivals, the Hôtel-Dieu Hospice (medieval hospital foundation) is the most important attraction and the most beautiful building in the city. This architec-tural gem, with colorful roof tiles, was built by Nicolas Rolin, the Duke's chancellor, in 1443 and is a testament to the history of the charity hospital in this region. A palatial compound for the poorest people, it is an outstanding example of Flemish-Burgundian architecture. The Great Hall of the Poor makes a memora-ble impact as you stand in front of the polyptych *The Last Judgment*, which Rogier van der Weyden created between 1446 and 1452. The nine oil paintings on wood still over-shadow any modern digital photograph in their intensity and physicality.

C FOR CLUNY

The Benedictine Abbey of Cluny, with the imposing Maior Ecclesia, was founded in 910 and grew into one of the most important educational, artistic, and religious centers, which radiated its influence throughout Europe during the following medieval centuries. The highest vaults in the Romanesque world still bear witness to the importance of this place, which is surrounded by extensive parks, a large forecourt with beautiful cafes, and a charming Old Town with a granary, city museum, and Romanesque houses. Long before the Dukes of Burgundy, who wrote European history in the fourteenth and fifteenth centuries, Cluny grew up in Burgundy with the founding of the orders of the Cluniac and Cistercian monks, who as architects, teachers, and farmers led Burgundian Romanesque into its golden era. It is a vivid example of the degree to which the monastery complex of Cluny changed an entire city, a region, and then all of Europe. By around 1100, some hundred other monasteries in France, Spain, Italy, and England belonged to Cluny, and its abbots had achieved incomparable power and independence. Its architecture and buildings still radiate timeless beauty.

TOURNUS AND VÉZELAY

The same is true of the neighboring city of Tournus, with its Saint-Philibert Abbey from the eleventh century. The city on the Saône River has an almost Mediterranean flair; here the bell towers rise over the pink-tiled roofs and help orient visitors in the narrow alleys of the dreamy

Old Town. With a larger gesture, the town of Vézelay emerges from the surrounding meadows and valleys atop a hill. The Saint Marie-Madeleine Basilica is a masterpiece of Romanesque architecture, a miracle of space, and rich in sculptures. Between the tenth and thirteenth centuries, emperors, kings, and common people made pilgrimages to the "Eternal Hill." It was from this early mass travel destination of the Middle Ages that the Second Crusade was launched. Then there are Perrecy-les-Forges, Paray-le-Monial, Fontenay, and Ronchamp, with their own rich histories.

CONSTRUCTION TECHNIQUES OF THE MIDDLE AGES

Hammering, beating, carving, and steaming, the craftsmen in Guédelon work quietly and almost meditatively; their intense focus radiates something spiritual. They have become one with an amazing project: a castle is being built in Guédelon, using the means and methods of the Middle Ages. The open construction site offers visitors a firsthand glimpse into the development of a castle complex. It will take around twenty years to finish. The 30,000 tons of required stone are taken from the nearby quarry and processed with tools from their own forge, and the lime is burned on-site. The colors come from the soil and plants, and the bricks are fired in their own kiln. The architect's thumb, hand, and cubit serve as measuring tools. www.guedelon.fr/en

MORE INFORMATION

Hotel de la Poste et du Lion d'Or, Place du Champ de Foire, F-89450 Vézelay; www.hplv-vezelay.com

18 TRUE BEAUTY—THE HOCHKÖNIG

CHEERS TO THE KING!

Schnapps for a euro, celebrity sightings, and a 20-mile (32-kilometer) "king's ski circuit" in the Königsrunde: the Hochkönig region invites skiing to your heart's content, with oversized king's thrones for resting and cozy huts with Jagatee—black tea and rum punch.

They have found each other: She is thirty-six years old and has ranked in the top thirty on the Freeride World Tour for years. He is slightly older, grew slowly during the Cretaceous period about 135 million years ago, and is also among the top thirty . . . of the most beautiful mountains in the Alps. Berber Semmelink, who grew up at 24 feet (7.3 meters) above sea level in the village of Heino, near Swolle in the Netherlands, has been a ski guide and ski instructor on the 9,649-foot-high (2,941 meter) Hochkönig Mountain for almost twenty years. "Together we are a dream couple," says Berber, who laughs and invites us to get started.

A full 20 miles (32 kilometers) of slopes spread over 21,900 vertical feet (6,700 vertical meters) are waiting: the "Königstour" or "king's tour."

ON THE ROYAL ROUND

The meeting point is the valley station at nine o'clock in the morning: the sun is shining, the snow is glistening, ice crystals are sparkling, and the sky is that wonderful deep blue that exists only in the mountains. Your stomach is tingling. In no time at all, or more precisely in ten minutes, the six-seater Hochmais chairlift is hovering over the World Cup route up to Gabühel. The first turns on the perfectly prepared slope are a pleasure.

THE WINTRY HOCHKÖNIG IN THE LIGHT OF THE RISING SUN (*ABOVE*)—BUT IT IS ALSO A DREAM IN SUMMER WHEN THE COWS GRAZE THEIR FILL ON THE MOUNTAIN PASTURES (*ABOVE LEFT AND BELOW LEFT*) AND THE ERICHHÜTTE MOUNTAIN HUT WELCOMES HIKERS ON THE ALMENWEG TRAIL (*BELOW RIGHT*).

The first of the targeted 20 downhill miles (32 kilometers) is tackled in a sedate fashion. The Königsrunde is only one section: the Hochkönig is one of five regions in the Skiwelt Amadé, with more than 528 miles (850 kilometers) of runs and 75 miles (120 kilometers) of slopes. The ratio of blue-level and red-level runs is balanced; black-diamond slopes are rather rare. The Königstour is particularly well suited for those who really enjoy skiing, and for whom skiing is just as important as the magnificent scenery.

"It's too early for that," Berber informs those who are thirsty, and points with her index finger at the Daumen (thumb). The Daumen is the nickname for the Sonnenstein, because of its shape. "That is where Mr. Red Bull, Dietrich Mateschitz, lives," she says. "He usually flies in by helicopter from Salzburg." By the way, Salzburg and the Sonnenstein are less than 62 miles (100 kilometers) apart.

SEE OVER SIXTY MILES

Along the well-marked tour route, the mighty Hochkönig is never out of sight. Oversized thrones invite you to take a royal break at the edge of the run. The air is thin and dry, but when you take in the panoramic view of the Steinerne Meer, your jaw will drop: on a clear day, you can admire peaks 62 miles (100 kilometers) away, as well as the two nearby 9,800-foot (3,000 meter) peaks, Großglockner and Kitzsteinhorn.

A skier sits as motionless as Buddha on the throne and seems to draw Alpine philosophical conclusions. The many Wi-Fi spots available, on the other hand, seem to inspire many young snowboarders at least as much as the royal Hochkönig surroundings do. (After all, the photos you have just taken or the scenes you recorded on your helmet camera have to be sent to your social media followers immediately!) Berber shows us her favorite free-ride slope as she glides by. Then she picks up the pace, because there are still a few miles to go on one of the longest ski routes in the Alps.

A FEELING FOR SNOW

A Ski World Cup competitor could complete the Königsrunde at racing speed in about thirty minutes—without lift time and hut stop. Skiers who do their turns in good form but are not quite that skilled will have to reckon with about five hours, including ascents, but without stopping for a break.

We have reached the village of Maria Alm, and it brings a surprise. On the slopes of the Hinterreit, Peter Hörl has been helping the international skiing elite achieve top positions in the World Cup for some twenty years. "His feeling for snow is sensational," says Berber. "There is no ski resort in the whole world where they can train undisturbed, as they can with Peter."

The guest book entries prove this statement. Downhill legend Hermann Maier said thank you, as did Bode Miller, Maria Höf-Riesch, and, of course, Marlies Schild, who comes from the Hochkönig area and, with thirty-five slalom victories, is the most successful racer in this discipline in World Cup history. Even when entire national teams arrive, be it from Switzerland, Austria, France, or the United States, the World Cup racers live and eat in the Haus Hörl guesthouse. Before or after the season, with a bit of luck, you might get to eat a tasty Kaiserschmarrn pancake with a world champion after the Königsrunde. Some may feel they've reached the ultimate emotional summit!

A GLASS FOR THE FINALE

It is 4:07 p.m., and at the Hinterthal valley station the sun has disappeared behind the mountains. The Royal Tour is completed. At the Urslauerhof hotel next to the slope, we work out the numbers in our head while sipping an Obstler (fruit schnapps) from the Schnapsbankerl (a shot glass holder shaped like a rustic bench): we've just traveled 28 miles (45 kilometers) on skis, 20 miles (32 kilometers) of which were downhill, and took a two-hour break and eighteen cell phone photos. At the end of the trail, the bottle of schnapps was waiting in a red cupboard outside the hotel, with glasses set next to it on a red bench, inviting us to enjoy a one-euro shot on the honor system. Where else in the world can you find all this? *Ein Hoch auf den König*—cheers to the king!

SNOW HIKING

Hiking isn't just for summer fun; it is a pleasure even in winter! The snow crunches under your feet, and you can cross a glittering winter landscape in peace and with plenty of time to look around. On the Hochkönig, 53 miles (85 kilometers) of prepared winter hiking trails await hikers, with beautiful views of the wonderful mountain ranges. Anyone who has never hiked on snowshoes can learn how on the snowshoe trail from the village of Mühlbach am Hochkönig. In addition, there are weekly guided snowshoe hikes available in Maria Alm: there is a half-day tour every Wednesday at 9:30 a.m.; meeting point is at the Maria Alm tourist office. Individually guided snow-hiking tours can be booked in almost every sports shop around the Hochkönig.

MORE INFORMATION

You can get there from Munich via Lofer and Saalfelden, Austria; distance is around 124 miles (200 kilometers). Snow report and further information: www.hochkoenig.at.

19 EXCITING UNDERWORLD — PETROVARADIN FORTRESS

LANDMARK ABOVE THE DANUBE

Directly across from Serbia's second largest city, Novi Sad, the Petrovaradin Fortress towers defiantly above the Danube River. The mighty structure makes an impression with its walls, moats, views over the city and river—and a vast underground network of tunnels. Not for claustrophobics!

VIEW OF NOVI SAD FROM THE PETROVARADIN FORTRESS (*ABOVE*); IN THE EVENING, IT IS IMPRESSIVELY STAGED WITH LIGHTS (*BELOW RIGHT*). A VAST TUNNEL SYSTEM RUNS THROUGH THE ROCK BELOW THE FORTRESS (*ABOVE RIGHT*).

The dark side is often the most exciting, and this proves itself once again at the Petrovaradin Fortress, which is among the largest structures of its kind in Europe. It towers high above the rocky banks of the Danube River. The fortress, built by the Austrians during the eighteenth century, conceals an astonishing, dark interior existence: over 12.4 miles (20 kilometers) of tunnel systems, once hollowed out by human hands for military reasons, then left to their fate. One of the most exciting vacation adventures in Serbia is a tunnel expedition by foot.

ON THE MOVE WITH THE "CITY GUERRILLA"

Off to the underworld! This is something you cannot do by yourself. The "city guerrilla" provides experienced guides for marching through the depths. Behind all this is an environmental initiative that has been running cleanup campaigns. This work has yielded a few dozen tons of rubbish, along with dog and cat carcasses. The head of the guerrillas is Leon Surbanovic, who, if he adds up his time in the tunnels, figures he has spent an entire year in the dark. He is practically the only person who can interpret the detailed tunnel map he has drawn up. He distributes photocopies before we set out. All the different levels, galleries, passageways, kinks, and intersections are confusing. "There are seventy entrances," says Surbanovic, who once wandered around underground for fourteen hours until he found the way out. Lovely prospects.

TOTAL SILENCE IN THE LABYRINTH

The countdown is on. Final instructions before the entry: the little group has to stay together. No going it alone. Those in front should warn those in back about ledges and holes in the floor. It gives you tingles to dive into this other world for a few hours. Stone steps lead down into the labyrinth, where total silence reigns. And darkness. No more cell phone reception. Temperatures range between 53 and 61 degrees Fahrenheit (12 and 16 degrees Celsius). Oxygen is not a problem because the air is mechanically circulated. The torch lights flicker eerily. The route goes deeper and deeper inside over hard-packed earth. Graffiti—there are reportedly around 1,500 works—testifies to the presence of humans.

Surbanovic stops. Thieves who once hid their loot here reported that there were way markers scraped into the walls or painted arrows for orientation. There are also vivid tales about love nests and battles between enemy gangs who tried to smoke each other out by using burning car tires during the 1970s. The only thing the tunnels haven't seen is acts of war. Dust hangs in the air, and the mud smacks under the soles of your shoes. One passage demands a crouching position; in another passage, you have to go past some bats at eye level, while keeping your distance. Surbanovic tells of finds that are kept at the guerrilla camp. Children's toys. A computer screen from the archeological early days of computer science. He recently found a tabletop soccer game that could fetch a few hundred dollars on eBay.

BACK IN THE FRESH AIR

Eventually you are spat out into the fresh air, and you realize it has also gotten dark outside. The walls form the backdrop along your way to a farewell view at the fortress clock tower, where love locks are fastened to the railings. The Danube sparkles, and reflections of lanterns and houses become blurred on the water's surface.

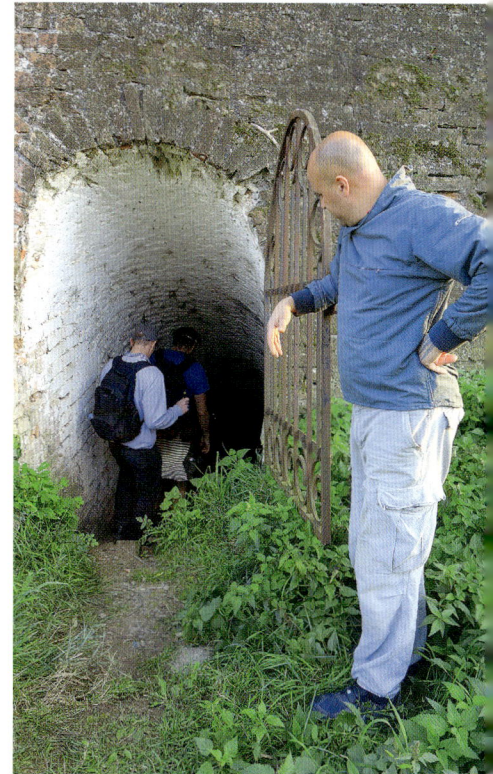

NOVI SAD DISCOVERIES

Life streams through the pedestrian zone in the heart of Novi Sad, which has almost 240,000 inhabitants and was named one of the European Capitals of Culture for 2021. Boutiques display the latest chic items, and locals meet on the terraces of lively outdoor cafés. The Town Hall, St. Mary's Church, and the theater are important buildings. Just outside the city, signs show the way to City Beach, a destination during the warmer months of the year. There you can plunge into the Danube torrent. At this historic beach, which has been there for over a century, the sand and meadow areas flow into one another. There is also a "second helping" of the Petrovaradin Fortress: the Exit music festival in July, a multiday celebration in the middle of the walled complex.

MORE INFORMATION

Travel information about Serbia: www.serbia.com

Novi Sad: www.visitnovisad.rs

20 IN THE FRAGRANT PARADISE FOR BEES—HVAR ISLAND

THE SUNNY ISLAND SHOWS ITS SUNNY SIDE

Tourism has a long tradition on Hvar Island. The turquoise-blue sea, wonderful coves, vineyards, olive trees, and fields of lavender began attracting the first vacationers almost 150 years ago. And then, as now, Hvar was pronounced "chvar"—with a rolling R at the end.

YOU CAN STILL SEE VENETIAN ARCHITECTURE IN HVAR CITY, WITH ITS LARGE HARBOR (*BELOW*). SMALL SANDY COVES INVITE YOU TO SWIM (*ABOVE RIGHT*); A FISHERMAN PATIENTLY MENDS HIS NET (*BELOW RIGHT*).

Six wooden boxes stand there, each holding 60,000 bees and one queen. Her diligent servants are still sleeping. Ivan opens the wooden boxes only at dawn, when the bees are starting to get restless. Today they will collect the nectar from rosemary, and from sage blooms in May, followed by lavender in June and July. This is how Ivan and another hundred island bee-keepers, with their 3,000 beehives, produce the famous honey from Hvar. "Rosemary honey is light, has a mild taste, and is one of the finest types of honey," explains Ivan. "Sage honey, on the other hand, has a beneficial effect on the respiratory organs." Lavender honey is the one most commonly sold on the island and has a calming effect, while meadow honey is cloudy and exudes a pleasantly mild fragrance. It is recommended for rheumatism, gout, and urinary tract infections. Archeological finds prove that beekeeping was already of great importance to Hvar in Roman times. Nowadays, however, people visit mostly to experience the sea and the island's coves, vineyards, olive trees, and lavender fields, and "certainly also eating the good honey for breakfast," adds Ivan.

AND NOW TO THE BEACH

Hvar is not only a sunny island, but it also has wonderful beaches. In Amfora Bay, Hvar's luxurious beach club features a renovated 1930s building and a pine grove as a backdrop, plus the private atmosphere of rental cabanas. Robinson Beach, by comparison, can be reached only on foot: this quiet pebble beach is halfway between Hvar and Milna. A distance of 1.2 miles (1 kilometer) west of Milna is Pokojnyi Dol Beach, which is child-friendly. Between Hvar and Stari Grad, you can reach Dubovica beach by foot along a steep trail; an idyllic cove with a pebble beach awaits you there. Nude swimming has been allowed since the 1920s at Pakleni Otoci, located in western Hvar and accessible by boat from the capital.

MORE INFORMATION

Accessible by ferry from Split. The best island seafood restaurant serving lobster is Passarola. (Beyoncé and Jay Z have already been there.) http://tzhvar.novena.hr/hr

FAME AND POWER

Hvar, located south of Split and the island of Brae, welcomes guests with its lush nature. The island stretches out like a line on the map and is oriented due south. It is called the "sunny island" for good reason. More tiny islets lie before it, like tufts of moss along a white border. Grapes, cherries, olives, and lavender grow here. And there are bees humming and buzzing wherever you go.

Hvar gained fame and power as part of the Venetian maritime empire. The lively city, with its cathedral and theater—the first municipal theater in Europe!—its clock tower, and its fortress, with the arcades of the Venetian city loggia, bears witness to this. Ferries land in front of the loggia, while the cruise ships prefer Stari Grad as a port of call. It was founded in 384 BCE and is thus the oldest settlement on the island, and cruise guests enjoy the harbor promenade, the city wall, and the stone alleyways and arcades. The serpentine route between Hvar City and Stari Grad is the most spectacular road on the island: 12.4 challenging, winding miles (20 kilometers) that offer wonderful vantage points.

TOOTING YOUR OWN HORN IS PART OF THE JOB

Vrboska has a unique feature: the windowless Sveta Marija church fortress with its two defense towers, dating from the sixteenth century. Jelsa, on the other hand, has a very beautiful town square and townhouses. The Lungomare promenade connects the bays of Jelsa and Vrboska along 0.9 miles (1.5 kilometers). The foundation stone for tourism was laid as early as 1868. That year, the island's first hotel opened and the first tourist association was founded. Apparently it did everything right. From today's marketing point of view, the only thing that should be improved on is the foundation's name: the Hygienic Society. This is of little interest to Ivan. He's waiting for his bees and enjoying some *istarska*. The soup, made from wine, olive oil, and toasted bread, is one of the island's specialties—"alongside honey, of course."

21 A DIAMOND IN THE ROUGH— KEFALONIA

RICHLY VARIED WORLD IN THE GREEK ISLANDS

An Ionian island that lies off the west coast of Greece—the largest and richest in contrasts—fascinates visitors with its imposing mountain region and alluring stalactite caves, its wonderful beaches and wild stony shores, and its wide range of landscapes and colorful coastal towns.

THE MELISSANI CAVE LAKE NEAR SAMI (*BELOW*) IS A POPULAR DESTINATION FOR BOAT TRIPS; THE CLASSIC AGIOS THEODORAS LIGHTHOUSE CREATES AN IMPACT AGAINST THE LIGHT OF THE SETTING SUN (*RIGHT*).

Kefalonia's look and feel features a highly articulated coastline comprising peninsulas with all kinds of completely different scenery, along with a mountainous interior. This large island has so far been largely spared from mass tourism, yet it inspires its visitors anew every year. On Kefalonia, dark fir forests extend up the slopes of the 5,338-foot-high (1,627 meter) Mount Enos. It has a steppe-like landscape, along with low table mountains and eroded valleys, and hills covered by dense olive groves where cypress trees stand out prominently, while the island's southern slopes are lined by long beaches. The best way to get to know the most-diverse facets of the island and to enjoy its breathtaking views is to take a personal exploratory tour, for which you definitely need a car.

WIDE RANGE OF LEISURE ACTIVITIES

Kefalonia's diversity is reflected not only in its landscapes but also in the wide range of activities available. These range from wine tastings in the best wine cellars on the Ionian islands, to hikes on Mount Enos and visits to fortresses and monasteries, to excursions by canoe or kayak. Nature lovers are not the only ones who will find a visit to the island's two caves worthwhile: the program includes the Drogarati cave and a short boat trip on the unique Melissani cave lake. The latter is

44 ON THE EDGE OF THE UNIVERSE — THE OREGON COAST

A JOURNEY THROUGH DENSE FORESTS, BETWEEN SKY AND SEA

Rough cliffs, picturesque lighthouses, small fishing villages, hidden artist colonies, wildly romantic beaches and sand dunes, fish, seafood, and sea lions—there is hardly a stretch of coastline in North America that is as diverse and dramatic as the Pacific Coast of Oregon.

The Pacific Coast Highway follows the Oregon coast for around 398 miles (640 kilometers). The Oregon section of the approximately 1,550-mile-long (2,500 kilometer) route between Los Angeles and Seattle is probably the most spectacular. Names such as Devil's Punchbowl and Cape Foulweather indicate how rough this coastline is. Huge monoliths, steep fjord-like bays, tree-covered sand dunes, and cliffs, as well as flat, inviting beaches, forests that reach down to the ocean, and wild, un-spoiled nature parks form an impressive backdrop along the Pacific Ocean that extends endlessly to the horizon. On the

edge of the universe—that's how you feel when you stand at one of the numerous scenic outlooks and gaze out over the ocean. Nutshell-sized fishing boats, but hardly any big ships, can be seen. The latter stay far away from the rugged, notorious coast. Several lighthouses warn seafarers in case of fog, darkness, and storms, but there are more than two hundred shipwrecks already "interred" along the coast.

If you come to the coast at the right time, you will witness an impressive natural spectacle: in early spring, whales migrate up to the north, to their summer home in Alaska, and they migrate south again in late autumn.

THE OREGON COAST AT ITS SCENIC BEST (*LEFT*). IT IS WILDLY ROMANTIC, ESPECIALLY AS THE SUN SETS ON HAYSTACK ROCK (*ABOVE*).

The stretch of coast between Northern California and Southern Oregon features underdeveloped redwood forests with fabulous giant trees up to 328 feet (100 meters) high and wild mountain rivers such as the Smith, Chetco, Pistol, Rogue, and Elk. The region is a paradise for water sports enthusiasts, who come here for rafting, kayaking, and canoeing, and also for anglers. Fly-fishing for salmon and steelheads, a migratory rainbow trout, is an especially popular pastime here.

IN THE BANANA BELT

Oregon's south coast is called the Banana Belt because of its tropical temperatures, but you will look for banana plants in vain. The region is the main producer of amaryllis bulbs. The warm temperatures are due to the so-called Brookings effect, a type of warm chinook wind that occurs particularly in autumn and winter, when winds from inland warm up over the coastal mountains. The region around the small, scenic port cities of Gold Beach and Brookings is also well known for a wide range of leisure activities, the abundance of salmon and oyster farms, and picturesque river valleys and dense coastal forests.

Between North Bend and Florence, nature itself is the undisputed main attraction: between the dense forests of the hinterland and the rocky Pacific Ocean coast, sand dunes rise up to 492 feet (150 meters) high. Some are protected as part of the Oregon Dunes National Recreation Area. In some regions, however, adventure is written in capital letters: dune riding takes you on a steep, up-and-down trip over the dunes at a fast pace in a dune buggy or ATV (quads)— open four-wheelers.

COASTAL ATTRACTIONS

In contrast, Florence, the City of Rhododendrons, with its lovingly restored Old Town and fishing port, is calm and tranquil. You can learn more about the coastal fauna in the Sea Lion Caves, about 12.4 miles (20 kilometers) north of Florence, where a sea lion colony makes its home in a sea-tossed grotto. Not far away, the Heceta Head Lighthouse highlights the curvy contours of the coast. Because of its fantastic location on the cliffs, it is rated as the most frequently photographed lighthouse in the United States and also functions as a bed-and-breakfast. The Oregon Coast Aquarium in Newport offers vivid and entertaining information about sea lions and other animals. In this unusual combination of aquarium, zoo, and park, sea otters, seals, and sea lions as well as all kinds of fish and sea birds cavort in modern habitats and aquariums. The small port town of Lincoln City is the central location on the northern coastline and especially popular because of its outlet shopping mall on Highway 101. In Tillamook, you will find excellent cheese and ice cream. Two cheese factories along the highway invite you for tastings: the small Blue Heron French Cheese Factory and the large Tillamook Cheese Factory. Finally, Bay City is a center of oyster farming; at Cannon Beach, the

IDYLLIC BAYS ARE INSPIRING IN THEIR BEAUTY, BUT THE WATER IS USUALLY TOO COLD FOR SWIMMING (BELOW). WHALE WATCHING AND WALKING ALONG THE BEACH; BEACHCOMBING IS POPULAR (RIGHT).

CHEERS!

An inconspicuous warehouse crouches under the mighty bridge that leads over the approach to Newport. This is the home of the Rogue Brewery, founded in 1988 and one of Oregon's best microbreweries. Brewmaster John Maier's beers have long been winning fame well beyond Oregon. In addition to its legendary Dead Guy Ale, the dark beers make the brewery famous. In addition to the Brew Pub in the brewery and another one at Newport Harbor, Rogue operates a number of restaurants across the United States, including in Portland and San Francisco. It also produces unusual whiskey, rum, and gin.

Rogue Brewery, 2320 OSU Dr., Newport, OR: www.rogue.com. Brewery and pub, plus restaurant and beer museum on the Historic Bay Front (748 SW Bay Blvd.).

MORE INFORMATION

http://visittheoregoncoast.com

rock pinnacles and mighty Haystack Rock, which lies in the Pacific right off the sandy beach, are an attraction for photographers.

THE LITTLE SAN FRANCISCO OF THE NORTHWEST

The city of Astoria is called the Little San Francisco of the Northwest for good reason. Anyone who has climbed its steep streets, passing lovingly restored Victorian houses up to the highest hill, Coxcomb Hill, will be reminded of San Francisco. From above, there is a spectacular view over the Columbia River estuary, and you can also see the wall paintings on the almost 131-foot-high (40 meter) Astoria Column, which was modeled on the Trajan Column in Rome.

In 1811, the place was the first permanent American settlement west of the Mississippi—more precisely as a fur-trading station—established by German-born trader John Jacob Astor. It lies in the delta of the Columbia River—the river, which forms the border between the states of Oregon and Washington, is still an important transport route and steeped in history. On November 7, 1805, the expedition led by US military officers Meriwether Lewis and William Clark finally reached the destination of their exploratory trip, the Pacific Ocean, after an arduous journey that took about a year and a half, traveling from St. Louis, Missouri. They were the first Americans to cross and explore the Northwest.

45 POETIC COWBOYS AND COWGIRLS—ELKO

A VISIT TO NEVADA'S BUCKAROO COUNTRY

About 7,000 visitors from all over North America flock to Elko in January to celebrate the American West and cowboy culture for six days at the National Cowboy Poetry Gathering. Replete with stories and songs, the festival is anything but a rambunctious Wild West event.

Outside the metropolitan areas of Reno and Las Vegas, the US state of Nevada consists primarily of vastness and wilderness, interspersed with ranches and gold, silver, and lithium mines. Here in the Great American West, the former homeland of the Paiute and Shoshone peoples, is where "living ghost towns," artists, miners, ranchers, and cowboys find a home.

COWBOY CULTURE IN ELKO

Northern Nevada is known as cowboy country, the home of the buckaroos. The term is derived from the Spanish word vaquero (cowboy); after all, it was Spanish Mexican settlers who started raising cattle here. There are still innumerable ranches in Nevada; many have been family-run businesses for generations, and they pride themselves on their traditions of the land—cattle, horses, and cowboys.

In the center of Buckaroo Country lies Elko, the region's main town of about 20,000 inhabitants. Elko's humble beginnings go back to the construction of the Transcontinental Railroad in 1868 and a camp at the Central Pacific Railroad stop. The town lies in the middle of the Great Basin, a barren,

ELKO, NEVADA, IS INEXTRICABLY LINKED WITH J. M. CAPRIOLA CO. (*BELOW*) AND THE NATIONAL COWBOY POETRY GATHERING, WITH PERFORMANCES AND TRADITIONAL CRAFTS (*BELOW RIGHT*). IT SITS IN THE MIDDLE OF THE GREAT BASIN (*ABOVE RIGHT*).

unpopulated high desert between the western foothills of the Rocky Mountains and the Sierra Nevada on the California border. The drainless Great Basin is crisscrossed by massive mountain ranges, such as the Ruby Mountains southeast of Elko, which are up to 11,155 feet (3,400 meters) high. In between lie valleys at an elevation of at least 3,900 feet (1,200 meters). Snow falls in winter, and summers are dry and hot.

The Western Folklife Center in the historic downtown Pioneer Building was established in 1980 to preserve the culture of the American West. Five years later, Hal Cannon, the first director of the cultural center, and local cowboy and poet Waddie Mitchell—still a driving force of the event—brought a meeting of cowboy poets to life. The Elko, as it was called at the beginning, was even declared a National Cowboy Poetry Gathering by a resolution of the US Senate in 2000. From a family get-together, it has long since developed into the granddaddy of 'em all, the biggest and most important cowboy culture event in North America. Those wishing to

participate must apply in writing and submit samples of their work. A committee reviews the registrations and mixes "oldies but goodies" with young talent. Many of the artists appear several times and in different combinations, and sometimes also in solo evening shows. During the three main days of the event, Thursday to Saturday, several events run simultaneously. Poetry, music, workshops, tours, cooking demonstrations, discussions, and lectures—it's not always easy to choose from the extensive program. Writing workshops for adults and young people are also offered, and poets such as Joel Nelson, Paul Zarzyski, and Randy Rieman take part in creative-writing courses at the local high school. During several open-mic events, young people and adults can gain stage experience by reciting their poems in front of an audience.

A FIRST-RATE POETRY SLAM

Everyone knows everyone else in Elko, despite the distances, and things are family-like. Artists and visitors meet at the long bar in the Pioneer Saloon or while shopping in the Mercantile, in front of the sales booths in the conference center, at Capriola's, or in the new Cowboy Arts & Gear Museum. Most artists are not full professionals but instead are cowboys or cowgirls, ranchers, rodeo cow-boys, or horse breeders or trainers with an artistic or musical bent. The fact that cowboys of all kinds take part—including African Americans and Native Americans, men and women, young and old—contributes to the broad range. Young, poetic cowgirls such as Annie Mackenzie, who hails from a ranch in eastern Oregon, sit on stage with Rod Nelson from North Dakota and other established stars of the scene. The humorous poems of "ranch wives" Patricia Frolander and Yvonne Hollenbeck regularly generate enthusi-asm, as does the creative work of Paul Zarzyski. He is considered the poetry slammer among the cowboy poets and is always a public favorite with his incomparable style of presentation and stage presence. However, there are also the

AS SOON AS THE SUN RISES OVER THE RUBY MOUNTAINS (*BELOW*), THE HORSES ARE SADDLED AND WORK BEGINS IN BUCKEROO COUNTRY (*ABOVE RIGHT*). YOU CAN FIND HANDMADE SADDLES AT CAPRIOLA CO. (*BELOW RIGHT*).

SHOPPING FOR COWBOYS AND COWGIRLS

J. M. Capriola Co. is more than a cowboy outfitter with some ranch supplies. On the upper floor, John Wright and his colleague Armando Delgado make saddles and leather goods. In 1894, the Mexican saddle maker G. S. Garcia, who specialized in the manufacture of silver bits, snaffles, and spurs, opened a shop on Elko's Main Street. In a roundabout way, it became Capriola, and this business is now owned by John and Susan Wright. Not only are they continuing the tradition, but they were responsible for opening the Cowboy Arts & Gear Museum in the neighboring former Garcia store in 2018.

J. M. Capriola Co.:
www.capriolas.com

Cowboy Arts & Gear Museum:
https://cowboyartsandgearmuseum.org

MORE INFORMATION
Information about NCPG:
www.nationalcowboypoetrygathering.org

Information about Elko:
www.exploreelko.com

thoughtful poets, such as Shadd Piehl, Joel Nelson, John Doffemyer, Randy Rieman, or the Crow Indian and rancher Henry Real Bird. In addition to everyday cowboy life, horses and cattle, the seasons, and nature, the themes of friendship and death, farewells, and change, as well as the everyday problems on a ranch, all are important topics.

TRADITIONAL WESTERN MUSIC
Plays on words on the one side; music on the other. Evening concerts in the Convention Center auditorium are popular, as are those in the smaller G Three Bar Theater in the Western Folklife Center. In addition, there are concerts and music workshops in the smaller halls at the conference center during the day, and spontaneous jam sessions are held in the legendary Pioneer Saloon, in the Western Folklife Center.

The musical spectrum is as broad as that of the poetry. Legends such as Riders in the Sky, Ramblin' Jack Elliott, Pipp Gillette, Mike Beck, or Michael Martin Murphy inspire the audience, as do "newbies" à la Andy Hedges, Adrian Buckaroogirl, or the Caleb Klauder Band. Cowboy Celtic from Canada stands out with a mixture of country and Celtic music (with harp!), along with out-of-the-ordinary musicians such as Dom Flemons and Brian Farrow from Washington, DC, who are reviving the music of the African American cowboys on banjo, bass, and guitar.

The performances of Wylie & the Wild West are among the highlights of the event. The horse breeder, trainer, and cutting cowboy Wylie Gustafson from Montana is a pleasure for both eyes and ears with his dancing and yodeling interludes. He represents an exciting mixture of cowboy and western music, traditional country and folk, rock 'n' roll and yodeling. In short, Wylie not only embodies pure western and cowboy music but also authentic cowboy culture as it is cultivated with great devotion in Elko.

STONE TOWERS AND NEEDLES, BATTLEMENTS AND ROCK WALLS (*BELOW RIGHT*)—BRYCE CANYON (*ABOVE*) IS KNOWN FOR ITS HORSE-SHOE-SHAPED AMPHITHEATER. TRIPS ON HORSEBACK THROUGH THE PARK ARE AVAILABLE FROM BRYCE CANYON CITY (*ABOVE RIGHT*).

46 INSIDE THE LABYRINTH—BRYCE CANYON NATIONAL PARK

A SPECIAL KIND OF AMPHITHEATER

There is no better place to study the forces of natural erosion than in Utah's Bryce Canyon National Park. Its strange stone towers, peaks, battlements, and rock walls are simply fascinating. Bryce Canyon is certainly one of the most beautiful destinations in the Southwest.

Wind and water have created a labyrinth of staggered, almost unreal-appearing towers and peaks, rugged edges, pinnacles, and folds that glow in the most-varied tones of yellow, red, and brown in the sunlight. If you approach Bryce Canyon from the west, the route initially runs through a rather "ordinary" mountain forest region at an elevation of 7,874 to 9,186 feet (2,400–2,800 meters). Suddenly the green thins out and an escarpment appears. If you stand here on the edge of the Paunsaugunt Plateau and look down some 1,969 steep feet (600 meters) into the Paria Valley, the view takes your breath away.

LANDSCAPE OF LEGENDS

Most visitors enjoy the sight of the stone theatrical scenery from one of the many parking lots and scenic outlooks along 18.6-mile-long (30 kilometer) Scenic Drive, a straight road that leads into the national park. The sunrise at Sunrise Point is an absolute highlight; its counterpart is the sunset at Sunset Point. Both natural spectacles make the legend of the Paiute people believable: it was here that Coyote, a cunning wizard and holy clown, is said to have turned villains into rocks. You can still see their faces, according to Native American Dick, a tribal elder, who in 1936 told a ranger that the figures were said to be painted exactly as they appeared the moment they were turned to stone.

CLEAR THE STAGE!

The horseshoe-shaped Bryce Amphitheater is the undisputed main attraction of the 90-square-mile (145 square kilometer) national park. Some fourteen so-called amphitheaters, semicircular formations that look like ancient theaters built into the slope, are clustered here on 9.3 square miles (15 square kilometers). It is possible to trace the impact of the forces of erosion and temperature fluctuations on these natural theater stages. After all, the region is free of snow for only a few months a year and is exposed to the widest possible climatic fluctuations: while the sun burns down mercilessly in summer and heats the area up to 104 degrees Fahrenheit (40 degrees Celsius), in winter the snow piles up on pinnacles and peaks. Water split the rocks as it froze and thawed and shaped them; heavy rains washed away whole pieces of rock. These processes are still going on, and it is assumed that within half a century the escarpment will slide half a meter farther into the high plateau.

LOUSY PLACE TO LOSE A COW

The Paiute had long been impressed by this natural wonder and spoke of a place "where red rocks stand like people in a bowl." The first white settlers, however, formulated their opinion less poetically. Thus, the Mormon Ebenezer Bryce, a nineteenth-century ranch owner and the man for whom the park is named, wrote of a "lousy place if you lose a cow in it." Admittedly, finding cattle in the tangle of canyons and cliffs may be difficult, but Bryce Canyon is a delightful challenge for hikers or riders. For a more detailed picture, venture into the winding world of pinnacles, folds, and canyons in this rugged natural wonder. There is a wide range of hiking and riding trails on which to do this. One of the easiest and most frequented is the approximately 3-mile-long (5 kilometer) Navajo Loop Trail, which leads from the parking lot at Sunrise Point down into the maze of rocks in the Bryce Amphitheater, past Thor's Hammer and back again, traversing an elevation difference of 525 feet (160 meters).

RUBY'S INN BECOMES A TOWN

It all started in 1916. Back then, Reuben C. "Ruby" Syrett, with some foresight, built a lodge and a few cabins on the edge of Bryce Canyon. When the national park was founded in 1928, he was able to harvest the first fruits in Ruby's Inn, which grew slowly into a supply station at the park entrance. In the years since, the third generation of Syretts has expanded the infrastructure by building the highly recommended Bryce Canyon Grand Hotel and Old Bryce Town (retail stores). The village has been called Bryce Canyon City since 2007; almost two hundred residents live here permanently, and mayor Shiloh Syrett comes from the founding father's family.

MORE INFORMATION

Bryce Canyon National Park:
www.nps.gov/brca

Bryce Canyon City, Garfield County:
www.brycecanyoncountry.com

Bryce Canyon Grand Hotel:
www.brycecanyongrand.com

A PROTECTED NATURAL MONUMENT SINCE 1911: THE COLORADO NATIONAL MONUMENT (*BELOW*) WITH IMPRESSIVE RED-ROCK NEEDLES (*TOP RIGHT*). THE REGION IS ALSO KNOWN FOR WINE (*BOTTOM RIGHT*).

47 THE "HEART OF THE WORLD"— COLORADO NATIONAL MONUMENT

A UNIQUE NATURAL LANDMARK IN WESTERN COLORADO

When John Otto (1870–1952) saw the Grand Valley in western Colorado in 1906, he was amazed by its beauty. He explored the canyons and mountains and rhapsodized, "For me this is the heart of the world." It was also Otto who campaigned for the area to be designated as a nature reserve.

With a lot of perseverance, John Otto succeeded in convincing the authorities and the public, and in 1911 the land was made a protected reserve as the Colorado National Monument. He was the first park ranger to be hired. Today the nature reserve is the main attraction in western Colorado, although it is still one of the lesser-known natural landmarks in the western United States.

RED-GREEN-WHITE—ROCK, NATURE, AND MOUNTAINS

The plateau, around 4,590 feet (1,400 meters) above sea level, captivates visitors with its bright sandstone formations, which have a color palette ranging from orange to red and purple to brown. For millions of years, the forces of nature have worked on the red sandstone of the Colorado National Monument and created deep canyons, steep rock faces, and curious sandstone sculptures.

THE BEST PEACHES AND BEST WINES

One of the top wineries in the Grand Valley is Colterris (www.colterris.com), whose owners, Scott and Theresa High, also manage High Country Orchards. Their peaches have such a good reputation that even the Obamas came to pick them. The wines are "100 percent estate grown" and made from Colorado's own grapes, and a strict distinction is made according to location. The winery's flagship products are its Malbec, the cabernet sauvignon, and a white cabernet sauvignon—this variety was first developed here.

Red Fox Cellars (www.redfoxcellars.com) is another winery in Palisade. It became known for wines that are sometimes aged in old bourbon barrels. The ciders made here in different flavors are also something special.

MORE INFORMATION

www.visitgrandjunction.com

Colorado National Monument: www.nps.gov/colm

Overnight accommodations: SpringHill Suites Grand Junction Downtown, www.marriott.com

The plateau builds up suddenly, 1,969 feet (600 meters) above the Grand Valley. It is densely overgrown with pine and juniper trees and is home to a large number of wild animals. Rim Rock Drive, which winds about 18.6 miles (30 kilometers) through the park in narrow sweeps, is like a lesson in geology and biology. You get to know the different climate zones of the Colorado plateau—from desert to high alpine regions—with their corresponding flora and fauna. There are always new dramatic views of the red rock formations from the scenic outlooks along the road. These rocks are an impressive contrast to the snow-capped Bookcliff Mountains in the background and the Grand Valley at your feet.

PEACHES AND LIQUOR

In the Grand Valley, originally inhabited by the Ute Indians, the Gunnison River flows into the Colorado River. The area is known not only for its variety of outdoor activities, which range from mountain biking and hiking to whitewater rafting and fishing, but also for its culinary diversity. In the late nineteenth century, the region comprising the villages of Grand Junction, Fruita, and Palisade developed into the leading fruit-growing region in western Colorado. Mainly plums and grapes wbut also cherries and other fruits are grown here, and wineries, schnapps distilleries, and breweries nestle among the orchards. Grand Junction lies in the center of the great valley. The small city—called GJ or the Junction for short—has around 60,000 inhabitants and a pretty city center with a traffic-calmed Main Street, lined with nice shops, bars, and works of art. The village of Palisade, a few miles east, is known as the Peaches & Wine Capital of Colorado. If you follow the Palisade Fruit & Wine Byway, you will find farms, orchards, and wineries and, in summer, roadside fruit stands. Palisade is also home to the Palisade Brewing Company and Peach Street Distillers, famous for their Jackelope Gin and Goat Vodka. Other high-proof products, distilled from produce from local farms, have also been added to the offerings. The Sprigs & Sprouts Lavender Farm is another example of the region's diversity. The farm offers its own lavender products, as well as lettuce and herbs from its aquaponic greenhouses. Suncrest Orchard Alpacas & Fiber Works specializes in alpaca wool and products. After a tour, you can visit the shop and feel how soft alpaca wool is and how it is especially suitable for allergy sufferers.

NEW ORLEANS IS NO TYPICAL US METROPOLIS. HERE THE MUSIC PLAYS ON EVERY STREET CORNER (*ABOVE*) AND THE MOTTO "LAISSEZ LES BONS TEMPS ROULER" (LET THE GOOD TIMES ROLL) (*RIGHT*) APPLIES ALL THE TIME.

48 LET THE GOOD TIMES ROLL!— NEW ORLEANS

THE BIG EASY HASN'T BEEN DEFEATED IN 300 YEARS

New Orleans has never been a typical American metropolis: climate and geography, architecture, cuisine, language and music, hippies and dropouts, eccentrics and artists, Cajuns and Creoles, unusual cemeteries and voodoo—the Big Easy is unique in every way.

May 7 is given as its unofficial founding date. However, no one knows exactly on which spring day in 1718 French nobleman Jean-Baptiste Le Moyne de Bienville laid the foundation stone for La Nouvelle-Orléans at a bend in the Mississippi on behalf of the royal Compagnie du Mississippi.

New Orleans is proud of its three-hundred-year history, marked by ups and downs such as the devastating flood disaster after Hurricane Katrina in August–September 2005. The "Old Lady on the Mississippi" has been through a lot—changing leaders, natural disasters, and fires—but it has never let itself be crushed. In 1762, to keep it out of British

hands, the French royal family handed the city to their Spanish relatives without much ado. By 1800 it was once again in French possession, but Napoleon sold all of the French lands on the western side of the Mississippi, together with New Orleans, to the United States three years later.

LIFE IS EASIER WITH A COCKTAIL

By the eighteenth century, colorful people were arriving in NOLA, as the locals call New Orleans: minor French noblemen, farmers from Germany, immigrants from the Canary Islands, traders from the Caribbean, local Native Americans and freed slaves, expelled French Canadians, Irish, and British. A casual attitude, tolerance, and eccentricity—all under the motto "Laissez les bon temps rouler," or "Let the good times roll"—are important character traits of the local people. With a sazerac, a hurricane, or a mint julep cocktail in your glass and a po' boy, a muffuletta, oysters, or jambalaya on your plate, you can live well. A jazz band on the next street corner provides entertainment, and a music or food festival is never far away. With these possibilities, who cares if the public transportation system doesn't appear to operate on any fixed timetable and the way to get air-conditioning in the legendary green street-cars that cross the Garden District along St. Charles Avenue is by opening the windows.

OLD AND NEW

Most visitors still crowd into the streets of the French Quarter—Bourbon Street attracts tourists with its bars and cheap drinks, while Royal Street features galleries and shops. Around central Jackson Square, with its dominating cathedral, artists offer their works and fortune-tellers their talents, and musicians give free concerts. Things are quieter in the green streets "upriver," west of the Old Town, in the Garden District. Wealthy Americans who moved here in the nineteenth century built splendid villas here, and the atmosphere is completely different.

In the meantime, more and more attractive new neighborhoods are emerging. For example, the former warehouse district on the other side of central Canal Street is developing into a desirable residential area with popular restaurants. Farther upriver, in the Lower Garden District, Magazine Street attracts visitors as a "mile" for strolling, with unusual shops and pretty cafés and bars. Other trendy areas are central city near St. Charles Street or midcity at the intersection of Canal Street and Carrollton Avenue. If you want to immerse yourself in the legendary nightlife of New Orleans, stroll down Frenchmen Street in the Faubourg Marigny, just a few steps downriver from the French Quarter. Music of all styles booms here from the hip music bars until the early hours of the morning.

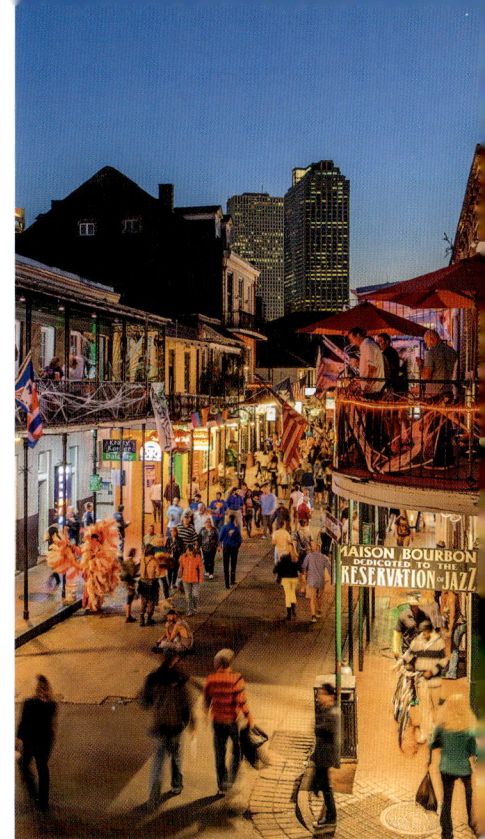

NOLA—A CITY FULL OF MUSIC

In Faubourg Marigny, a stone's throw from the French Quarter, is the Louisiana Music Factory (www.louisianamusicfactory.com). This long-established music shop offers information on hip clubs and concerts, T-shirts, and posters, but above all a huge selection of CDs and LPs and listening stations. The focus is on music from NOLA and Louisiana, from jazz to brass bands to swamp rock, blues, Cajun, and zydeco. The small but fine Brieux Carré Brewing Company is just around the corner (www.brieuxcarre.com). For staying overnight in New Orleans, we recommend the chic Jung Hotel (www.junghotel.com) on Canal Street.

MORE INFORMATION

www.neworleans.com

WHERE MEN BECOME GODS— TEOTIHUACÁN

THE THIRD-LARGEST PYRAMID IN THE WORLD

The pyramids of Teotihuacán lie north of Mexico City and are simply breathtaking. They bear up to a comparison with the famous pyramids of Giza.

THE SUN PYRAMID OF TEOTIHUACÁN IS ONE OF THE LARGEST PYRAMIDS IN THE WORLD (*BELOW*). MYSTERIOUS BEINGS ADORN THE PYRAMID OF THE DEITY QUETZALCOATL (*ABOVE RIGHT*). THE PERFORMANCES AND DANCERS IN TRADITIONAL COSTUMES ARE MEMORABLE (*BELOW RIGHT*).

Your T-shirt sticks to your soaking-wet skin. The thermometer shows only 72 degrees Fahrenheit (22 degrees Celsius), but it feels 10 degrees hotter. It's hazy, but the sun burns down mercilessly. Then there is the high elevation: breathing becomes more difficult at 7,500 feet (2,300 meters). Teotihuacán—which means "where people become gods" in Aztec—was once a city with 200,000 inhabitants and is not easy to explore, especially if you want to climb high up and scale its core structure: the 213-foot-high (65 meter) pyramid with its five mighty steps and countless steep stairs.

A STRUCTURE OF SUPERLATIVES

In terms of volume, this is the largest pyramid in the world after Giza in Egypt and Cholula near Puebla. It was built using 2 million tons of stone and earth. When you get up to the top, you don't think about your wet shirt or your short breath anymore. You are overwhelmed: the view of this city, which was laid out according to astronomical principles, is one of the most impressive outlooks over an ancient site that our world has to offer.

There are more temples and pyramids along the 2.5-mile-long (4 kilometer) Road of the Dead, which runs from the south past the

PYRAMIDS AND PISTOLS

Mexico recorded 39 million tourists in 2017—more than Thailand (37 million) and Germany (35 million)—and was surpassed only by France (92 million), the United States (78 million), Spain (75 million), Italy (61 million), China (59 million), and Great Britain (42 million). Yet, the responsible authorities simply failed to provide one thing in their rose-colored view of their 187 archeological zones, 182 national parks, and thirty-four UNESCO World Heritage Sites: security warnings. However, the Federal Ministry of Foreign Affairs has published them and warns travelers to be careful, such as in the evening in Cancún, on the Acapulco coast, and on the trip to Teotihuacán. Hence the advice to visit the pyramids only in an organized group.

MORE INFORMATION

A passport is sufficient for entry. You can usually pay in US dollars. Most of the rain falls from May to September.
www.visitmexico.com

Pyramid of the Sun to the north and the slightly smaller Pyramid of the Moon. "We don't know anything about the builders," says a tourist guide. "The Aztecs chose the names and thought the pyramids were royal tombs. When they came, Teotihuacán had already been deserted for around seven hundred years."

ONE OF THE LARGEST CITIES IN THE WORLD

On the basis of the excavations that have been ongoing since 1900 and have not yet been completed, scientists are assuming that Teotihuacán must have been the most powerful city in Central America during the first 650 years of our era—and one of the largest cities in the world. The area is estimated at 12.4 square miles (20 square kilometers). There was a residential area with multiroom apartment houses for the lower classes and, separated by high walls, a residential area for the upper classes. Of course, there were also temples and places of sacrifice as well as graves. At the south entrance, the small museum at parking lot 1 presents timetables and exhibits to provide visitors with a good overview of the entire

area, which has been a UNESCO World Heritage Site since 1987. It is assumed that Teotihuacán had existed since the year 100, which is around 2,600 years younger than the pyramids of Giza in Egypt. But there is also the thesis that there could have been an Age of Pyramids in the world's high cultures. And it is possible to note some parallels, such as the layout and number of the pyramids.

DETOUR TO TULA

Unfortunately, the way from Mexico City to Teotihuacán is just as arduous as the climb up the Pyramid of the Sun. It sometimes takes two or three hours to travel 31 miles (50 kilometers) from the city center. But every minute you spend in a traffic jam is worth it. Especially since there is another excavation site well worth seeing, only about 12.4 miles (20 kilometers) away from Teotihuacán, which is mostly free of traffic jams. This is Tula, the cultural center of the Toltecs, with its almost 16-foot-tall (5 meter) warrior statues. These imposing Atlases crown the Pyramid of the Morning Star. Two of the colossal statues are, however, reproductions; you can admire the originals in peace in the National Museum in Mexico City.

BELIZE IS FAMOUS FOR ITS FANTASTIC BEACHES AND RAINFOREST (*ABOVE*), A HUGE, INTACT CORAL REEF (*BOTTOM RIGHT*), AND RELAXED ATMOSPHERE—EVEN THE JAGUARS TAKE IT EASY (*ABOVE RIGHT*).

50 TROPICAL RELAXATION—BELIZE

AT THE GREAT BLUE HOLE

Belize offers fantastic beaches and impressive Mayan ruins, tiny islands and vast coral reefs, and a delightful mix of Asian, European, and South and Central American cuisines. The people are friendly, and (petty) crime is kept within limits.

The time has finally come! A question that has been burning since childhood needs a plausible explanation: "Why are bananas curved?" It will be answered in Belize, a real banana republic, where more than 70 million tons of bananas are harvested each year. Banana plantation guide Daniel was just waiting for this question. He laughs! "It grows straight down at first," he explains. "Only later does it seek the sun. And for that the fruit just has to grow in a curve." Politically, Belize is anything but a banana republic. The only country in Latin America in which English is the state language and Queen Elizabeth II is still formally the head of state, it has a constitutional monarchy as its form of government and is part of the Commonwealth.

(NOT) A BANANA REPUBLIC

Otherwise, the former British Honduras (until its independence in 1981) is a country with African roots and a melting pot of cultures. The Maya people have also left their traces behind; these are best seen in Lamanai and Xunantunich. The city ruins of Lamanai, in particular, have a mystical atmosphere, especially toward late afternoon, when the tourists disperse and howler monkeys outnumber people.

A WORK OF ART BY NATURE

Belize has abundant rainforest and a tropical climate. This is why the rainy season is much longer than the dry season from February to May. In fact, the rainy season doesn't mean that it rains continuously from morning to evening. The people are helpful, interested, and relaxed. Belize is probably the safest country in Central America after Costa Rica. Nevertheless—as almost everywhere—it isn't a good idea to display valuables. Traveling individually and renting a car is no problem. Prices in general are low. The country's biggest sensation is the Great Blue Hole: this marine sinkhole has a 984-foot (300-meter) diameter and lies in the middle of the sea, right in front of the second-largest barrier reef in the world. In theory, even a large cruise ship could anchor in it! From the air, this UNESCO World Heritage Site looks like a contemporary work of art: its round, royal blue surface is surrounded by light-turquoise water. The play of colors arises because an underwater cave collapsed 12,000 years ago at this spot, 43.5 miles (70 kilometers) from the coast, and therefore deeper and shallower waters meet here. In any case, the only way to get a perfect view of the almost circular hole is from the air. Flights in small propeller planes are available on a regular basis.

ISLAND DREAMS

The Belize Barrier Reef is the largest in the world after Australia's Great Barrier Reef. It is a good 155 miles (250 kilometers) long and stretches from the north, from the Mexican Yucatán Peninsula and the island of Cozumel, along the entire coast of Belize to Honduras. Here you will find beautiful islands with wonderful palm trees, powdered sugar-like sand on the beaches, spectacular bright-blue water, and a largely intact underwater world. The corals are still colorful, even though Belize has not been spared from coral bleaching. If you snorkel there, you are almost guaranteed to see large turtles, manta rays, and sharks.

An amazing phenomenon can also be observed at the Jaguar Reef: bioluminescence. This term describes the ability of living beings to generate light, by themselves or with the help of symbionts. Fireflies are the best example of this.

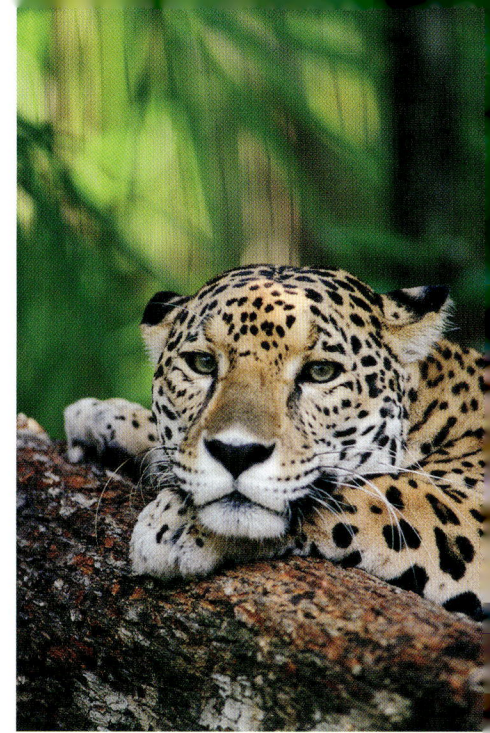

A NIGHT IN A TREE HOUSE

Anyone who thinks that the night in the jungle is very quiet is greatly mistaken. Things whistle, bubble, crackle; there are noises that have never been heard before—constant, piercing, and sometimes a little scary. And when there are howler monkeys around, it gets really loud. Nevertheless, you should treat yourself to at least one night in a Belize tree house! Some of the tree houses, mostly built on stilts, offer the luxury of an outdoor shower; others don't even have windows, but there are always mosquito nets. And if there is no net, insist on one. Otherwise you can forget having a restful night. There are many options available, but the prices are higher than they are for staying overnight on the ground. Good tree house accommodations cost around $100 per night.

MORE INFORMATION

To protect against malaria and dengue fever, wear long clothes in the evening, sleep under the net, and bring mosquito repellent! www.travelbelize.org

DENSE RAINFOREST COVERS THE PUNTA
GORDA REGION IN BELIZE.

WHERE COLUMBUS ONCE LANDED—ISLA ROATÁN

BELOVED BY CRUISE SHIPS

The crime rate is very high in mainland Honduras. The situation on the island of Roatán, which is part of Honduras, is very different. Cruise ships call at the main town of Coxen Hole almost every day and ensure the safety of their guests.

BOATS AWAIT GUESTS AT TABYANA BEACH (*BELOW*); **DIVING WITH DOLPHINS IS A SPECIAL EXPERIENCE** (*ABOVE RIGHT*). **LIONFISH ARE AN INVASIVE SPECIES IN THE CARIBBEAN AND ARE CONSIDERED POISONOUS PESTS** (*BOTTOM RIGHT*).

Columbus discovered Roatán in the Caribbean a good five hundred years ago, but—for many—this island off the Central American coast is still something of a secret. For most people, Roatán, with an area of around 52 square miles (83 square kilometers), is simply a blank slate. This also applies to the small cays east of the island: Morat, Barbaretta, Pigeon, and Barefoot Cay. On a clear day you can see the more distant neighboring islands of Útila in the west and Guanaja in the east. When it comes to the Caribbean, postcard images come to mind of palm trees, sand beaches, and a turquoise-blue sea. All of this is true of Roatán, in places such as West Bay. In addition, there are the parrots up in the trees, loudly drawing attention to themselves, and the hummingbirds, which flaps their wings so fast that they can hover in one place. And the interior of the island has dense jungle and hiking for nature lovers. The mountain ridge, covered by tropical vegetation, ultimately shapes the profile of the island. "Green, green, so much green," Columbus is said to have exclaimed enthusiastically. The largest natural

THROUGH THE BLUE SEA IN A BLUE HULL

Most guests visit Roatán Island for the first time during a cruise—and this inspires guests to come back, wanting to discover more of this little gem of an island. Cruises are available that dock in various must-see Central American locations, such as Roatán, Cozumel, Costa Rica, and Panama.

MORE INFORMATION

Be sure to bring good mosquito repellent and sun protection. People speak Spanish and English.
http://tourismroatan.com

treasure of the island, however, lies out to sea: the large coral reef that is surpassed in size worldwide only by the Australian Great Barrier Reef. Divers love the warm, crystal-clear water; the large variety of corals; and the spectacularly colored walls, small canyons, and caves. Your diving experience is complemented by the presence of mighty bass, moray eels, turtles, rays, and also whale sharks in the spring months.

CALM IS RESTORED IN THE EVENING

Hectic activity prevails in Coxen Hole once again. Two ocean liners have docked at the same time. The island has to deal with up to 5,000 visitors on the absolute peak days. Most of them, however, have booked their shore excursion in orderly fashion, so that the crowd is distributed in a fairly controlled way across the island. This is the disadvantage of Roatán: if there are any cruise ships moored in Coxen Hole, you can kiss solitude goodbye while the ships are docked from 9:00 a.m. to 5:00 p.m. Yet, as soon as they have cast off again, the cozy island atmosphere returns.

Crime is not a foreign word on Roatán, 40 miles (65 kilometers) from the mainland, but it is manageable. Even the taxi drivers are good fellows. Haggling is not necessary because the authorities set the fares.

ORDERLY TRAFFIC

The main street, lined with wooden houses, is busy today. The bars pour streams of beer, the souvenir stands offer everything handmade, and the policeman regulates the traffic and makes sure that the moped drivers don't use the many pedestrians as slalom poles. After all, there are now around 250,000 visitors a year, the majority of them cruise passengers who don't stay overnight. Only one-fifth of that number of people actually live on the island. They originally came from the Caribbean island of St. Vincent and were resettled on Roatán by the British, then the colonial rulers, at the end of the eighteenth century. A few come from Caracol and the Cayman Islands. Honduras has been independent since 1821; the last colonial power was Spain.

52 NICARAGUA'S PEARLS OF THE CARIBBEAN—THE CORN ISLANDS

BIG CORN & LITTLE CORN

One big, one small—the Corn Islands are Nicaragua's Caribbean dream in duplicate. Big Corn Island and Little Corn Island are two beautiful partner islands, although no one grows corn here any more. But you can see palm trees, beaches, and a sea of flowers.

A few centuries have passed since the islands served as pirates' nests. This is where the notorious bands hid out and procured provisions. Today travelers are looking for other kinds of treasure: the beaches, diving and snorkeling areas in the crystal-clear water, the easygoing Caribbean lifestyle, and freshly caught lobster at a beach restaurant in the evening. The Caribbean Sea bobs up in down in colors ranging between turquoise and light green, spanned by an endless blue sky. Just as you imagined it would be in a fantasy world. And for once, here is proof that reality measures up to mental images—and even surpasses them.

Together, the islands cover an area of just 8 square miles (13 square kilometers). Big Corn Island is densely populated, and it is estimated that 13,000 people are now clustered there; Little Corn Island has only a fraction of that number. Fishing and tourism are important sources of income. There are accommodations for every budget on both islands, be it in hotels or hostels.

FAR FROM THE MAINSTREAM

Since the Corn Islands were a British protectorate until the end of the nineteenth century and then were leased by the United States for some time afterward, their English

ON A BIKE TOUR YOU CAN FIND THE MOST BEAUTIFUL SPOTS ON BIG CORN ISLAND (*LEFT*); THE SUNSET IS ALMOST TOO BEAUTIFUL TO BE REAL (*ABOVE*).

167

A RAY HOVERS OVER THE CORALS LIKE A CREATURE FROM ANOTHER WORLD (*BELOW*). BEACHES INVITE YOU TO LINGER (*ABOVE RIGHT*), AND COLORFUL HUTS PROVIDE A POP OF COLOR BETWEEN BANANA PLANTS (*BOTTOM RIGHT*).

name is still more common today than the Spanish Islas del Maíz. Corn crops used to be widespread here; hardly any remain, but the soil is as fertile and rich as ever. The typical abundant vegetation includes banana groves, mango trees and coconut palms, bougainvilleas and hibiscus bushes—a fantastic rush of colors. In many places the locals' painted houses—orange, purple, lemon yellow—make

their contribution. The Corn Islands are somewhat remote. From the nearest mainland town, Bluefields, the crossing can be made by boat, which requires a tough stomach, but the most common way to get there is the almost one-hour flight by propeller plane from Nicaragua's capital, Managua. The runway on Big Corn Island takes up a significant part of the northwestern part of the island. Little Corn Island is 7 nautical miles away and can be approached by sea only from the larger island.

BY BIKE ON BIG CORN ISLAND

On Big Corn Island, where taxis operate at moderate prices, a round trip by rental bike is recommended. If you are in a hurry and pedal hard, you can circle the island in less than an hour. But who's in a hurry here? The Caribbean stands for a special feeling of nonchalance that is contagious. The locals' everyday accommodations can be seen everywhere and reinforce this vibe: a hammock and a rocking chair. Rental-bike provider Frankie Campbell is in his forties, was born on the island, and is already a grandfather. He lives not far from the runway, next to a huge mango tree, and is happy to give visitors good tips for exploring the island. He also confirms: "We live here peacefully." There is no crime.

The most beautiful island beach is at South West Bay; the crescent-shaped strip of sand spreads out about 0.6 miles (1 kilometer) long. A loop tour of the island by bike takes you right through its everyday life. Hibiscus hedges with colorful flowers surround outhouses next to banana trees; women are scrubbing on washboards, and families are out and about under their parasols. Strangers are greeted warmly everywhere. The "highlands" are hardly worth mentioning, and on long sections of the roads you are at sea level. Evidence of history and culture is in short supply, apart from churches of various faiths, cemeteries, and

WELL BEDDED

Arenas Beach Hotel offers attractive accommodations on the southwest part of Big Corn Island. A dead-end street with little traffic separates the facility from South West Bay. This is an easy and safe way to get into the water, and you can walk or jog on the beach. The hotel does not meet luxury standards, but there is a choice of eleven comfortable rooms in the main building, all with a balcony, and twenty additional rooms spread out among bungalows with hammocks and communal terrace areas. Families with children can have a wonderful vacation here. All rooms and bungalows have air-conditioning. There is drop-off and pickup service to the nearby airport. A pleasant beach restaurant is connected to the hotel, where you can have breakfast or sit and enjoy the views.

MORE INFORMATION

"Live your dream on Big Corn Island," as it says on the Arenas Beach hotel home page— the photos are confirmation. https://arenasbeachhotel.com

remnants of the so-called slave wall in the northeast of the island. Slavery was abolished in the mid-nineteenth century, and this is commemorated on August 27 every year. A particularly beautiful stretch of road leads along the sea near Sally Peachie and then to the Catholic church and school, before coming full circle to Frankie's bike rental.

DISCOVERIES ON FOOT ON LITTLE CORN

Little Corn Island, its neighbor island lying within sight and accessible by scheduled or private boat from Big Corn Island, is traffic- and road-free. There is nothing else to be done here, except to move away from the main town, simply called the village, on foot. One route takes you past swampy areas in the east to lonely Kelly Gully Beach. It's not one of those dream beaches like you find in

the catalog, but that doesn't matter. From there, walk farther north around the palm-fringed coastline, along more stretches of beach, and over the heights back toward the village. Lizards scurry across the path. Dragonflies dance in the sun. Hibiscus grows like weeds. Reggae sounds drift from huts at the edge of the urban center. There are overnight accommodations, simple restaurants and bars, and a school.

HARD TO SAY FAREWELL

It is hard to say farewell to the islands. First Little Corn Island becomes a blur from the back of the boat. Then it's off to the tiny Big Corn Island airport, where luggage is handled by hand and a sign in the check-in hall declares that Jesus is Lord of the island.

LONELY ARCHIPELAGO IN LAKE NICARAGUA—SOLENTINAME

ISLANDS FULL OF PEACE AND TRANQUILITY

To get to the Solentiname archipelago in Lake Nicaragua, you first travel by land for hours to the small town of San Carlos, near the border with Costa Rica, and then continue by boat. You are rewarded for all the effort by these peaceful and tranquil islands, where nature is beautiful and people are friendly.

THE ISLAND LOOKS PARTICULARLY PEACEFUL AT SUNSET (BELOW) AS THE GLOWING COLORS OF BOATS (*ABOVE RIGHT*) AND CARVINGS BLEND INTO EACH OTHER; COLORFUL MACAWS ADD TO THE EFFECT (*BELOW RIGHT*).

The Solentiname archipelago is a peaceful idyll. Except for the fact that the archipelago is located in the vast Lake Nicaragua, it has nothing in common with Ometepe and the Isletas de Granada—these islands are easily accessible and therefore more frequented. Solentiname, on the other hand, is a tourist sideshow. And that's good. Anyone who comes here presses the "off" button.

REMOTE AND IDYLLIC

Solentiname is a remote archipelago, comprising thirty-six islands and islets. If you calculate all the land areas together, you come up with about 25 square miles (40 square kilometers). About a thousand people live on this archipelago. During the boat trip from San Carlos, cormorants and pelicans, fishing boats, and herons appear. Then the first wooded miniridges of the widely scattered archipelago emerge more clearly.

OLD PIRATES' RIVER—THE RÍO SAN JUAN

The pleasant little town of San Carlos is more than just the stepping-stone to the Solentiname Islands. Scheduled boats also run eastward on the Río San Juan, which flows out from Lake Nicaragua just before the San Carlos promenade. Pirates from the Caribbean once crossed the river to reach Lake Nicaragua and attacked Granada, a rich Spanish colonial city on the northwestern edge of the vast waters. When people became aware of the danger, fortifications were built in the area of the Río San Juan. The Castillo de la Inmaculada Concepción de María, built in 1675, is particularly impressive. The fortress towers over the town of El Castillo, which is connected to the riverboat network. El Castillo also features river rapids.

MORE INFORMATION

Nicaragua's official website is a good source of information and has many photos. www.visitanicaragua.com

One of the islands where travelers find overnight accommodation is Mancarrón. No car engine noise disturbs the silence, because there are no roads—and therefore no pollution and no traffic. Instead, there are chirping birds. Hummingbirds buzz over flowers and dip in their long beaks.

Here you can see the hanging nests made by Montezuma oropendola birds. There are huge trees covered with epiphytes; a light breeze passes through the papaya bushes. In the 1960s, Nicaraguan priest and poet Ernesto Cardenal founded a Christian community here, and the church and a small library still exist. Iguanas rustle in the nearby bushes. Somewhere in the background a rooster crows.

BALSA WOOD CARVINGS

A concrete path runs past simple houses, overflowing greenery, giant bamboo, banana trees, and bougainvilleas. The path ends at the island school, from which happy children in uniform emerge. Islanders who get sick go to the tiny health center; the nearest hospital is on the mainland in San Carlos. Conventional electricity? No such luck. Generators or solar modules provide electricity, which also powers television and the internet. The friendly people here do not live entirely cut off from the world. The sign in front of a shop says: "Top up your cellphone calling card here." Balsa wood carvings are on offer too. The designs are mainly birds painted in bright colors that reflect the surrounding nature—green, red, yellow, turquoise. Tourism is a moderate source of income; otherwise people fish and farm. There are cornfields and plots of beans.

PARADISAICAL ATMOSPHERE

San Fernando is another island where nature has poured out its cornucopia. Water turtles slide off stones. Hibiscus hedges create bright splashes of color. Mango trees whet your appetite for the juicy fruit. A trail runs across the green heights of the island, over a root system and through a cattle pasture to a boulder with petroglyphs; the spiral pattern could represent a stylized figure. Leaf cutter ants are working busily in their columns. Butterflies dance over grass. Along the way to the nearby scenic outlook, small waves are lapping on the lakeshore. This is paradise; you don't ever want to leave!

54 PURE CARIBBEAN FEELING— TORTUGUERO

WHEN A CROCODILE HAS SEX . . .

. . . it's impossible for visitors not to take notice! Costa Rica's coast along the Caribbean Sea is 132 miles (212 kilometers) long. Two-thirds of it is inaccessible, but the rest packs a punch! You can probably see more animals in Tortuguero National Park than anywhere else in Costa Rica, which is rich in animal life.

What were things like years ago? "We used to get water from the well, wash our laundry by hand, and live without the internet or cell phones. I've been in Tortuguero for twenty-three years," adds Barbara Hartung. She studied biology in Tübingen, Germany, and São Paulo, Brazil, specializing in zoology and rainforest biodiversity. Of course it sounds a bit wistful, because now Tortuguero has water mains, washing machines, the internet, and cell phones here in the swampy forest with innumerable water channels and lagoons, which encircles a large part of the coastal town. But there are no connections or roads anywhere. Not even a dusty runway. Tortuguero, in the northern part of the Costa Rican Caribbean, can be reached only by boat or bush plane. "And to be honest, we also don't want a road link, because this would endanger the park and the ecological system," says the head of the Tortuguero National Park, Sara Zúhiga Calderón.

WHEN ADAM GETS HANDED A MANGO

A horde of howler monkeys are roaring in the trees, a crocodile dozes on the riverbank, and Jesus lizards have a competitive race for insects on a lagoon. They are called that

THE BOAT TRIP TO TORTUGUERO NATIONAL PARK TAKES YOU THROUGH DENSE GREENERY (*ABOVE AND ABOVE LEFT*) POPULATED BY RED-EYED TREE FROGS AND CURIOUS CAPUCHIN MONKEYS (*BELOW LEFT*).

IN TORTUGUERO YOU CAN LIVE RIGHT BY THE
WATER (*ABOVE*); FINE SANDY BEACHES AND
COLORFUL CORAL REEFS ARE FOUND NEAR
CAHUITA AND IN THE ADJACENT NATIONAL
PARK (*RIGHT*).

because they can skim across the water on their broad feet, and Jesus is said to have walked on water. There is something new to discover every minute.

If Eve were to hand Adam an apple in a paradisiacal setting these days, it might have been a mango and the setting might be Tortuguero. In any case, you quickly get the impression that in large parts of the area along the channel, hardly anything has changed since the arrival of Christopher Columbus in 1502—if you disregard the washing machines, cell phones, and excursion boats. These latter are particularly noticeable when a cruise ship has moored in Puerto Limón, 62 miles (100 kilometers) away, and the passengers have booked Tortuguero as a day trip.

TWO OCEANS IN ONE DAY

Sara and Barbara know from experience how tourism develops in such a remote area—and from the statistics. The thirty-four-year-old Sara has been working in the national park for ten years. It is her life. "We have a park here where many endangered species live, like our

sea turtles that come ashore to lay their eggs," she says. She therefore sees the figures as sobering: "In 1996 there were 13,031 visitors. By 2006 it was already 103,121. And ten years later the number increased to 136,699." An unbelievable increase of a good 1,000 percent in just twenty years. What will it look like in 2026?

On Costa Rica's Pacific coast, residents laugh at these numbers. There, visitors from all over the world are already creating mass tourism. At the narrowest point in the country, the two oceans, the Pacific and the Caribbean (or the Atlantic), are only about 62 miles (100 kilometers) apart as the crow flies. Breakfast with reggae on the Caribbean side and dinner with salsa on the Pacific side: that's how it is in Costa Rica!

IN THE LAND OF THE TURTLE HUNTERS

Tortuguero means "turtle hunter," because for centuries the small coastal town lived from the trade of the turtles' shells, eggs, and meat. It wasn't until 1975, when the national park was established south of Tortuguero, that this business was stopped.

Today the 1,200 residents, largely cut off from the outside world, work mainly in tourism, as does Barbara Hartung: "In Costa Rica, I first worked in various national parks, including in Tortuguero. I have meanwhile become self-employed, including to offer an alternative to mass tourism. Instead of sailing through the rainforest in noisy motorboats, I paddle a canoe and take small groups on walks through nature, which is the only way to experience it authentically. Because if you don't open your senses, you cannot get to know the fascination of the rainforest."

TI AMO!

It smells moldy, of swamps and mangroves. Only a few birds can be heard. Slowly, very slowly, it comes closer. The back prongs cut through the water, making it ripple. A second reptile is approaching. The excitement grows. "Now it's about to start," says Barbara quietly. Indeed, the two crocodiles, 6–10 feet (2–3 meters) long, quickly attack each other. They strike out with their tails so that the water splashes for meters away. The movements are so fast that you can hardly take pictures. "Why are they fighting?" asks a visitor. "It goes on like this for five minutes," Barbara replies. "Only then will it be quiet for a few seconds. The two aren't fighting." A pause. "Crocodiles don't just doze off all day or lurk waiting for prey. Sometimes they also have to do something for propagation. People! They are having sex right now!"

In such primal moments, you know that Tortuguero is a unique place. "The biodiversity is incredible," says Barbara. "You can see spider monkeys, capuchin monkeys, sloths, iguanas, herons, toucans, kingfishers, parrots, darter birds, river turtles, and, more rarely, anteaters and coatis and, very rarely, wild cats such as the shy and exclusively nocturnal jaguars"—or even crocodiles when they are making love.

COLORFUL CAHUITA

The Pacific coast is lined with hotels. On the Caribbean side there are simple wooden lodges with a hammock and rocking chair, especially in the south, from Cahuita along the beautifully curved, sandy beaches fringed with coconut palms and rainforest leaning toward the sea. Fortunately, Cahuita and Puerto Viejo have not yet attracted hordes of visitors. Costa Rica's southern Caribbean coast is stuck somewhere between the backpackers and package travelers. It is a place where the world turns a little more slowly than it does anywhere else. As is well known, on the water people dream more of the past than of the future. And in Cahuita they still live in a wonderfully multicolored Caribbean way.

MORE INFORMATION

Costa Rica is a safe country for travel.
www.visitcostarica.com

55 EXCITING DISCOVERIES IN THE WETLANDS—RÍO TEMPISQUE

ABUNDANT WILDLIFE IN COSTA RICA'S NORTHWEST

The sparsely populated banks of the Río Tempisque are classic Costa Rican wetlands and have a large share of wildlife, especially birds. In this region, which is also used for cattle breeding, floods during the rainy season are normal.

COSTA RICA'S WETLANDS (*ABOVE*) ARE AMONG THE MOST BIODIVERSE REGIONS IN THE COUNTRY. AT RIO TEMPISQUE THE CROCODILES SUNBATHE ON THE RIVERBANK (*BELOW RIGHT*); THE DIVERSE BIRDLIFE INCLUDES GREAT BLUE HERONS (*ABOVE RIGHT*).

If you turn off the Pan-American Highway in northwestern Costa Rica and pass the modern bridge under which the Río Tempisque flows into the Gulf of Nicoya, the route runs behind it and to the right, through sparsely populated areas. And right into the middle of everyday life in the countryside. Farms, cattle pastures, cowboys, and cornfields are all to be seen. Small properties are scattered in the landscape, sometimes with parabolic antennas on their roofs. There are rocking chairs on the front porches. Or hammocks. Freshly washed laundry is hanging to dry on fences. Near the village of Puerto Humo, where there is a school, a church, and

a soccer field, a junction leads to the Rancho Humo Estancia. Welcome to solitude! The ranch classifies itself as an "ecological boutique hotel" and is a wonderful address, situated in a vast terrain. Exciting exploratory trips in four-wheel-drive vehicles take you from the premises through the animal-rich wetlands and to the Río Tempisque, where you change to a boat to press on into the countryside.

FOCUS ON SUSTAINABILITY

Rancho Humo Estancia is a typical example of eco-friendly Costa Rican tourism. In 2005, when William J. Salom and his family bought the land, they planned to establish a cattle farm. But it quickly became clear that the area, surrounded by wetlands as well as the Río Tempisque and the Palo Verde National Park, presented an opportunity for a gentle form of ecotourism. It was important at the same time to maintain a balance between economic interests—cattle breeding on the partially abandoned pasturelands, and the preservation of the wetlands that had disappeared elsewhere in Costa Rica due to development. In 2015 the Rancho Humo Estancia officially celebrated its opening.

BIRD ISLAND AND MANGROVES

The wetlands flood in the rainy season, leaving the trees and fences deep in the water, but the cattle escape to higher slopes on a kind of dike. These are barely passable amid the water. The green belts extend to the Río Tempisque. Apart from the peace and quiet in harmony with nature, the highlights here are the excursions starting at the Rancho

Humo Estancia under expert guidance—be it a ride in an all-terrain vehicle through the wetlands or a boat trip on the Río Tempisque, including circumnavigating the Isla de los Pájaros, or bird island. You have to slather on insect repellent if you don't want to become a food source for the mosquitoes, which are unfortunately part of the wildlife. The mangroves along the riverbanks, as well as the Jerusalem thorn trees (*Parkinsonia aculeata*), are distinctive representatives of the regional vegetation. Called *palos verdes* in Spanish, these thorny trees have yellow flowers.

CROCODILES, IBISES, IGUANAS

The Río Tempisque and the adjacent wetlands are the habitats of crocodiles, wood storks, cormorants, turkey vultures, parrots, and ibises. There are also huge numbers of herons and spoonbills. Almost more spectacular than the Montezuma oropendolas are their gourd-like nests. And spotting iguanas quickly becomes a pleasant diversion.

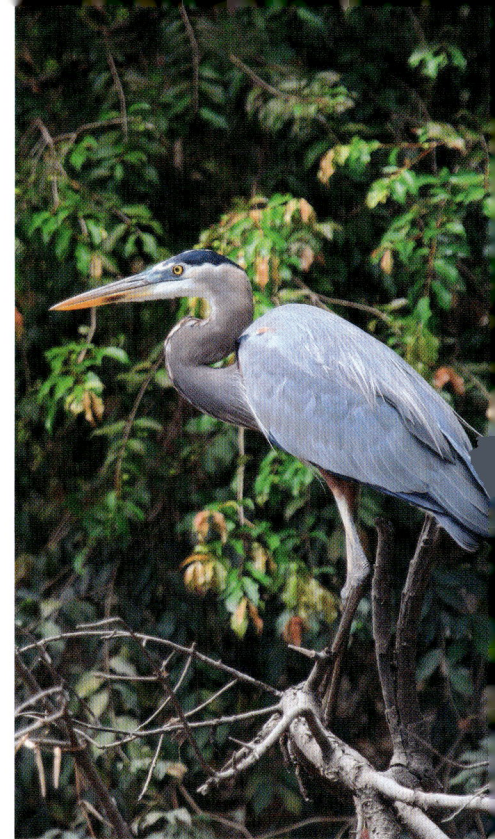

PALATIAL ACCOMMODATIONS

From a standard room to a family suite, Rancho Humo Estancia offers upscale lodging. Air-conditioning, private bathrooms, terraces, wireless internet access, comfortable beds, and velvety down comforters contribute to your enjoyment amid the solitude. The feel-good ambience is further enhanced by service from the well-trained staff, common rooms decorated with works of art, a restaurant, a small pool, and abundant greenery. Prices correspond to the exquisite atmosphere. Even if you're not a hotel guest, however, you can purchase day passes for excursions from the Rancho Humo Estancia.

MORE INFORMATION

In addition to accommodations, the Rancho Humo Estancia website lists the available tours. http://ranchohumo.com

56 THE CANAL AND MORE— EXPEDITIONS IN PANAMA

COLORFUL AND RICH IN CONTRASTS

Oh, how exciting Panama is! Not only along the legendary Panama Canal, but also in the highlands and on the Pacific Ocean islands. The capital, Ciudad de Panamá, is rich in contrasts. Take time for colorful expeditions to these places. It's worth it.

What an incredible colossus! Gently, almost silently, the *Limari* approaches a ghostly chain of "mountains" made by container ships. In the southern part of Lago Gatun, Panama's largest lake, a cargo ship has completed half the trip through the Panama Canal. The 50-mile-long (80 kilometer) passage between the Pacific and Atlantic oceans costs it a quarter of a million dollars but saves a trip around Cape Horn.

Captain Fermín pilots the *Róbalo* along the same route. Compared to the heavily loaded ship, his excursion boat looks like a flyspeck. Fermín's boat has a different mission: to steer its freight of passengers in search of wildlife into the fingers of the lake as quickly as possible. Islands of grass rise up on the horizon; the hilly green of the rainforest lines the shore like an honor guard; the canal traffic is suddenly far away. Guide Gilberto searches the banks with binoculars and finds some "prey" for watching. Howler and capuchin monkeys. A fasciated tiger heron and a toucan. Ahead, a young American crocodile is lying on a tree trunk, its mouth open. The minireptile lets the boat get close and then splashes into the water as if to prove what Gilberto has to say: "Believe me, it's not made of plastic."

MODERN OFFICE TOWERS DOMINATE THE SKYLINE OF PANAMA'S CAPITAL CIUDAD DE PANAMÁ (*BELOW*). THE LOCAL KUNA PEOPLE WELCOME VISITORS TO THE SAN BLAS ISLANDS IN THE CARIBBEAN (*ABOVE AND BELOW RIGHT*).

INDIGENOUS WORLDS

In the Canal Zone, an ethnotourism trip takes you to the Emberá people. They emigrated from Panama's border region with Colombia and provide insight into their community in the village of Emberá Querá, built in 2007. "We are ambassadors for our culture," emphasizes Mayor Jobel Dogiramá, with a mixture of seriousness and pride. "We want the world to know that ancient peoples live on in Panama with their traditions. The tourists make us feel important and honored." A visit is not cheap; the fixed price includes pickup service in a large motorized canoe to cross the Gatun River. Other Indigenous worlds open up on the San Blas archipelago in the Caribbean. There the Kuna people have embraced tourism as a controlled source of income and welcome visitors to such islands as El Porvenir.

MORE INFORMATION

The official tourist website gives a good over-view of the country's diversity.
www.visitpanama.com

HIGHLAND FRESHNESS AND GRINGOLAND

Fields of red cabbage at an elevation of 5,577 feet (1,700 meters)? In Panama? Strange, but true. A change of location and scene leads to the highlands in the far west. Where the 9,843-foot-high (3,000 meter) Mount Barú displays its volcanic slopes, poinsettias grow like weeds, orange-red flame trees are sprinkled amid the green, and everything imaginable flourishes on the soil around the town of Boquete: strawberries and blackberries, avocados, lemons, oranges—even red cabbage along the hiking trail to the lonely El Tatica waterfall in the Don Chaco nature reserve. At the same time, Boquete stands for the phenomenon of "gringoization." Several thousand Americans, mostly retirees, live in the extended area around the town. Not necessarily out of love for Panama, but because of the climate, which is good for their health.

THAR SHE BLOWS!

Worlds away from Boquete—and yet only 62 miles (100 kilometers) distant—lie the Pacific islands in the Gulf of Chiriquí. The "pacific" ocean is seldom peaceful. The waves rage around sandbanks and volcanic islands; the tour boat that started at Boca Chica is tossed up and down. Bottlenose dolphins frolic in the water; then we hear, "Thar she blows!" Humpback whales surface. "A mother with a calf," calls nature guide Miha and estimates the size of the "baby" to be 13 feet (4 meters).

"The whale season here is from the beginning of July to the end of October," says Miha, who joins the birdwatching and mangrove excursion in early evening. High in the trees of nameless islands, pelicans and cormorants have switched off to sleep mode, while frigate birds and white-bellied boobies glide around. Silver-and-blue herons can be seen in the muck along the shore. Instead of postcard kitsch, the sky darkens at sunset. Layers of clouds and the lead gray of a distant veil of rain create a striking atmosphere.

BLEND OF MANHATTAN AND COLONIAL OLD TOWN

Last but not least: Ciudad de Panamá, the capital city of Panama. Planned development has produced a Manhattan on the Pacific—a big mosaic of bank, office, hotel, and residential towers. Things are completely different in the colonial Old Town, a UNESCO World Heritage Site. There is a great amount of historical infrastructure, and also need for renovation. While the plaster is peeling off some facades, other buildings have been spiffed up beautifully and glow in their old-new splendor.

57 IN THE FOOTSTEPS OF CAPTAIN SPARROW—ST. VINCENT AND THE GRENADINES

WHERE DOES HAPPY ISLAND LIE?

Sailing is often expensive. Fortunately, the prices in St. Vincent and the Grenadines are reasonable—and this is one of the best sailing areas in the world.

Andale makes the trip exciting: "We're on board for a week. And we call not only at Happy Island, but also some other happy islands," he says. The thirty-nine-year-old skipper with an athletic, broad-shouldered build laughs. "The people on our islands still don't have dollar signs in their eyes yet."

Our destination on this snow-white sailing yacht with the seductive name *My Mistress* is the southernmost of the thirty-three islands of the Caribbean state of St. Vincent and the Grenadines, which has been independent since 1979. For every 100,000 inhabitants,

some 100,000 sailors also come every year, but there is room for everyone on the country's 249 square miles (400 square kilometers).

MIRAGE AT SEA

The sails billow in the wind and the 50-foot (15-meter) yacht's bow cuts into the deep-blue water. Petit St. Vincent remains on our starboard side; who would want to go to a resort island, when there is a lonely sandbank glittering on the horizon as if it were a mirage? Mopion is the name of this barren sand structure, which can even move: a single palm-thatched umbrella, firmly anchored in

TAKE THE DARE: JUMPING DOWN INTO THE MIDDLE OF THE FALLS OF BALEINE IN NORTHERN ST. VINCENT (*ABOVE LEFT*). IF YOU ARE LOOKING FOR FANTASTIC BEACHES, YOU WILL DEFINITELY FIND THEM IN THIS SMALL CARIBBEAN COUNTRY (*ABOVE AND BELOW LEFT*).

THE TOBAGO CAYS ARE A POPULAR DESTINA-
TION FOR SAILORS—BESIDES, CAPTAIN
SPARROW WAS MAROONED HERE (*ABOVE AND
RIGHT*). PORT ELIZABETH IS ANOTHER POPULAR
MARINA ON BEQUIA, AN ISLAND IN THE
GRENADINES (*BELOW RIGHT*).

concrete, shows how the sand is shifting.
"Sometimes the umbrella stands to the right;
then it is again on the left," Andale says while
picnicking on this 164-foot-long (50 meter)
patch of sand in the Caribbean Sea. A film crew
filming a commercial on Mopion had a lot of
trouble, because the shoot lasted three days
and each day the sandbar looked completely
different in shape.

"Don't fight the yacht," recommends Andale
after a shrimp-and-mango sandwich. "Treat her
gently and strictly at the same time—like a
woman." Macho Andale senses the accusing looks
of the female passengers and charmingly gives in:
"I was just kidding!" The wind smacks the canvas;
the light breeze has freshened up. Union Island
comes into view. Union is sailor central in this
neck of the woods. In the village of Clifton, gossip
replaces newspapers, going to church is compulsory, and there is no prison. For anyone who
forgot to bring an item, Union has it all! Baguettes
and beer, expensive vegetables, even an
award-winning shoemaker, and, above all, Happy
Island lying offshore.

ONE MILLION FOR AN ISLAND

Happy Island was originally just a sandbar.
Six years ago, however, four sailors posed for

a photo on it, beaming with joy and holding
up an SOS sign. Janti Ramagi, a picture-
perfect Rasta and the Union Island
environmental officer at the time,
remembered that event when he was tasked
with removing small mountains of conch
shells from the island's beaches. Janti
decided to build an SOS spot for stranded
sailors by transporting 3 tons of conch shells
to the sandbar. The first simple hut has
turned into a bar where yachties sailing in
the area stop by for a rum punch or snack.
Rasta Janti now lives and loves on his Happy
Island; he smokes marijuana the way others
smoke cigarettes, and says, "Happy Island is
built of marine mollusks, muscles, and
intelligence." A sailor once offered him a
million US dollars for his island, "but who
would sell his own paradise?" he asked.

$20 FOR A LOBSTER

Salt Whistle Bay on Mayreau Island is another
small paradise, or at least one of the best
anchorages in the area. As soon as a yacht
enters the wide round of the bay and its
anchor chain rattles to the bottom, Mr.
Bushman appears: "How about a lobster?
Small or big?" A crustacean wriggles in each

hand, and another six lobsters are crawling in the hull of the barge. "OK, $20 apiece, grilled and served with garlic butter. Is eight o'clock OK?" Bushmann doesn't just sell his lobsters as they do in other anchorages, but also prepares them as requested. That—even experienced yachties say—is something unique in the world. Along with it, a cool Weisse beer, the slight rocking of the boat, and the countless stars in the sky.

While the sailors indulge in comfort and romance, the islanders just need good ideas to earn their livelihood. The fields of sea island cotton no longer yield anything. Yet, Careenage Beach, on the east coast, provides some people with a week's income in one day. There the current, always the same, drives precious flotsam and jetsam onshore: dinghies, canoes, surfboards, and everything that has not been properly moored on the Tobago Cays. Many a hobby sailor has been able to recover his lost boat in Mayreau. There might be a prankster who believes that the knots tying up many a dinghy might occasionally be loosened a bit at night.

WHERE JOHNNY DEPP WAS MAROONED

Jumping into the sea in the morning is like diving into happiness. Yet, things can get even better, such as swimming with turtles in the light-blue lagoon of the Tobago Cays. It is the animals' living room, and many of the beaches are the nursery. To this day, turtles bury their eggs there in the warm sand. This is not the only reason why the Tobago Cays are a national park and a must-see. This group of four small, uninhabited islands is protected by the Horse Shoe Reef and creates an image fit for a screensaver. Petit Tabac, which is within sight just outside the reef, on the other hand, is just the right backdrop for every joke about a man on a desert island or pirate movie. So, in *Pirates of the Caribbean*, the villain Barbossa maroons Captain Sparrow, played by Johnny Depp, and the pretty Elizabeth on Petit Tabac. There are a few palm trees, some scrub, a white sandbar that juts out into the sea like a tongue, and all around is water in colors ranging from light blue to ink blue. Andale was right. There's not just one Happy Island in the Grenadines.

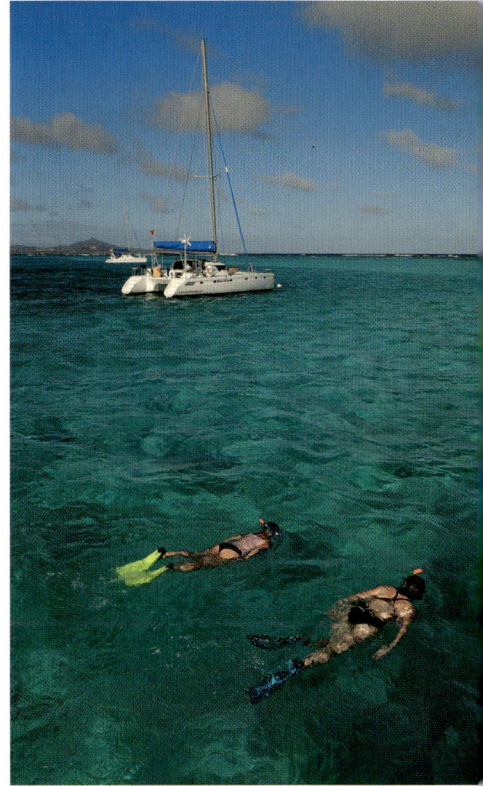

READY TO PUT OUT TO SEA?

Prices for a sailing yacht with two cabins for four guests and a galley start around $2,000 per week, plus a skipper for $765 and a 10 percent tip, and insurance for $220 per week. Dishes, bedding, and towels are included in the price. Drinks and meals are extra. The best thing to do is to stock up on enough bottled water, juice, lemonade, beer, and wine or rum for the evening on the day you sail. Supplies for breakfast, midday snacks, and meat for the non–fish eaters should be bought before first casting off. In the evening, things are planned so that you can go to a restaurant on the nearest island or be supplied with fish and lobster from hawkers. The passengers do the dishes. The best time for sailing is November to February.

MORE INFORMATION

A passport is sufficient for entry. Sun protection is definitely necessary. The skipper takes care of all sailing arrangements.

ASIA

Camels, Royal Cities, and Boiling Geysers

74 POOR AND NOUVEAU RICHE— BAKU

CITY IN FLAMES

Azerbaijan is a country of great contrasts. Some of the oldest oil fields in the world lie before the gates of its capital, and yet there is visible poverty. In Baku, meanwhile, people live in luxury.

AZERBAIJAN HAS THE LARGEST NUMBER OF MUD VOLCANOES IN THE WORLD, WHICH THROW METHANE GAS AS WELL AS COOL MUD INTO THE AIR (*BELOW*). THE HEYDAR ALIYEV CULTURAL CENTER WAS DESIGNED BY STAR ARCHITECT ZAHA HADID (*ABOVE RIGHT*). AN OIL BATH IS SAID TO SOOTHE ALL KINDS OF AILMENTS (*BELOW RIGHT*).

He's short and well dressed; a nice young man who may be a little shy. He usually sits in the back of the tour bus and is as quiet as a mouse. The tour guide, microphone in hand, speaks loudly and apparently openly about all kinds of things, but he does not introduce the young man. The visitors come from different countries. They are curious and well traveled and want to be able to include Azerbaijan in their list of checked-off countries under the letter "A," after Argentina and Australia. One of them, Jean-François from a small village in central France, asks the young man a question during a photo stop—speaking in English with a wonderful French accent: "Tell me, young man, are you actually our KGB minder?" The KGB no longer exists in Baku; however, the State Ministry of the Interior and Security occupies the same address that the KGB had. And the same people likely are still working in the terrifying sand-colored, eight-story building as long as a city block. Some young people have surely been added to the staff since 1991, when Azerbaijan got its independence from the Soviet Union. People like the young man,

Baku shows off its wealth ostentatiously against the backdrop of a desperately poor country, as revealed in a trip outside the city limits. After the polished center comes a belt of desolate prefabricated apartment buildings, and finally the land, dusty and cordoned off where there are oil fields, as on the Absheron Peninsula. Lada cars rumble around, and sometimes even a horse and cart. Many people are self-sufficient. Villages typically contain only a grocery store and a tea room, and in Naftalan is an odd wellness spa where you can try an oil bath. Naftalan crude oil is not suitable for industrial use and is used exclusively for healing purposes; for example, as a treatment for ulcers and nettle rash.

MORE INFORMATION

Azerbaijan has four seasons with mild winters and hot summers. Very few people speak English, and a group tour is recommended. http://azerbaijan.travel

perhaps? He looks calmly at Jean-François and says, "No. I'm just a helper in case we run into problems on the way." Then his cell phone rings. The conversation is over.

WELCOME TO THE ALIYEVS' BAKU

The first surprise comes at the domestic airport. The boarding pass shows Heydar Aliyev, not Baku, as the destination. This is the name of the father of the current head of state of Azerbaijan, Ilham Aliyev. The second surprise comes on arrival—the sight of every building in the Aliyevs' Baku shimmering in a string of lights. One high-rise—the Flame Tower—is actually spewing fire. This complex of glass and steel has been a symbol of Baku since its completion in 2013 and presides over the city. Three flames blaze around 656 feet (200 meters) high into the black night sky by the Caspian Sea. They consist of more than 10,000 LEDs and were designed by Osram to resemble oil and gas flares, a symbol of the rich natural resources that brought Azerbaijan to prosperity. Meanwhile, the young man is typing in a bored way on his cell phone.

A HALTED TOWER

On Friday evening, the Bentleys and Porsches, Ferraris, and Mercedes cruise the streets of Baku. Even the police are behind the wheel of new 5 Series BMWs. Well-off women, dressed to the nines, go out in the company of their husbands. The cityscape has changed completely over the past ten years, as the bigger-higher-better mindset spread from the nearby Gulf region. The small Old Town, dating from the twelfth century, with its roughly 4,900 feet (1,500 meters) of largely intact city wall, is a UNESCO World Heritage Site. For a long time, however, a very large project, the construction of the Baku tower on the artificial island of Khazar, seemed more interesting. The tower was supposed to be 3,445 feet (1,050 meters) high and thus surpass Dubai's Burj Khalifa by 728 feet (222 meters). But the construction project was canceled. Nobody talks about why; politics are rarely discussed in the Aliyev State.

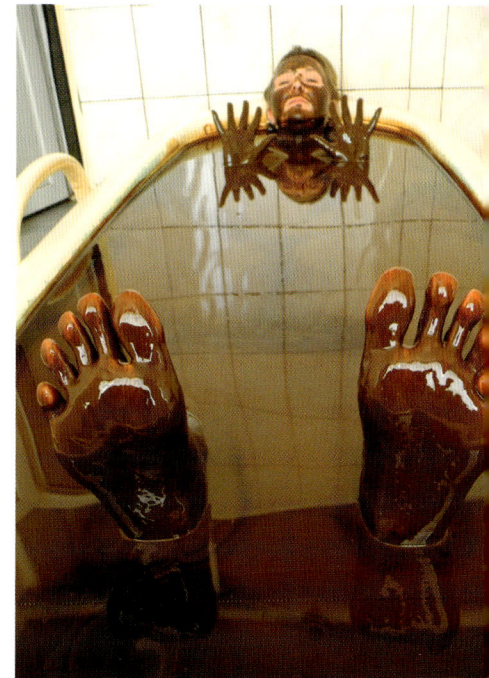

75 HISTORY-STEEPED JORDAN— WADI RUM AND PETRA

ARABIAN DESERT FROM A THOUSAND AND ONE NIGHTS

Wadi Rum is a grand desert landscape on the border with Saudi Arabia, which was made famous in the film *Lawrence of Arabia*. It is based on the memories of the Englishman T. E. Lawrence, who organized the Arab Revolt against the Ottomans in Aqaba during World War I.

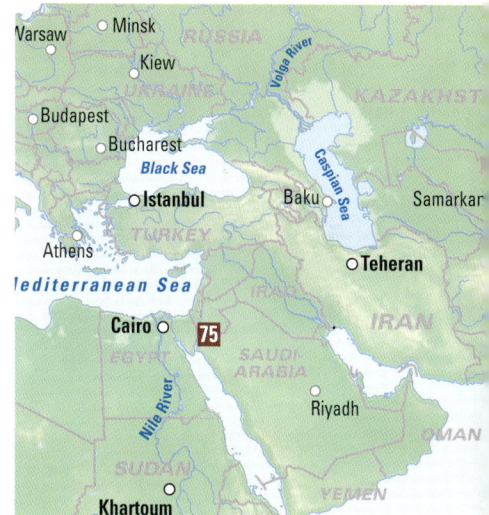

One of the most fascinating landscapes on Earth lies east of the Red Sea, between Israel and Saudi Arabia. This is the Jordanian desert, with the breathtaking Wadi Rum. Along this wadi (dry valley), the biggest in the country, huge rock massifs rise from the sandy desert in vertical rock walls up to 2,625 feet (800 meters) high.

DISCOVERIES IN WADI RUM

Most visitors to Wadi Rum are day-trippers who stop at the entrance to the village near the Rest House. From here you have a wonderful view of the vastness of the desert and can take a delightful walk into the small and unremarkable village of Rum. The inhabitants are hospitable Bedouins— "Welcome to Jordan" is not a hackneyed phrase here, but an authentic greeting. Many live as seminomads; they have permanent housing, but from time to time they move with their flocks of goats and sheep through the barren desert, where they live in camps. For travelers, however, it is worth taking the time to dedicate more than a day to exploring the area in more detail. One possibility is taking exciting hikes through the numerous siqs (narrow gorges) that cut through the massifs. You can admire Nabataean rock carvings on a tour through the large siq at

A BEDOUIN STANDS WITH HIS DROMEDARIES IN FRONT OF THE ROCKS OF JEBEL RUM (*LEFT*); THE VIEW OF DESOLATE WADI RUM EXTENDS FAR TO THE HORIZON (*ABOVE*).

Jebel Khazali. This is recommended on particularly hot days because it is always pleasantly cool inside the gorge. However, be aware that the siqs can fill with water quickly and are dangerous during storms.

Fascinating day tours also take you to the sand dunes at Jebel Um Ishrin or to the Pillars of Wisdom mountain formation. More-distant destinations such as the rock bridges at Jebel Burdah and Um Fruth can be explored on a dromedary or—more conveniently—in an off-road vehicle. And you can enjoy real desert romance in the Barrah Canyon: spending the night under the starry desert sky is an experience that you will never forget!

ALONG OLD BEDOUIN TRAILS

Some trails lead to the high massifs where the Bedouins used to follow their animals to watering places. One particularly well-known trip on these ancient trails is the traverse of Jebel Rum along Sheikh Hamdan's Route, which leads over the highest point in Wadi Rum at 5,755 feet (1,754 meters) in elevation. Traversing Jebel Rum is one of the most

impressive mountain hikes in the world and is a challenge—not so much because it is physically arduous, but because it is difficult to say oriented and find the route. The old Bedouin route is extremely varied, running through countless canyons, which you cross on rocky ridges or that connect with each other. Here you sometimes have to scramble along ledges. Finally, on the summit plateau, you have to cross a vast area with countless peaks that resembles a gigantic maze. Right up to the end of the trail, you are constantly questioning whether you are on the right track. If you don't dare take this hike on your own, you can book a guide.

ADVENTUROUS CLIMBING ON HIGH SANDSTONE WALLS

Wadi Rum, with its neighboring dry valleys, is one of the most formidable desert-climbing areas in all of Arabia. The sandstone massifs, which range from red to white, yellow, purple, and mother-of-pearl and come in all conceivable shapes and colors, rise up on a base of granite and offer alpine climbing in gigantic dihedral and crack systems. The area became internationally known to the climbing scene in 1984 because of the Englishman Tony Howard—today there are more than 400 mostly self-secured routes of all levels of difficulty in the extensive area around Rum. However, because of the rigorous safety measures, climbing is reserved for advanced climbers. And so, it is not surprising that despite its reputation, there are relatively few rope teams in this climbing area.

PETRA—CAPITAL OF THE NABATAEANS

An hour and a half northwest of Wadi Rum, close to the village of Wadi Musa (Valley of Moses) in the Edom Mountains, lies the world-famous ancient rock city of Petra. The area, south of the Dead Sea, has been inhabited since ancient times and is known for its archeological treasures. From around the fifth century BCE, the nomadic Nabataean

PREPARING TO COOK: A BEDOUIN WOMAN LIGHTS THE FIREPLACE IN HER TENT (*BELOW*). **THE ROCK BRIDGE OVER THE JEBEL BURDAH IN WADI RUM IS A WORK OF NATURE** (*ABOVE RIGHT*); **HUMANS CARVED THE AD DEIR TEMPLE IN PETRA OUT OF THE ROCKS** (*BELOW RIGHT*).

MAGICAL PETRA BY NIGHT

If you spend several days in Petra and Wadi Musa, don't miss Petra by Night. After dark, the entire entrance gorge is illuminated with tea lights for almost 0.9 miles (1.5 kilometers) along the way to Khazne al-Firaun. Visitors are encouraged to walk in a line and in silence through the narrow gorge, which creates a mystical atmosphere. Arriving at the treasure house, everyone gathers in a circle around a storyteller who tells of the legacy of the Nabataeans. Mint tea is served. A Bedouin accompanies the talk on his lute, and you can hear typical Arabic tones. After the cultural performance, you walk back to the starting point—a magical experience that you will remember for a long time.

MORE INFORMATION

General information about Wadi Rum: www.wadirum.jo

Petra by Night: www.visitpetra.jo

people were living here. They skillfully controlled the incense route and gained great prosperity. Starting from the third century BCE, they began to erect permanent structures in Petra, and in the second century BCE, they made it the capital of their empire.

During its heyday, Petra comprised more than a thousand buildings, some of them monumental. Most were carved into the colorful sandstone cliffs. Today this is a UNESCO World Heritage Site and considered one of the new seven wonders of the world. The most famous buildings carved out of the massive rock include the Ad Deir rock temple, the thirteen tombs of the King's Wall, the Roman theater, which is estimated to have had a seating capacity for 9,000, and the 131-foot-high (40 meter) Treasure House of the Pharaoh, the Khazne al-Firaun.

The city also had a sophisticated water supply system made up of countless aqueducts and cisterns. Well protected by the 3,937-foot-long (1,200 meter) and 262-foot-high (80 meter) gorge (siq), for 600 years Petra was an important way station for caravans on their way from Asia to the Mediterranean and was an important trading center for spices, incense, and luxury goods such as ivory and silk. Due to political and economic developments under the Romans, by the third century the city had lost its importance. Beyond this, severe earthquakes damaged many of its structures and caused most of its residents to leave the city. Starting from the Middle Ages, Petra became completely deserted—today it is the most visited attraction in Jordan and is considered the most famous attraction in the Middle East.

76 THE YOUNGEST KINGDOM— BAHRAIN

INTO THE FUTURE AT FORMULA 1 SPEED

Oil and gas deposits have brought visible wealth to Bahrain. However, those natural resources are becoming scarce, so its future prosperity is increasingly dependent on trade, banking, and tourism.

THE PRAYER ROOM IN AL-FATEH MOSQUE, ONE OF THE LARGEST MOSQUES IN THE WORLD (*ABOVE*), COMPLETED IN 1988. IN CONTRAST, THE CARVED DOOR ON THE SHEIK BIN ALI HOUSE IN MUHARRAQ, WITH A FRIENDLY GENTLEMAN IN THE TRADITIONAL DISHDASHA (*ABOVE RIGHT*), DATES BACK TO THE EIGHTEENTH CENTURY. HIGHWAYS AND MODERN HIGH-RISE BUILDINGS DEFINE THE CITYSCAPE OF THE CAPITAL MANAMA (*BELOW RIGHT*).

An Islamic State fighter is boxing. His right fist punches out, fast as lightning, and strikes Uncle Sam head on. "Yeah, give it to him," calls out one of the crowd watching the fight. But Sam strikes back. "Yes, finish this butcher!" cries another person. The rest of the group watches the fight with humor. After all, a young Tamil is holding the two fighters in his hand, and they are puppets. The puppeteer wants to make some money with the political figures. Therefore, in this show-fight-for-sale in the souk, the bazaar in the center of Bahrain's capital Manama, everyone takes a beating equally. The idea is

to amuse the audience and customers, not alienate them. The Tamil knows that the country's mood is divided.

A BIT OF THE USA IN THE GULF

The 5th Fleet, with its 3,000 American sailors, is stationed in the port of Manama. Bahrain sleeps better knowing that the United States has its back. Most people have a Western lifestyle. On the wide highways, bulky limousines roll along sedately, as do even-bulkier SUVs. Men and women indulge their desires in huge, air-conditioned shopping malls and order drive-in burgers as if they were in the States. If it weren't for the men's white dishdashas and the women's black hijab headscarves and abaya robes, you might think you weren't in Arabia at all.

Bahrain—independent since 1971, with 1.5 million inhabitants and 99 miles (160 kilometers) of coastline—is a traditional trading state. However, it has also established itself as a financial center and is considered one of the most liberal countries in the Middle East. International trade on a large scale has given many residents a small amount of freedom. Word of Bahrain's progressivism got around. It generates income through regular invasions from neighboring Saudi Arabia. Every year, three million vehicles roll along the 15.5-mile (25 kilometer) King Fahd Causeway connecting Bahrain and Saudi Arabia across the Persian Gulf. And the more than seven million annual visitors spend a lot of money here. Bahrain has movie theaters, restaurants, clubs, and pubs serving alcohol, as well as Russian women who provide other amusements. Meanwhile, the Saudi women who traveled along with the men lose themselves in the shopping centers or the gold souk.

FROM CAMEL TO FERRARI

Since 2004, King Sheikh Hamad bin Isa bin Salman Al Khalifa has been bringing his country into the spotlight once a year through the Formula 1. By investing 150 million euros to build the racetrack and paying a rumored twenty million euros to consultant Bernie Ecclestone, the F-1 boss at the time, Bahrain has outwitted agile Dubai. The Bahraini people have exchanged their camels for Ferraris.

OFF TO THE DESERT

Bahrain isn't a particularly pretty island; it is flat, sandy, and covered with pipelines. It doesn't have stunning attractions, apart from the world's largest cemetery, with 85,000 burial mounds in the shape of a sugar loaf, where the dead and their belongings were buried. They lie on the outskirts of A'ali, as far as the eye can see. The grave cones reach heights of 148 feet (45 meters), with a diameter of up to 165 feet (50 meters). And there is another attraction: the world's first oil well, which began to bubble on June 1, 1932. However, Oil Well No. 1 was not the first oil well to be drilled. That happened as early as 1858, surprisingly in Wietze, 10.5 miles (17 kilometers) west of Celle in Germany.

MORE INFORMATION

Anytime other than the hot summer is a good time to travel. Visitors receive a visa upon entry; English is spoken almost everywhere.

THE DESTINATION OF OPEN DOORS

Travel to the Arab world these days? Yes, when it comes to Oman. The people who live there practice Ibadi Islam and have nothing to do with the conflicts between Sunnis and Shiites. In the geological wonderland of the Hajar Mountains, you can also get to know traditional village structures and ways of life.

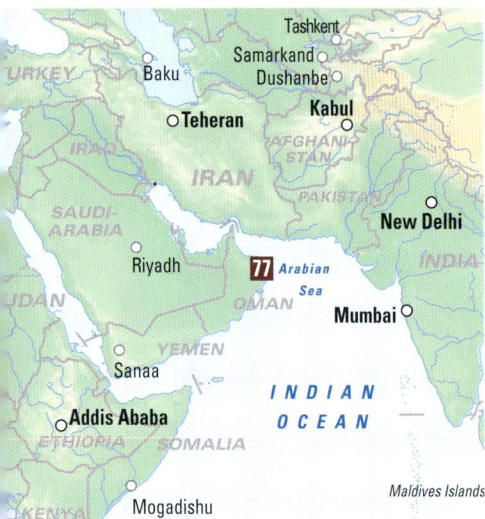

THE OLD FORTRESS OF HISTORIC NACHL IN THE WESTERN HAJAR MOUNTAINS HAS BEEN FULLY RESTORED (*BELOW*). THE MOUNTAINS RISE TO 9,800 FEET (3,000 METERS) (*RIGHT*).

Suddenly the gate opens. The tourist couple looks puzzled and quickly apologizes for their curiosity. The two of them had peeked through a small crack into one of the inner courtyards in the city of Nizwa. The man in his snow-white and smoothly ironed dishdasha, who opened the door from the inside, is also surprised but then says, "Please come in. I would be happy to show you our majlis." This refers to the open living room, or rather a meeting room, where people discuss serious matters or cheerfully laugh at them. The women meet to gossip, the men to smoke water pipes. The couple is offered fresh tea.

BIZARRE AND BREATHTAKING

The late sultan Qaboos bin Said Al Said decided that his subjects should show the greatest possible courtesy to tourists. So that is how things are done. In the souk of the capital, Muscat, there is no groping or harassment. You get the impression that even the most hidden, darkest corner of the bazaar is the safest place in the world. This is how things are done in Nizwa and high up

into the Hajar Mountains. They rise up to 9,800 feet (3,000 meters), and the mountains look like ridges of the Alps where the rain hasn't come for ten years. The mountain range is considered a wonderland for geology, because nowhere else is it possible to explore a cross section of all the layers of rock as easily as in this rugged, stony area. The views in the Hajar range, with its canyons, plateaus, and bizarre rock formations, are simply breathtaking. In some places there is a vertical descent of 6,500 feet (1,981 meters), and on the other side you can see terraced farming. The Aflaj Irrigation System has been part of the UNESCO World Cultural Heritage of Humanity since 2006. There are inhabited and abandoned villages, goats, and donkeys. But the most important thing is that despite their cell phones and satellite dishes, people generally live in the traditional way. And part of that tradition is hospitality with a capital H.

THE SULTAN WOULD BE PROUD

The oases have date trees, including Nizwa, the former capital and oldest city in the country, which lies in the middle of the Hajar Mountains. Don't miss the fort with its mighty round tower. With a diameter of almost 148 feet (45 meters) and almost 100 feet (30 meters) tall, it is the largest tower in Oman.

But less than 18.6 miles (30 kilometers) farther on, in Bahla, the disappointment is great: the doors of the UNESCO World Heritage Site of Hisn Tamah, a mighty Omani clay brick fortress, are tightly locked. You can't even look inside through a slit. A passerby notices the visitors' confusion and calls out, "The castle is closed at eleven on Fridays. So there is no point waiting. Come to my house. We'll have tea together." During the conversation, the man says he doesn't have a blood brother, but "we Omani are all brothers nevertheless." Sultan Qaboos would be proud.

AFTER THE MOUNTAINS, THE DESERT

The last foothills of the Hajar extend to the port city of Sur in the east, which was the former center of the slave trade and the home of the dhows. South of the Hajar Mountains there are still some villages, such as Ibra, which has a women's market, before the eternal, desolate stretch of desert. The dunes of the Al-Wahiba Desert, which are more than 328 feet (100 meters) high, rise just 62 miles (100 kilometers) south of Sur.

UNFORGETTABLE LOOKOUTS

Sitting at an elevation of 6,500 feet (1,981 meters), the Anantara Al Jabal Al Akhdar mountain resort is one of the highest-situated luxury resorts in the world. However, it has only two stories, making it unique in the high-rise Arab hotel industry. The young resort ducks down, brown and inconspicuous, in the equally brown but spectacular landscape of the Hajar Mountains. The view reaches 6,500 feet (1,981 meters) deep into the Grand Canyon of Oman, the Green Mountain gorge. Those who treat themselves to a pool villa 33 feet (10 meters) from the abyss will not forget this hotel for the rest of their lives. From there you can enjoy the bizarre mountain world for hours—and of course the comfort of a fantastic, five-star resort. https://jabal-akhdar.anantara.com.

MORE INFORMATION

Visas are supplied upon entry. Warm winters, hot summers, cool high altitudes. www.omantourism.gov.om

243

78 PILGRIMAGE TO THE HOLY LAKE—PUSHKAR

FESTIVAL OF LIGHTS ON THE NIGHT OF FULL MOON

Devout pilgrims, venerable saints and emaciated ascetics, vigorous showmen, clever fortune-tellers and amazing magicians—they all celebrate Pushkar Mela. The two-week festival is both a religious celebration and a huge camel market that attracts farmers, traders, and beggars.

People have stowed all their belongings on camel and buffalo carts or on their backs. Goats, buffaloes, horses, and especially dromedaries are to be seen, because Pushkar is also the largest camel market in the country. The festival consists of two different events: it starts with the Pushkar Mela, the largest camel market in the world, and then goes on to the Pushkar Puja, one of the most important religious celebrations honoring the god Brahma.

The highlights of the Pushkar Mela include the camel games, races, beauty pageants, and a dance competition. But there are also competitions for those sporting mustaches and for

tying turbans, plus dance performances by schoolgirls in brightly colored uniforms. Ferris wheels provide a thrill, loudspeakers boom everywhere, and noisy announcements continue till late at night. In the narrow streets, women have simply stacked their fruit and vegetables on the ground, while cart-pulling traders and camel sellers pass the displays.

A CITY FOR PILGRIMS

During the last four days before the November full moon, all of Rajasthan seems to be concentrated in this single place. Everyone wants to experience the big festival—it is simultaneously a pilgrimage to the holy lake, a

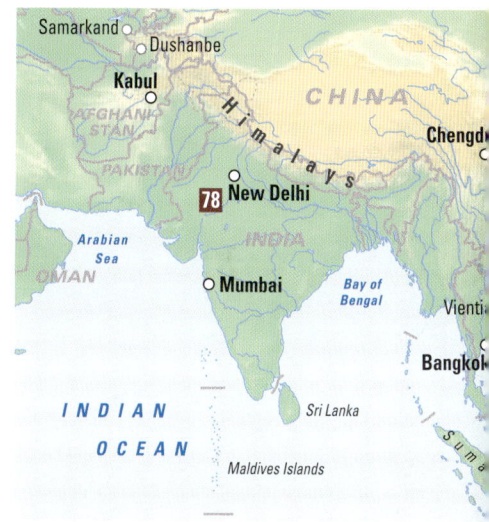

DELICACIES ON OFFER IN THE PUSHKAR MARKET (*ABOVE LEFT*); BEGGARS, WHO FORM A SEPARATE CASTE, AND SADHUS (HOLY MEN) IN THEIR ORANGE ROBES ARE AN INTEGRAL PART OF THE PUSHKAR MELA (*BELOW LEFT*). A MAGICAL ATMOSPHERE PRESIDES OVER THE CAMEL MARKET IN PUSHKAR IN EARLY MORNING (*ABOVE*).

camel market, a marriage market, a social get-together, and a picturesque tourist meeting place. Since the many pilgrim hostels cannot cope with the rush of more than 100,000 visitors to the Pushkar Mela every year, the desert area around the city is transformed into a huge camp, right up to the Aravalli Range. Several large camps will also be set up for foreign tourists during the festival and be provided with comfortable living tents and large dining tents, fully equipped with electric lighting and even flush toilets in the middle of the desert. The lake, named after the lotus blossom (push-kara), is deeply rooted in Indian mythology as a sacred place and was mentioned in the *Mahabharata*. India's great heroic epics, the *Mahabharata* and the *Ramayana*, depict the pilgrimage of the five Pandava princes and King Rama to Pushkar. According to the founding legend, Brahma was said to have chosen this place for his sacrificial ritual. To make the sacrifice, he needed his wife, Sarasvati.

However, she made him wait too long for her arrival, so the impatient gods looked for a replacement. In a hurry, Indra, king of the gods, could find only a herd girl, Gayatri—according to local belief a cowherd from the Gujar tribe. Brahma quickly married her, and the sacrifice began. However, when Sarasvati finally appeared at the sacrificial site and understood the situation, she condemned the gods who had robbed her of her position. As a consolation she was given her own temple southwest of the lake, on the top of Ratna Gir, the Jewel Hill. A narrow footbridge leads up to it.

THE GHATS

At any time of the day, the stairs along the shore, called ghats, are overcrowded; devout pilgrims stay in the holy water for a long time with their hands folded, hoping they will experience a better rebirth and redemption from earthly hardship. Real and false saints, cunning fortune-tellers, self-proclaimed astrologers, and literary experts set up their stands on the shore, most of them under a parasol. Ascetics are immersed in deep meditation; naked yogis hold strange contorted positions or do headstands. Saints bless the pilgrims and consecrate all sorts of amulets; charlatans praise obscure potions and miracle pills based on alleged Ayurvedic formulas; barbers not only shave off beards but also pull rotten teeth with rusty pliers or bleed the sick. The fifty-two ghats, where sacrificial ceremonies take place, were built with the money of wealthy donors. But the Islamic rulers who lived here for a long time abhorred this "idol worship." Mughal Emperor Jahangir, for example, preferred to pursue his passion for hunting, which in the eyes of the Hindus was blasphemy. He even had a sculpture of Varaha, the boar incarnation of the god Vishnu, thrown into the lake. Bathing in the lake is just as effective as bathing in the Ganges near Varanasi. The men often swim out quickly with rapid thrusts and circle the small

AKBAR'S PALACE IN NAGAUR FORTRESS IS AN EXCELLENT EXAMPLE OF THE RAJPUT-MUGHAL ARCHITECTURAL STYLE (*BELOW*). PUSHKAR LIES DIRECTLY ON THE HOLY LAKE (*ABOVE RIGHT*), WHERE SACRIFICIAL CEREMONIES TAKE PLACE ON THE GHATS, THE STAIRS ALONG THE LAKESHORE. A FERRIS WHEEL IN THE FAIR-GROUNDS SHOWS THAT PUSHKAR MELA IS NOT ONLY A RELIGIOUS FESTIVAL (*BELOW RIGHT*).

CATTLE MARKET IN NAGAUR

Every year in January and February, thousands of villagers travel with their herds to the cattle market in Nagaur from near and far. The colorful, lively Nagaur Fair is far more traditional than the market in Pushkar. The colorful men's turbans and women's costumes gleam splendidly with their embroidered veils, mirror-decorated bodices, and wide swinging skirts. The women proudly display the rich silver jewelry on their arms and ankles, on their fingers and toes, in their ears and nose, and on their chest and forehead. A tent city will be built to accommodate the tourists—but Nagaur is also a rewarding destination at other times. The Rajput city, picturesquely enclosed in a 4.7-mile-long (7.5 kilometer) wall, and its Ahhichatragarh Fort and two Hindu temples, is definitely worth seeing.

MORE INFORMATION

Pushkar: Raj Resorts, tent camp, telephone +91 141 238 51 41; www.rajresorts.com

Nagaur: Royal Tents Camp, telephone +91 291 257 23 21; www.royaltentsnagaur.jodhanaheritage.com

island with the chhatri pavilion, which the Thakur of Khimsar rebuilt in 1848. The women remain on the lowest front stairs, where they can stand in the deeper water and dip under the water in their brightly colored saris. At every passage to the lake, people press flowers into your hand, while also hinting that you should get the fortunate blessing of a Brahmin on the steps down to the water, which of course includes a donation. Doing business with ignorant foreigners is profitable, because they love to enjoy the exotic ritual at a bathing lake in the open air.

KARTIK PURNIMA

The bathing rituals reach their climax on the night of the full moon, or Kartik Purnima, when they are particularly beneficial. Bathing on this day should also free you from illness and unhappiness. The bathing ceremonies last until dawn, after which the pilgrims crowd to the Brahma temple and the other shrines in the

temples to pray. Temple music sounds all night long, and the temple bell strikes incessantly. Taking photographs at the ghats is forbidden.

But this night holds another special highlight in store: the Festival of Lights. After the hustle and bustle of the previous days, now a more mysterious atmosphere emerges: Pushkar is a particularly romantic sight on this night because there are large leaves floating on the water, which hold rose petals and small lights. Believers let their little homemade boats, made of leaves decorated with flowers and oil lamps, drift out into the lake as an offering to the gods. The lights wink like the stars in the sky, and their glow is reflected in the lake. It is an event you will never forget.

79 SWAYING ON A CAMEL'S BACK — THROUGH THE THAR DESERT

BALM FOR THE SOUL UNDER A SPARKLING DESERT SKY

Camel trekking in the desertlike steppe landscape of the Thar, in the Indian state of Rajasthan, means almost unbearable, oven-temperature heat starting at sunrise and a marked coolness at night. It is an experience of silence and loneliness, and only the soft plodding of the dromedaries can be heard.

THE LONG RIDE THROUGH THE THAR DESERT WEST OF BIKANER (*BELOW*) IS AN ALMOST MEDITATIVE EXPERIENCE. CAMELS ARE FESTIVELY DECKED OUT BEFORE THE CELEBRATIONS (*ABOVE RIGHT*). WOMEN BALANCE HEAVY CLAY POTS ON THEIR HEADS IN A DESERT VILLAGE (*BELOW RIGHT*).

Camel trekking is for early risers. If the single-humped dromedaries are saddled up and packed up by sunrise, there is a nervous optimism. The animals, who always appear to be in a bad mood, protest loudly, roaring, gurgling, puffing, and gasping. The camels are not beautiful. Their small heads on a long neck look a bit strange, they have tiny ears, their eyes are surrounded by bulges, their teeth are crooked and an unsightly yellow color, and their jaws continuously grind tough grass. But dromedaries are skilled actors. They flinch at every hand movement, and the

show they put on when they are being loaded up or when they stand up is ripe for the stage. They also have large, deep-set eyes that look a bit haughty from under their long eyelashes.

THROUGH THE DESERT ON CAMELBACK

The first few minutes on the back of a young camel are pure horror. It stands up abruptly, using its hind legs, so that my upper body lurches forward. It stretches out its front legs, and I tip backward again. Then it extends its hind legs to their full length and I immediately slide forward. The whole thing has the impact

YOU'LL ARRIVE AT THE NEXT CAMPSITE BY SUNSET, AT THE LATEST (*BELOW*). THE LANDSCAPE OF SAM, NEAR JAISALMER, FULFILLS ALL THE MENTAL IMAGES OF A SAND DUNE DESERT (*BOTTOM AND BELOW RIGHT*). GIRLS TAKE ON HOUSEHOLD CHORES AND CHILDCARE TASKS FROM AN EARLY AGE (*ABOVE RIGHT*).

of a rear-end collision without a headrest. However, the ride becomes a meditative experience after the first swaying steps. It is an indescribable feeling, sitting high on the animal, which boldly sticks its nose into the wind and then rides out into a sea of shimmering sand, with the steel-blue sky on the horizon. At first the trip goes through stony terrain bearing sharp-leaved plants and thorny bushes. The hard-baked ground is ocher to yellow brown. The camels accelerate their pace and head for the sand dunes. Except for their quiet footsteps, no sound can be heard. I am surprised to find that the surrounding area is by no means as devoid of life as I thought, because I hear little bells ringing. A herd of black-and-white goats suddenly appear and immediately disappear again in a cloud of dust and haze. My camel's fluffy red-brown ears listen to the sound of the bells. The monotonous movement of a camel ride and the steady rocking of the "ship of the desert" closely resemble the rhythms that Muslims use for their devotions when reading the Koran. This vastness, this silence—you can almost physically feel it, lose yourself in it and amid this wasteland, and think of yourself as the only person on earth.

SONGS AROUND THE CAMPFIRE

Some travelers prefer to walk for a few miles in the glowing sand to relieve their aching backsides. But they do not keep up with the speed of the dromedaries, 3.7 miles (6 kilometers) per hour, for long. By now the walkers have also suffered blisters on their sensitive feet. A number of diminutive huts indicate that we have reached Bodana, our stage destination for the day. According to the traditional code of conduct for the desert, we get off the camels outside the village and lead the animals along the dusty village street. After all, you don't look disrespectfully down at the residents in their homes from the back of the dromedaries! The next morning we oversleep. Shortly before seven, we crawl out of the tents where we slept on the mostly hard floor. Shadowy figures scurry past in the semidarkness of the blue morning shadows. Barely has the sun risen over the sand dunes when small fires start flickering. The travelers crowd around, muffled in the morning coolness. Slowly a red sheen on the eastern horizon paints the first tentative dab of the

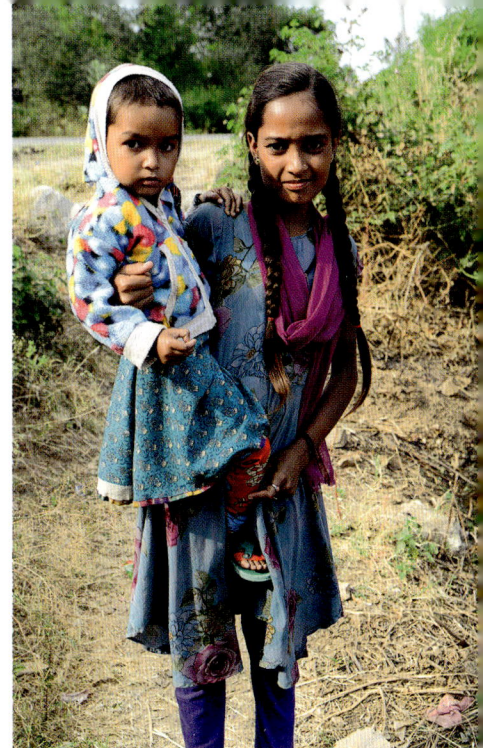

starting day. At the end of another day on camelback, we spend the night near the run-down desert nest of Berla.

I look forward to these evenings around the campfire. A singer from our accompanying group gives his best to songs about the shepherd's loneliness, a favorite camel, painful love, and the hardships of desert life—monotonous music, just like the vast desert of Thar. The drums beat out the rhythm, and a jaw harp fills the starry night with melancholy and longing. After a three-hour ride the following Sunday morning, we reach Akeli. The water boils on the campfire for our black tea, which we gratefully sip. It is seasoned with cardamom, ginger, black pepper, or camel milk, depending on your preference. After a short midday rest we continue riding toward the setting sun. The only sound is the plaintive singing of a camel driver, songs about lost love and daring exploits. We set up our tents on a sand dune before the handsome village of Baroo. The fire crackles and the flames blaze into the starry

sky while we lie on our mats, listening to the music of our Indian companions. When the fire dies out, the drivers wrap themselves in their woolen blankets. Millions of stars twinkle in the heavens.

TASTE OF THE SILK ROAD

After a strenuous seven-hour ride, we finally reach Tota the next day. In front of the red-hot disk of the setting sun, the camel's heads go up and down, and the humps sway back and forth—an image of surreal power. After the long day, we almost fall out of the saddle from tiredness. The cook is silent and prepares our evening meal, made of tomatoes and garlic, coriander and chili, delicious vegetables, potatoes, and eggs. This scene could also have played out six hundred years ago, when long-distance traders on the old Silk Road and adventurers such as Marco Polo were making their way to Jaisalmer. The full moon has shrunk to a thin sickle and watches over this night, which I wish would never end.

THE DUNES OF SAM

Around 25 miles (40 kilometers) southwest of Jaisalmer, a dune landscape extends almost infinitely to the horizon. The Sam Sand Dunes, which are popular with tourists, satisfy all the clichés of a sandy desert—in a different way than the Thar Desert, which is actually a steppe landscape. However, visitors will inevitably find themselves among numerous other dune addicts who want to have the same experience. The first thing that catches your eye, however, is not just the camel drivers with their animals, but also intrusive musicians and souvenir dealers. You have to walk away a bit to be alone with yourself and nature. Then the excursion becomes an experience of silence and meditation.

MORE INFORMATION

Adventure Travel Agency,
telephone +91 29 92 25 25 58;
www.adventurecamels.com

Trotters Tour & Travels,
telephone +91 982 89 29 974;
www.trottersjaisalmer.net

80 PAINTED GODS— THE AJANTA CAVES

WINDOW INTO EARLY TIMES

Monks carved the Ajanta Caves into the mountains. With their detailed murals and large Buddha sculptures, the caves are a surprise for visitors. From an artistic-technical point of view, these works show a much-higher level of development than European art at that time.

THE CAVE MONASTERIES AND TEMPLES OF AJANTA, WHICH ARE UP TO 2,200 YEARS OLD, ARE ADORNED WITH ELABORATE WALL PAINTINGS AND SCULPTURES (*ABOVE*). CHAITYA CAVE 26 CONTAINS THE FAMOUS, 23-FOOT-LONG (7 METER) FIGURE OF THE BUDDHA AS HE IS ENTERING NIRVANA (*BELOW RIGHT*). ENTRANCES TO THE ELLORA CAVE TEMPLES ARE ALSO DECORATED WITH FIGURES (*ABOVE RIGHT*).

We can distinguish among twenty-nine cave monasteries (viharas) and five cave temples (chaityas), which date from 200 BCE to 650 CE. Most of the twenty-nine caves, which were abandoned in the seventh century and only accidentally rediscovered in 1819, are in good condition and are still among the highlights of the tourist attractions in India, while remaining almost unknown. The paintings on the walls and ceilings are not frescoes; they were applied to a dry base consisting of earth, cow dung, and finely ground limestone. A design was then sketched on top; next it was outlined in black paint, and finally the painting was covered with varnish.

CAVES OF INTEREST TO TOURISTS

There are eight caves of interest to tourists. You absolutely have to see Monastery Cave 1, because its wall paintings are among the best in Ajanta. The most beautiful are probably the pictures of the black princess and of the dying princess. Two bodhisattvas (beings striving for the highest knowledge) frame the sanctuary—on the left Padmapani holds a lotus flower, and Avalokiteshvara is on the right. Tales from the old Buddhist legends (Jataka) also adorn the walls. One of the most beautiful monastery caves is Cave 16, which possibly served as the entrance to the entire complex. Its best-known picture represents the dying Sundari. The wife of Buddha's half brother Nanda died after learning that her husband wanted her to return to an earthly state in order to become a nun. Cave 17 is also fantastic: it shows, among other things, an expedition of Prince Vijaya, the mythical progenitor of the Sinhalese (543–505 BCE), to Sri Lanka.

The famous Cave 26 is a chaitya hall stupa, a meeting place and sanctuary for monks. On the left wall there is a 23-foot-tall (7 meter) representation on a pedestal of Buddha entering nirvana, while his disciples mourn him. The demon Mara is also depicted in this cave; he used his pretty daughter to seduce Buddha—unsuccessfully, of course.

Unfortunately, many paintings in Cave 2 are badly damaged. The ceilings are painted in addition to the walls, which depict the Jataka stories and scenes from the life of the Buddha. In the left shrine on the back wall you can see fat yakshas (demigods of lower rank) and their servants, as well as female believers, such as a princess of the Nagas (sacred snakes) on a swing. The largest cave, no. 10, dates from the first century BCE and the first century CE and was allegedly discovered by Englishmen out hunting. Here, too, the paintings are in poor condition, smeared with graffiti. They present themes from the previous life of the Buddha. Temple Cave 9, with its octagonal columns, dates from the first century BCE and is thus one of the oldest caves in Ajanta. In the Hinayana school of original Buddhism, Buddha was never represented personally, only through symbols (a footprint or the wheel of the law). On the west side in front of the almost-perfect Temple Cave 19, there is a beautiful stone figure of the Naga king, with seven cobras snaking around his head. The stupa features a striking, horseshoe-shaped window and is decorated inside with an image of the Buddha.

THE ELLORA CAVES

The thirty-four Ellora Caves are located 18.6 miles (30 kilometers) northwest of Aurangabad. These Buddhist, Hindu, and Jain cave temples, with their huge sculptures and rich iconography, were carved into the rock and constructed from top to bottom so that no scaffolding was required. They date from the fourth and thirteenth centuries and are newer than the Ajanta Caves. The most interesting Buddhist complexes (nos. 1 to 12) are Caves 10, 11, and 12. Of the Jain caves (nos. 30 to 34), no. 32 is particularly worth seeing. More impressive than the Buddhist and Jainist temples, however, are the Hindu temples (nos. 13 to 29)—especially temples 14, 15, and the Kailasa Temple (16).

MORE INFORMATION

Accommodations: Rama International, R-3 Chikalthana, Aurangabad, telephone +91 240 663 41 41

81 RAJAN'S REALM — THE ANDAMAN ISLANDS

BEYOND INDIA

By now, divers and anglers, end-of-the-world seekers and travel dreamers, and snake and bird specialists all are coming to the Andaman Islands, which belong to India. Some are attracted by the jungle and king cobras, while others are lured by the remote island beaches or large fish such as sharks and marlins.

Rajan has done it. He has climbed the long career ladder from lumberjack to actor and a Bollywood career—in the Andaman Islands. Translated, Rajan means "the royal." And that's just how he looks: strong, large, with dazzling white teeth.

As is so often the case in story-book careers, however, things didn't go so well at first. Rajan was brought from the Indian mainland to the Andamans to work in the jungle. Every day he toiled in the forest; the heat was unbearable, the food scarce. Until one day a film scout from Mumbai showed up at the remote camp. Bollywood needed a star, and Rajan was discovered: 8.2 feet (2.5 meters) tall, about 13,000 pounds (6,000 kilograms), and about 20 feet (6 meters) long—a mighty elephant who also had particularly long tusks. Rajan was the first Bollywood star in the islands.

NON-INDIAN INDIA

By ship, the trip to the Andamans takes fifty-six hours from Kolkata, formerly Calcutta, the closest major city on the Indian mainland. And tourists taking the plane have to get up early and catch all connecting flights to arrive at their bungalow on Havelock Island by the afternoon. That is how isolated the Andamans are in the Indian Ocean. There are 572 islands covered in dense jungle; simple, noticeably untouched island villages; and an ugly capital.

A BANANA DISPLAYS ITS BLOSSOM ON BARATANG ISLAND; THE BLOSSOMS ARE EATEN AS VEGETABLES (*LEFT*). THIS PRISTINE BEACH IS NEAR HUT BAY, THE MAIN TOWN ON LITTLE ANDAMAN (*ABOVE*).

Port Blair—in earlier times, a prison camp of the former colonial power Great Britain—is now a catch basin for immigrants from mainland India.

Culturally, the Andamans have at best a rudimentary connection to Indian traditions. And so Port Blair seems completely non-Indian. There is hardly any temple life, no sadhus are to be seen, and cows are not part of the street scene. There is no child labor, no beggars, no homeless people.

THINGS THAT CREEP AND FLY

Havelock Island has the most beautiful beach in the archipelago: Beach No. 7 is curved like a sickle, with light sand and about 0.6 miles (1 kilometer) long. Beaches and villages do not have names, but numbers—the same ones that the lumberjack settlements once had. In the elephant camp near Beach No. 3 you can see how the pachyderms are trained for their hard work in the logging camps. Take a stalk of bananas with you; these strong guys will do almost anything for a banana.

Havelock offers the best resort in the archipelago, the Barefoot at Havelock Jungle Resort. The bungalows, built in the lush jungle, are about 656 feet (200 meters) away

from Beach No. 7. Indian law requires this distance to the sea. And if you don't leave your doors and windows closed, your comfortable cottage will quickly be filled with creeping and flying creatures: fist-sized flying beetles, crickets, cicadas, and unfortunately mosquitoes. Until a few years ago, Rajan would sometimes stroll by.

FROM FILM STAR TO PHOTOGRAPHER'S MODEL

Bollywood cleared out at some point—back to distant Mumbai. But Rajan stayed on. He was lucky; after the film shoot, the owner of the resort bought the elephant and made him a star again. Rajan liked to swim in the sea, and after an English photographer took sensational underwater photos of him, amateur photographers from all over the world started traveling here to take a picture of Rajan. The pachyderm was allowed to live out his remaining life as a model, so to speak; he died in 2016. Everyone is still talking about him, and Bollywood couldn't have written a better script for Rajan.

Overall, tourism in the Andaman Islands is still in its infancy. Since 1997, the islands have been only partially accessible to visitors, and tourists are now allowed to spend the night on eight of the islands. The majority of the guests are Indians from the mainland or backpackers who find happiness in the simplest of inexpensive little huts. Most of the islands are closed to visitors, because there are self-sufficient ethnic groups living there. They live outside modern civilization, as nomads, hunters, fishermen, and gatherers and maintain their traditional way of life without the assistance of technology or other modern achievements. The Indigenous people of the Andaman Islands belong to the oldest population stratum in South Asia. They now comprise only about five hundred of the island's more than 300,000 inhabitants but once numbered in the thousands. The extreme population decline is a result of colonization: the people were attacked by

INDIAN WOMEN IN BRIGHTLY COLORED SARIS STROLL THROUGH THE COASTAL FOREST AT RADHANAGAR BEACH ON HAVELOCK ISLAND (*BELOW*); THIS CLOTH MERCHANT, A SIKH, RUNS HIS SHOP IN THE ANDAMAN ISLANDS CAPITAL OF PORT BLAIR ON SOUTH ANDAMAN ISLAND (*BELOW RIGHT*). THE REEFS OFF THE ISLANDS ARE GREAT SPOTS FOR SNORKELING (*ABOVE RIGHT*).

the English and decimated by the diseases that were brought in. However, they survived the tsunami of December 26, 2004, unscathed, in contrast to the rest of the island's population, who mourned some 5,000 victims. The Indigenous population knew how to correctly interpret the natural signs, such as the behavior of the animals and the extraordinarily strong ebb of the water that preceded the tsunami. They quickly sought out higher elevations.

THE LAST OF THEIR CULTURES

Today around three hundred Jarawa, around a hundred Onge and Sentinelese, and around forty peaceful Greater Andaman people live in reserve-like areas on Strait Island. They all are closely related linguistically, culturally, and genetically but in some cases have developed different survival strategies. The Sentinelese deliberately refuse any contact and also militarily defend North Sentinel Island, where

they live. A few years ago they killed two fishermen who apparently fell asleep, drifted off course, and landed on their island. Such killings are not prosecuted by the Indian authorities. When anthropologists released a pig on South Sentinel Island, it was also killed because the Sentinelese did not want the strange animal in their territory. The Onge, on the other hand, love piglets and peacefully share their Little Andaman Island with plantation workers from Bengal. The color red plays an important role for the Jarawa. Jarawa men stopped buses running on the Andaman Trunk Road, which connects North and South Andaman Islands and runs through their country, because some passengers were wearing red shirts. The Jarawa took the shirts, without words, as well as all the other red items, even the little rubbish bin by the driver's seat. Since then the road has been mostly closed. Every two hours, vehicles form a convoy escorted by the police.

SNORKELING ALONG THE EDGE OF THE REEF

Of course, everyone wants to see the big boys: sharks, marlins, yellowfin tuna, grouper, and snapper, as well as rays and sea turtles. But even small fish can be fascinating when they appear in schools of thousands. Off South Button Island, such schools of fish create constantly changing formations that look like works of art. South Button is the center of a comparatively small and uninhabited marine national park of less than 0.4 square miles (1 square kilometer). A trip by boat to Henry Lawrence Island is also worthwhile. Here at high tide you can snorkel over intact branch coral, sponges, and brain corals to the edge of the reef, which suddenly breaks off into the inky blue of the open sea. An encounter with the big boys is not to be ruled out.

MORE INFORMATION

All roads run via Kolkata or Chennai. You need a visa for India and can get a special visa for the Andamans in Port Blair.

www.andamantourism.gov.in

82 BELOW THE SUMMITS OF THE GODS—BHUTAN

IN THE LAND OF GROSS NATIONAL HAPPINESS

Bhutan is full of myths, legends, and spirituality: of its 750,000 inhabitants, every fifteenth person is a monk or nun. This appreciation of intangible values is also reflected in the politics of this small kingdom. Here, people strive to increase the Gross National Happiness.

MONKS WALK THROUGH THE INNER COURT-YARD OF THE PUNAKHA DZONG MONASTERY FORTRESS (*ABOVE*). THE TIGER'S NEST MONASTERY, CONSECRATED IN 1692, IS SITUATED ABOVE PARO ON THE EDGE OF A STEEP, 2,953-FOOT-HIGH (900 METER) ROCK FACE (*ABOVE RIGHT*). COLORFUL PRAYER FLAGS SEND PRAYERS TO HEAVEN; RELIGION PLAYS AN IMPORTANT ROLE FOR EVERYONE, NOT JUST FOR THE MONKS IN THE MONASTERY (*BELOW RIGHT*).

And now another eight hundred steps—after two hours of climbing steeply uphill. Mostly without talking, because the air is thin. The goal of the trip is Tiger's Nest, at 10,236 feet (3,120 meters) almost 3,300 feet (1,000 meters) above the Paro valley. This temple complex built into a steep rock face is the country's postcard motif. Once at the top, Saamdu Chetri says, "May this visit bring us joy, peace, harmony, love, and happiness." In the main temple, his students dramatically throw themselves to the ground, yet this gesture of humility seems awkward. His students are Dutch, and Saamdu Chetri is not just their guru. He has been a monk for over two years, and everyone in Bhutan knows him as the country's manager of happiness.

A GURU? A TEACHER!

Gross National Happiness. What a term! It is more important than the gross domestic product, as the King of Bhutan stated in the 1970s, because economic development must go hand in hand with Bhutan's culture, nature, and Buddhist values. The king set up a commission for Gross National Happiness, with Saamdu Chetri as its director. "Yes, we were ridiculed for our concept of happiness," says the happiness guru during the descent. "But we were also invited by the UN to explain it."

THESE SCHOOLGIRLS IN PUNAKHA, IN WESTERN BHUTAN, ARE IN A GOOD MOOD (*BELOW*); IN THIS REGION, THE SEVEN-TEENTH-CENTURY PUNAKHA DZONG IS THE SECOND-LARGEST FORTRESS MONASTERY IN THE COUNTRY (*BELOW RIGHT*). CHAM DANCES, WITH THEIR COLORFUL MASKS AND COS-TUMES, ARE AN IMPORTANT ELEMENT OF THE TSECHU RELIGIOUS FESTIVALS (*ABOVE RIGHT*).

Guru means nothing other than teacher. And the teacher is now speaking nonstop, because it is easier going downhill. He lectures on the thirty-three indicators in nine categories, such as health or education, which define Bhutanese happiness and environment in very practical terms. He points to the rubbish lying along the way. "Take a look around; all consumer waste! Cans, tubes, plastic." He picks up an empty Coke can and looks at it as if it were the symbol of unhappiness: "Use cola as a bug spray. It works! Marinate a piece of meat in cola. The next day it's gone! And nevertheless, everyone drinks the stuff!" The sixty-two-year-old doesn't say it is a witches' brew—that would be un-Buddhist.

SLIPPERS IN THE SNOW

Happiness sometimes seems elusive down in the valley. Many apartments don't have heat, and road workers still hammer construction stones by hand. And it is not just in the beautiful Gangtey plateau that some people wear only felt shoes or even slippers when walking in the snow, because winter shoes are too expensive. Saamdu Chetri knows that. Nevertheless, he sees his small country, wedged between the giants of China and India, as being on the right track.

Gross National Happiness is not achieved easily. Much of it has to do with Buddhism, which is deeply rooted in the country. To an outsider, it looks like a lot of religion mixed with a little social romanticism, a desire to be more "green," and a dash of the Attac movement. Advertising for consumer goods is not allowed, distributing plastic bags is prohibited, cigarettes are available only under the counter, and fast-food restaurants are unknown. There is not a single traffic light, the houses are a maximum of five stories high, and the national dress is compulsory in offices, in temples, and at work. The national sport is archery, and you many ascend the country's peaks only as high as 19,600 feet (6,000 meters) in elevation, because the higher elevations belong to the gods. This means that the last of the world's 19,000- and 20,000-foot (6,000 and 7,000 meter) summits that remain unclimbed are in Bhutan. If it sounds like another world, it is, because Bhutan, the size of Switzerland, was completely isolated until the 1960s. It had no currency of its own, no telephones, no post office, and no schools, hospitals, or roads. So happiness was given a helping hand.

MIDFIELD IN THE MATTER OF HAPPINESS

Today every second monk is fiddling with his cell phone, including Saamdu. "These things are not happiness, just an aid. We also have television, and there are no blocked websites. Bhutan knows what is going on outside it," he says. "And we have largely opened up to tourism." The roads are still under construction, and the mountainous routes can be uncomfortable.

It is only since 1974 that Bhutan began admitting between what started as 5,000 and most recently has become 34,000 visitors each year, although they have to pay a considerable daily rate averaging $250. Backpackers and cheap trekkers stay away from this country, which rises like a staircase from 656 feet (200 meters) in elevation in the south to the eternally snow-covered peaks of the Himalayas. In between, there are rural scenes of rice terraces and cattle and villages with mud brick houses. Everywhere the prayer flags flutter, the prayer wheels turn, and monks walk, dressed in wine-red robes. They live in the so-called dzongs, which can offer a home to up to three hundred monks. The sound of mighty drums thuds dully from the dzongs, some of which are mighty fortress monasteries, while the mantras sound monotonous. It seems that hardly anything has changed since the seventeenth century, when the Dzong of Paro was built. To see and experience all of this is daily happiness for the visitor. "There is still a lot to be done on a small scale," says Saamdu, also with regard to tourism, "but on a large scale we are well positioned." The numbers speak for themselves: in the United Nations World Happiness Report, Bhutan ranks in the midfield at seventy-ninth (Norway is first), while it ranks significantly lower worldwide in terms of gross national product (first is Luxembourg). Seen in this way, you would like to hope that Gross National Happiness will be setting the tone in wonderfully beautiful Bhutan for a long time to come.

"AMAN" TRAVEL

"We also have to work sustainably in tourism," says happiness manager Saamdu Chetri. And here the Amankora is in the front row: a luxury hotel with four annexes, scattered in five different valleys, each one with an individual character and a magnificent mountain backdrop. In Paro, the hotel is built like a Bhutanese village house; in Gangtey and Bumthang you live in mountain lodges; Punakha is like a royal residence, and Thimphu is stern and powerful, like a dzong. Since the minimum daily rate tourists pay for services is not always comfortable even for middle-class travelers, consider booking a private Bhutan tour with flights, a guide, Aman accommodation, meals, and comfortable vehicles, which partly compensate for the poor road conditions. www.amanresorts.com

MORE INFORMATION

In Delhi or Bangkok you have to change to Bhutan's Drukair Airlines to Paro. Visa required. The best time to travel is spring. www.tourism.gov.bt

83 CITY OF A THOUSAND PAGODAS—BAGAN

ON YOUR WAY IN OX CARTS

Myanmar is considered the most pristine country in Asia and the most beautiful in terms of landscape and art history. Even when it was the British colony of Burma, it was a Shangri-La for nostalgics and enjoyed great popularity as the "land of the pagodas" when you followed in the footsteps of Rudyard Kipling.

YOU CAN ENJOY A BEAUTIFUL VIEW OF THE ENTIRE COMPLEX FROM THE TWO-STORY TAYOKPYE TEMPLE, INCLUDING OF THE RARELY VISITED PAYATHONZU TEMPLE (*ABOVE*). NO NEED TO TRAVEL IN AN AIR-CONDITIONED BUS: YOU CAN ALSO GET TO SOME OF THE SIGHTS IN AN ENVIRONMENTALLY FRIENDLY OX CART (*BELOW RIGHT*). THE WOODEN YOKESONE KYAUNG MONASTERY IN SALE HAS BEEN A MUSEUM FOR BUDDHIST ART SINCE 1995 (*ABOVE RIGHT*).

The most stylish way to visit the city of Bagan is by boat on Ayeyarwady River, if the water level allows it. On the eleven-hour journey, you get to know people and the landscape at an unhurried pace, and you can take in the most-varied impressions in peace. At the intermediate ports of call, fish are offered for sale, chickens tied by the feet land on the hard ship planks, and large banana plants and fruit baskets are handed over from the riverbank and stowed on board.

Bagan's greatest attraction is visible from the ship: the golden zedi of the Shwezigon Pagoda. The broad landscape, spanned by a radiant blue sky, features dry, yellow-brown earth; stupas built of dark-red brick; and shining, golden temple domes. Starting from late morning, all of it lies under a huge umbrella of heat and dust. In any case, the best way to travel is to rent a carriage, bike, or electric scooter, because this way you can experience the landscape up close and much more intensely than from behind the tinted windows of a tourist bus.

LIVELY MARKETS AND QUIET TEMPLES
The markets are particularly worth seeing in the morning. While strolling along the

displays, you can enjoy the scent of fruit, vegetables, and spices, which are available in great variety; the market women are colorfully dressed, some calmly puffing on huge cheroot cigars. You can enjoy the warm light of the late afternoon during a romantic ride in a horse-drawn carriage or an ox cart. The fine haze softens the light and envelops everything in a delicate veil. You look at the pagodas with their stupas glistening gold in the hot sun in astonishment and awe. They have either cone-like roof structures or, like the Shwezigon Pagoda, bell-shaped domes. The temples are also architecturally diverse. Some have a central shrine, others a square tower—such as the Ananda Temple with its corn cob-shaped stupa—or a pyramid-shaped tower like the Mahabodhi Temple. You walk countless times through dark, narrow corridors and climb the steep, narrow steps onto the terraces. Friendly girls stand along the side of the landing and advise visitors to take their time: "Slowly, soooo slowly."

FINE HAZE AND DELICATE MIST

The best way to enjoy the sunset is to climb the temple Thitsawadi, the only one you are allowed to climb. There are four other temples—Pyathatgyi, Shwesandaw, Myauk, and Taung-Guni. The whitewashed Shwesandaw Pagoda is particularly well known. You can watch the sun set from its five stacked terraces. However, since it is overcrowded, it is usually better to pay a visit at sunrise. For those who don't mind getting up early and paying the high fee, another highlight is a balloon ride. From above, the pagoda landscape looks like a soft pastel painting. While the balloon hovers silently over the landscape, still covered by a thin morning mist, the sun unfolds its warming halo and with its light awakens the countless temples and stupas to new life. A new day begins in a magical country.

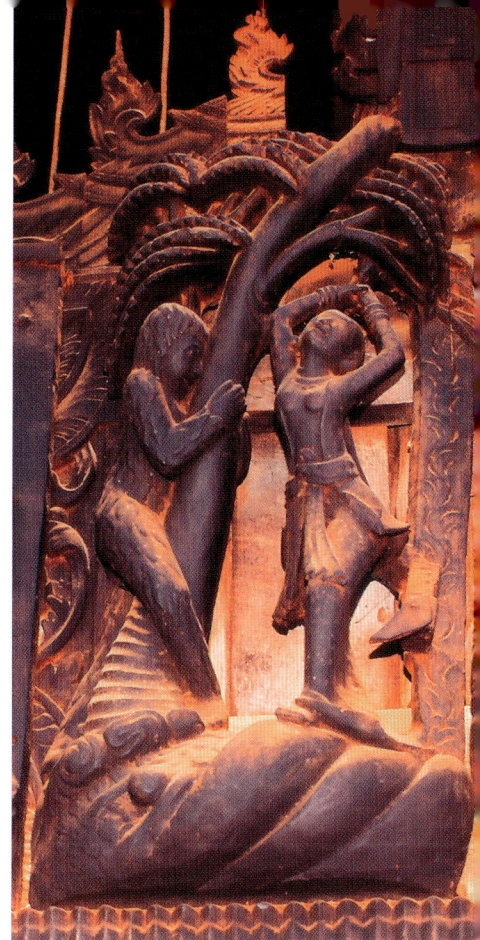

SALE (SA LAY)

The town of Sale near Bagan is barely known among tourists, although it has some must-see attractions. These include the Yokeson Kyaung wooden monastery, built in 1882, with its staircase adorned with snakelike dragons. The forty-five wooden sculptures on the balustrade of the outer veranda are interesting; these show scenes from court life and the *Ramayana* and the Jataka stories. The Man Paya Shrine is also worth a visit. Its 10-foot-tall (3 meter) Buddha figure is said to have been made around 1300, using a gilded lacquer. Legend has it that the figure swam across the Ayeyarwady from Monywa to Sale.

MORE INFORMATION

Entry visas cost about $18 (15 euros) and are valid for one week. A bike costs $1 to $2 per day, an electric scooter costs $6 to $11 (5 to 10 euros) per day, and horse-drawn carriages are $17 (15 euros); a balloon ride is $335 to $450 (300 to 400 euros).

263

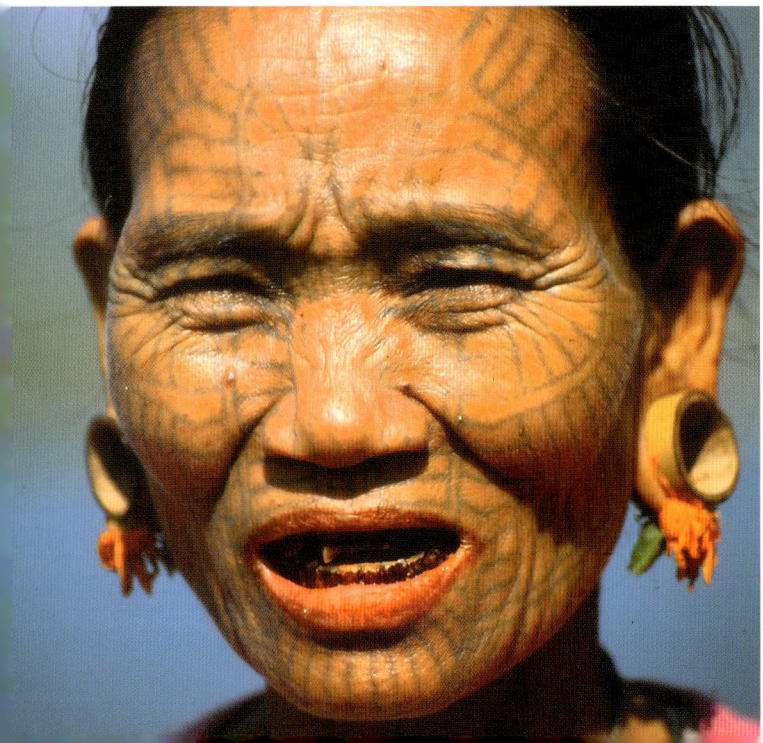

84 THE ANCIENT RAKHINE ROYAL CITY—MRAUK U

TEMPLES AND SOLITARY SANDY BEACHES

Mrauk U was the capital of the ancient Rakhine Kingdom and was once a magnificent metropolis. With its countless temples and pagodas, it is one of the most beautiful sights in Myanmar. The southwestern part of the country also attracts visitors with its fantastic endless and almost-deserted beaches.

Mrauk U is the main attraction of today's Rakhine State and can be reached only by water from Sittwe, which was once considered the richest and most beautiful port city of Myanmar. The ferry to Mrauk U sets off very early. The trip on the Kaladan River to what used to be the center of the formerly powerful Kingdom of Rakhine is around 43.5 miles (70 kilometers) long, and ships need five to seven hours to cover this distance.

About an hour from Sittwe, Ponnagyun is the first port of call for some ships.

Situated on the 16-mile-long (26 kilometer) Island of the Pandits, Ponnagyun was an important military and naval post and also boasted a palace. The seventeenth-century Uyit Taung Pagoda rises toward the sky from a hill. It contains the forehead bone of a pundit, a religious scholar, as a relic. The boat trip continues along the Kaladan River. Hobby ornithologists can watch a large variety of waterfowl in peace and quiet, because Siberian wild geese, wild ducks, and different species of storks and herons

KOTHAUNG TEMPLE IS ALSO CALLED THE TEMPLE OF 9,000 IMAGES BECAUSE OF ITS MANY STATUES (*ABOVE LEFT*). WHILE OLDER CHIN WOMEN HAVE FACIAL TATTOOS AND LARGE EARPIECES, MOST OF THE YOUNGER CHIN GIRLS NO LONGER FOLLOW THIS CUSTOM (*BELOW LEFT*). FROM OUTSIDE, THE HTUKKANT THEIN TEMPLE LOOKS ALMOST LIKE A FORTRESS (*BELOW*).

all have found a reserve in this water-rich and sparsely populated region. Schools of river prawns flee the sound of the approaching ship along the mangrove-covered riverbanks, and the nets in the river with their wriggling prey testify to the abundance of fish.

Old-fashioned sampans and junks loaded with people and goods keep crossing our path. Almost endless, lush green rice fields line the banks, and water buffaloes with powerful horns are seen again and again. In between, there is a flashing glimpse of a village here and there, with houses on stilts in palm groves and whitewashed pagodas amid the dense green. The journey continues, always northward, until the ferry finally reaches Aungdet by afternoon. The little village lies on the Henkayaw River, a tributary of the Kaladan. From there, it is only a few hundred meters on foot to Mrauk U.

THE CORRIDOR OF THE KOTHAUNG TEMPLE IS DECORATED WITH MANY BUDDHA FIGURES OF DIFFERENT SIZES (BELOW). WHILE FISHERMEN BRING IN THEIR CATCH ON NGAPALI BEACH IN THE LATE AFTERNOON, THE WIDE SANDY BEACH WITH ITS SHADY PALM TREES OFFERS TOURISTS ALMOST UNDISTURBED REST AND RECREATION (ABOVE AND BELOW RIGHT).

THE OLD ROYAL CITY

Mrauk U, with its more than seventy temples and pagodas, is one of the most impressive destinations in Myanmar. A main attraction in the old royal residence city is the Shitthaung Temple, which looks like a fortress. Its terraced structure with ornamental zedis is reminiscent of the famous Borobudur Temple complex on Java. The two inner galleries contain innumerable niches holding figures of the Buddha—Shitthaung's familiar name, the Temple of 80,000 Images, alludes to them. Of particular interest, however, is the outside gallery, which contains Buddhist depictions of the 550 Jataka tales, as well as of Hindu gods such as Brahma, Vishnu, and the elephant-headed Ganesha. The representations were carved out of sandstone and partially painted. If you leave the Shitthaung Temple through the main entrance, you will see the Htukkhant Thein Pagoda opposite. This elongated structure with a semicircular end has narrow windows that look like loopholes. Thus, the temple almost reminds you of a fortress from the outside. You reach the east entrance via a staircase, which leads to a spiral passage with beautiful stone relief carvings. From there, the way goes to the left into the pagoda interior, through an arched corridor where you can see 146 sandstone Buddha figures set in niches along the sides.

Only 100 feet (30 meters) north of the Shitthaung is the octagonal Andaw Temple, surrounded by small, round brick pagodas. Inside, two openwork walkways lead from the eastern vestibule around the closed core of the building. The walkways contain many niches, holding thirty-two Buddha images. When you leave the Andaw Temple and turn left, you will reach the Ratanabon Pagoda. There is a beautiful view of the Htukkant Thein Pagoda from its platform. The pagoda has no decorations; not a single Buddha statue can be found. However, if you follow the road straight ahead from the intersection, after a short

THE BAY OF BENGAL COAST

A 0.6-mile-wide (1 kilometer), gently curved bay featuring the finest sand, with tall palm trees and crystal-clear water, where schools of colorful coral fish swim about—this is how you imagine a tropical paradise. Ngapali Beach fulfills those dreams. Mass tourism has not yet reached this small piece of Earth, and the 1.9-mile-long (3 kilometer) beach is almost deserted. Its landmark is the stone mermaid, who sits enthroned on a small group of rocks in the middle of the beach. There are numerous hotel complexes near the palm-lined beach, and you can get delicious seafood in the restaurants along the narrow street behind it. When an ox cart trundles by in the evening and the sun sets in a blood-red spectacle in the sea, your beach dreams come true.

MORE INFORMATION

Joint website of Myanmar's tourism industry: www.tourismmyanmar.org

walk through the fields you will come to the Kothaung Temple, the Temple of 9,000 Images. The name refers to the innumerable small Buddha figures carved into the walls of the galleries. According to astrologers, the temple was to be built in six months. But the workers did not have time to fetch the sandstone blocks from the coast, so they also used bricks. As a result, the temple quickly fell into disrepair.

ETHNIC DIVERSITY

Myanmar is a multiethnic state, and some Tibetan-Burmese ethnic groups live widely scattered in the western mountainous regions of the Rakhine state, which are crisscrossed by fast-flowing rivers. Tourists can visit their villages, such as Kyichaung or Konchaung.

The remote villages of the Tibeto-Burmese Chin can be reached by small motor boats on the Lemro, a tributary of the Kaladan. The Chin are among the largest ethnic groups in Myanmar and are also native to the neighboring regions of India. Traditionally, Chin women adorn themselves with facial tattoos and large ear pieces, but tattooing is practiced less and less. In recent times, however, there have been brutal clashes between the Myanmar army and the Arakan Rohingya Salvation Army (ARSA) Islamic militia in Rakhine. Therefore, trips to the villages of the Rohingya, who do not have Myanmar citizenship, are on hold. However, a booming tourism industry in Mrauk U and Ngapali is expected to emerge.

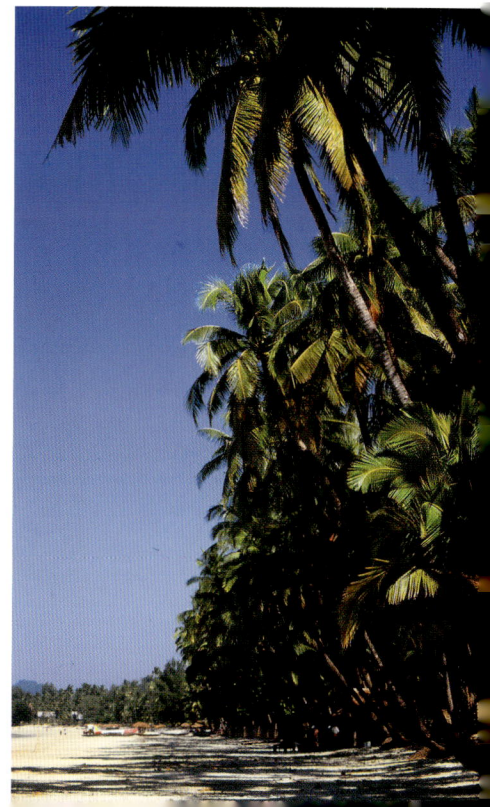

85 FASCINATING CITY OUTSIDE BANGKOK—NAKHON PATHOM

TO THAILAND'S LARGEST CHEDI

Around 50,000 people live in Nakhon Pathom—and on Buddhist holidays a similar number flock to the Phra Pathom Chedi in this city west of Bangkok. The huge, ancient Buddhist structure is beyond question the cultural highlight of western Thailand.

Sunthorn Phu means to the Thais what Shakespeare means to the British and Goethe to the Germans. Many consider him to be Thailand's greatest poet, because during his lifetime—1786 to 1856—he was the first to reference man-made objects in the country's literature. Previously, religious motifs and stories dominated Thai poetry. In "Nirat Phra Pathom," Sunthorn Phu describes a trip to Nakhon Pathom. He walks reverently clockwise along the temple terrace around the chedi, which was then under construction. Today, the 417-foot-high (127 meter) structure is considered the most sacred chedi in the country. In one passage Sunthorn writes: "This must be the way to heaven when we die," referring to the building's square top, which is interpreted as a sanctuary standing above the earthly realm.

BIGGER THAN THE SHWEDAGON PAGODA

The Phra Pathom Chedi in Nakhon Pathom, which is visible from afar, rises 417 feet (127 meters) into the sky. It is not as tall as the barely 505-foot-tall (154 meter) wooden Tianning Pagoda in Changzhou, China, but taller than the world-famous Shwedagon

GLEAMING GOLDEN PHRA PATHOM CHEDI IS THE TALLEST AND ONE OF THE OLDEST BUDDHIST STRUCTURES IN THAILAND (*BELOW*). A COLORFUL TRAIN RUNS BY THE KWAI RIVER AND THE INFAMOUS BRIDGE (*TOP RIGHT*). A WOMAN BRINGS OFFERINGS TO THE TEMPLE (*BOTTOM RIGHT*).

RIVER TRIP IN WESTERN THAILAND

Pierre Boulle wrote the novel *The Bridge on the River Kwai*, which became world famous through the Hollywood classic directed by David Lean and with William Holden in the lead role. The story has a deadly serious background: during World War II, more than 100,000 forced laborers and prisoners of war taken by the Japanese lost their lives here due to the inhumane conditions. Yet, western Thailand has much more to offer: rafting on bamboo rafts on the Kwai Noi, the Kwai Yai, or the Mae Klong Rivers through a wild natural landscape. People have settled in floating houses on some sections of these rivers. Tourists also have the option of spending the night on jungle rafts on the river. There is no electricity—a bit of oil-lamp romance is preserved.

MORE INFORMATION

The trip from Bangkok by bus takes just under two hours. Tourists can stay overnight on the water in the Antique Boat Hotel. www.tourismthailand.org

Pagoda of Yangon in Myanmar, which measures almost 328 feet (100 meters), almost as high as the diameter of the impressive dome of the Phra Pathom is wide.

The Holy Chedi of the Beginning is also one of the oldest Buddhist buildings in Thailand. Its origins go back to the third century BCE, when the Indian king Ashoka commanded a powerful Buddhist empire and sent monks to Nakhon Pathom to preach the religion in what is now Thailand. The foundation of today's temple was probably built in the fourth century CE but has undergone many changes over time. The structure was rebuilt into today's gleaming, golden-brown chedi just over a hundred years ago. The bell-shaped chedi consists of two chedis. An ancient, 128-foot-high (39 meter) chedi dating from the fourth century was discovered by archeologists. Built in the style of the Mon people, it was a testament to the prosperity of an important ancient Mon kingdom based in Myanmar and Thailand. Nakhon Pathom was an important trading town and had the right to mint coins. At that time, the settlement still lay directly on the sea coast, but because the coast has increasingly collected silt, the sea has retreated by more than 31 miles (50 kilometers) over the years. At the beginning of the eleventh century, the Khmer built a prang or temple tower over the sanctuary, which was already 279 feet (85 meters) tall. But its glory did not last long: the Burmese destroyed the monumental building as early as 1057. Today's chedi was not completed until 1870, after seventeen years of construction.

REVERED BUDDHA STATUE

The great Buddha figure of Nakhon Pathom is only 26 feet (8 meters) tall but enjoys the highest level of veneration. The statue, designed in Sukhothai style, is one of numerous Buddha images lined up along the promenade on the terrace. In each of the four viharne, the assembly halls for the members of the order, the life of Siddhartha, Buddha's birth name, can be roughly traced by means of groups of figures. However, Buddha manifests himself differently each time: in the southern viharn, he is protected by a snake; in the western one, he is resting; in the eastern one, he shows himself beneath a bodhi tree; and in the northern one he is standing. Next to the eastern viharn, the attached museum displays a particularly interesting exhibit: a stone wheel that symbolizes the teachings of the Buddha and dates back to 150 BC.

86 THAILAND'S AMAZING NORTHEAST—THE ISAN

A POORHOUSE WITH A RICH CULTURE

Ban Chiang is regarded as a cultural cradle of mankind, and Phimai as one of the most important temples in Southeast Asia. But nowhere is Thailand poorer than in the rural northeast. There are few dimly lit nightclubs or sophisticated infinity pools in the Isan region, and above all there is no hectic rush.

The visiting monks are almost competing with each other to snap pictures. Some laugh; others are amazed. For them, as for all other cultural tourists, the Phimai Temple complex is a sight to see. Phimai has no religious meaning for them and is also not a place for meditation.

Phimai is one of the most important temple complexes in Thailand and is located 31 miles (50 kilometers) northeast of the inconspicuous provincial capital of Nakhon Ratchasima. If you are coming from Bangkok, the city is considered the gateway to Isan, and also to the Phimai temple complex, the Angkor Wat of Thailand, although Phimai is significantly smaller than the fairy-tale temple in the Cambodian jungle and is number two in the Khmer hierarchy. However, Phimai houses by far the most important collection of Khmer art in Thailand and presents the Hindu cosmos in perfect symbolic form. It is still unknown whether the ruined city was destroyed or slowly decayed over the course of what could have been eight centuries. The only certainty is that the high Khmer culture of Phimai was replaced by the Sukhothai period in the thirteenth century, and during the following Ayutthaya period from the fourteenth century onward, Buddhist culture and architecture finally prevailed.

THE MAIN PRANG (TEMPLE TOWER) OF THE IMPORTANT PHIMAI KHMER TEMPLE COMPLEX (*LEFT*). THE GREAT ELEPHANT FESTIVAL IS CELEBRATED IN SURIN IN NOVEMBER (*ABOVE*).

THAILAND'S RURAL POORHOUSE

The Isan region is rich in history and culture. And although 20 percent of the total population grows 50 percent of the country's rice harvest here, the northeast is still considered the "poorhouse" of the country. Until a few years ago, children, mainly girls, were sold to Bangkok. To this day, people sell their votes for money to alleviate the worst kind of misery. Various governments have poured hundreds of millions of baht into development programs, ranging from the establishment of cooperatives to land grants. Despite these efforts, the standard of living in the troubled northeast is still the lowest in the kingdom. A rural exodus could not be stopped, even by the reintroduction of Mutmee weaving. Precious Mutmee silk is created by a weaving method that has its traditional home in Isan. Individual threads are stretched, intertwined, and dyed several times before the weaving begins.

A CULTURAL CRADLE OF MANKIND

In the 1970s, archeologists excavated stone agricultural implements in Ban Chiang in the far northeast. They demonstrate that rice was probably grown there thousands of years ago—likely long before the Chinese grew it.

Even before the Mesopotamians began forging weapons, the people had figured out how to make them. They also kept domestic animals and created ornate ceramic vessels.

The findings of Ban Chiang were so groundbreaking that archeologists are still not certain whether the oldest cultures in Asia were actually native to present-day China. That in turn would mean that Ban Chiang might have been the site of one of humanity's cradles of culture. Anyone who is interested in these human origins should visit Ban Chiang, even though the remaining original finds are presented in a style worthy of a high school exhibit. The most important finds were long since taken to the United States and to the National Museum in Bangkok.

THE TEMPLE WITH A BORDER CROSSING

Some 372 miles (600 kilometers) south, you can make your way over a border crossing, along 6,500 feet (1,981 meters) of footpath, and up 341 steps and four floors, to visit Khao Phra Viharn, a purist Hindu temple that was disputed before the International Court of Justice in The Hague in 1962. According to the judgment, Khao Phra Viharn is no longer on Thai land, but rather Cambodian, but for the Thais, it is still home. From the seventeenth century until the Indochina War, Thailand had occupied the entire area on a large scale. In addition, the mountain's feet are on Thai territory. Only the overhanging rock on which the temple stands protrudes into Cambodian airspace. Cambodians concede the territorial technicality but defiantly argue that "Khao Phra Viharn is still ours!" The temple comes close to the ideal Khmer complex. Because it is situated on a rock plateau, however, the only way to visit it is from Cambodia. There are no border formalities of any kind, but signs on both sides of the 1.2-mile-long (2 kilometer) access road remind us that both countries have fought

AT THE SURIN ELEPHANT FESTIVAL, SOME TWO HUNDRED ELEPHANTS FROM ALL OVER THAILAND ARE TESTED FOR THEIR DEXTERITY, ENDURANCE, AND OBEDIENCE (*BELOW*). **THE MANDAPA (LINTEL) IN THE PHIMAI TEMPLE COMPLEX SHOWS REPRESENTATIONS FROM THE HINDU EPIC THE** *RAMAYANA* (*ABOVE RIGHT*). **THE HANDS OF THE BUDDHA FIGURE IN WAT PA NANACHAT IN UBON RATCHATHANI ARE FORMED IN THE GESTURE OF THE TEACHER, THE DHARMACHAKRA MUDRA** (*BELOW RIGHT*).

AT THE FORTUNE-TELLER

Samruam Mosumried is forty-two years old and has been a fortune-teller for ten years. He is one of countless prophets of good and bad fortune who ply their trade in front of almost every moderately important temple in Thailand. The former rice farmer felt called one day to predict the future and read the lunar calendar. Now he advises his clients for one hundred baht per session. "It is better to just put ninety-nine baht or some other odd number in the mug with the lucky sticks," says the appointed person, since that already brings you good fortune. He asks for your date of birth, which he converts into the corresponding year of the Buddhist lunar calendar. Then he assesses the customer's strengths, weaknesses, and other characteristics—quite specifically, and sometimes surprisingly well.

MORE INFORMATION

All larger towns in Isan can be reached by bus from Bangkok. Try Isan cuisine, such as noodles à la Phimai style (spicy!).

wars against each other in recent history. The areas to the right and left of the road are still mined. The constant friction sometimes escalates, so it is best to look into the current situation at Khao Phra Viharn shortly before you visit.

The Prasat Phanom Rung temple complex is worth its own cultural trip. After a row of 130 half-height columns, five increasingly narrow stepped terraces rise up before you. The sanctuary presides above; from there, you can enjoy a magnificent view over the rice fields. In the warm evening light, the relief sculptures seem to come to life: here the sleeping Vishnu, there the meditating Brahma, and Shiva seems to be dancing. This Hindu temple dates from the tenth century. Apart from the extraordinary cultural sites—many are repositories of Khmer art, and some objects still lie undisturbed underground in this region—you will find wonderful peace in the Isan. The great stream of tourists has not yet reached this area, with one exception: thousands of visitors flock to Surin on the third weekend in November. More than a hundred elephants are presented in parades and competitions, and tourists snap thousands of photos.

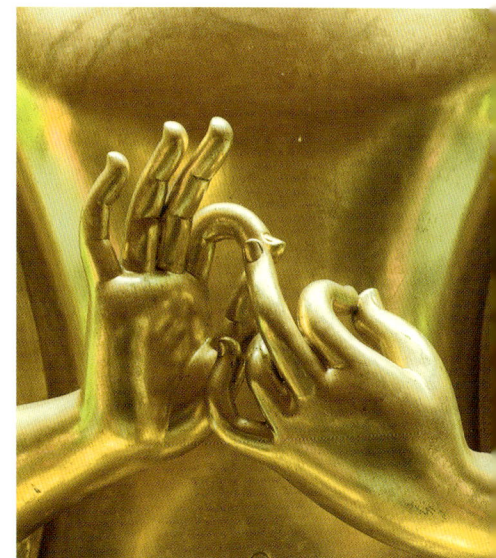

87 MAGICAL KARST LANDSCAPE— DRY HALONG BAY

GROTTOES, TUNNELS, AND THE OLD ROYAL CITY OF HOA LU

In contrast to Halong Bay, the limestone cliffs in the Dry Halong Bay don't rise from the sea, but from rice fields. Fairy-tale trips in a sampan and bike tours through the amphibious landscape are part of the "absolute must" program.

FROM THE CAVES IN TAM COC (THREE GROTTOES) THE VIEW REACHES TO THE STRIKING LIMESTONE CLIFFS (*ABOVE*). A DRAGON MEETS YOU ON THE STAIRWAY TO A TEMPLE NEAR TAM COC (*BELOW RIGHT*). THE HISTORIC CAPITAL, HOA LU, IS THE SCENE OF TRADITIONAL CELEBRATIONS AND CULTURAL FESTIVALS (*ABOVE RIGHT*).

In this fantastically beautiful landscape about 56 miles (90 kilometers) south of Hanoi, the bizarre limestone cliffs are not surrounded by the sea, but by waving fields of rice. And the grottoes are not stalactite caves, but so-called tunnels created by water that has washed its way through the rocks for thousands of years.

ON THE NGO DONG

You can navigate the shallow Ngo Dong River in simple bamboo boats, on trips two to three hours long. The destination of Tam Coc (Three Grottoes) is only the last of countless small highlights that add up to one of the most beautiful day trips in northern Vietnam. The dark tunnels measure an impressive 427, 230, and 131 feet (130, 70, and 40 meters), but the real attractions are on the riverbanks. Here, farmers trudge through the muddy field behind their plows. Water buffalo carry children on their backs, and flocks of ducks waddle across the dams, brought into line by herding boys with sticks. It is a soothing ride through a piece of Vietnam that has remained as it originally was.

Ninh Binh, capital of the province of the same name and gateway to Dry Halong Bay, is now a calm city with 150,000 inhabitants. More churches than anywhere else in a town of this size indicate the high proportion of Christians, mostly Catholics, in the region. After the city was almost completely bombed out by the Americans, for the first few decades the cathedral ruins were left standing as a memorial but then were torn down. Today the Phat Diem Cathedral near the village of Kim Son, 18.6 miles (30 kilometers) south of Ninh Binh, is considered the center for Catholic Christians in northern Vietnam. A visit to the oversized complex is worthwhile; the altar was carved out of a boulder, and gold-lacquered pillars support the huge nave.

FROM CHURCHES TO PAGODAS

Many temples and cultural sites stand out in the ancient landscape of the Red River delta. The Keo Pagoda in the neighboring province of Thai Binh to the east is important in terms of culture and history and is part of an especially beautiful landscape. It belongs to the richly traditional Buddhist monastery of enlightenment. The monastery venerates a monk who cured a king of serious disease over nine hundred years ago. To honor him,

an annual festival with processions and boat races is celebrated around the middle of the ninth month.

The pagodas of the Emerald Grotto of Chua Bich Dong, southeast of Ninh Binh, also mark one of the many cultural highlights of this particularly fascinating region. The temples, with their curved roofs, look very Chinese. Two other places in the neighborhood let you look even deeper into Vietnamese history. The large bronze drums on display in the Hanoi Historical Museum come from the archeological excavation site of Dong Son, which is considered the cradle of Vietnamese civilization. In contrast, the history of the former capital Hoa Lu goes back "only" about a thousand years. Little remains from the time of the first kings of the Dinh dynasty. But it is worth going to see the beautiful temples and the oldest royal tombs in the country from Ninh Binh. The ideal way to cover the 7.5 miles (12 kilometers) is by bike, which doesn't take too much effort. Almost every hotel in Ninh Binh rents out bikes.

ECO-FRIENDLY LODGE WITH A PHILOSOPHY

The La Ferme du Colvert lodge is part of an ecotourism project. Located 25 miles (40 kilometers) south of Hanoi and easily accessible via National Road 6 in the direction of Hoa Binh, it offers ten bungalows set around Dap Dom Lake. Each one is individually designed and appointed with locally made furniture made of granite, bamboo, embroidery, and wood from the trees in the neighborhood. Farmers pass by on their way from the rice fields and offer a friendly wave. Guests have many options: watch the gardener fishing in the pond, take a pleasant raft ride, visit a village festival, or warm up in a *hamam*, which has steam that smells of bamboo leaves, lemongrass, and coriander.

MORE INFORMATION

Vietnam Aventure:
www.vietnam-aventure.com

88 VIETNAM'S LARGEST ISLAND—PHU QUOC

MANY-FACETED DISCOVERIES IN THE GULF OF THAILAND

At almost 373 square miles (600 square kilometers), Phu Quoc is Vietnam's largest island. Discovery tours take you to wonderful beaches, pepper plantations, and port towns.

PHU QUOC IS THE LARGEST ISLAND IN VIETNAM. VISITORS ESPECIALLY LOVE THE BEACHES WHERE FISHERMEN MOOR THEIR BOATS (*RIGHT*), BUT THE MODERN BUDDHIST TEMPLE COMPLEX IS ALSO AN ATTRACTION (*BELOW*).

In An Thoi, the southernmost port on Phu Quoc, an unvarnished everyday life prevails. Women wave the flies away from the strips of freshly slaughtered meat hanging in street stands. Armadas of mopeds rattle toward the harbor, where fishing boats arrive early in the morning. Crates filled to the brim are taken ashore by human chains, and ice blocks weighing several hundred pounds go back on board. The atmosphere invades your senses. It smells of fish in various stages of decay. People carrying loads and pushing carts whiz around; dogs dig in the rubbish. After their work is done, sailors soap up on deck and rinse off with a hose. The foamy sludge runs off into the harbor basin.

But in the background, the structure of the world's longest over-the-sea cable car emerges from the tropical green. If you are keeping an eye on the various resort megaprojects, you might know that Vietnam's

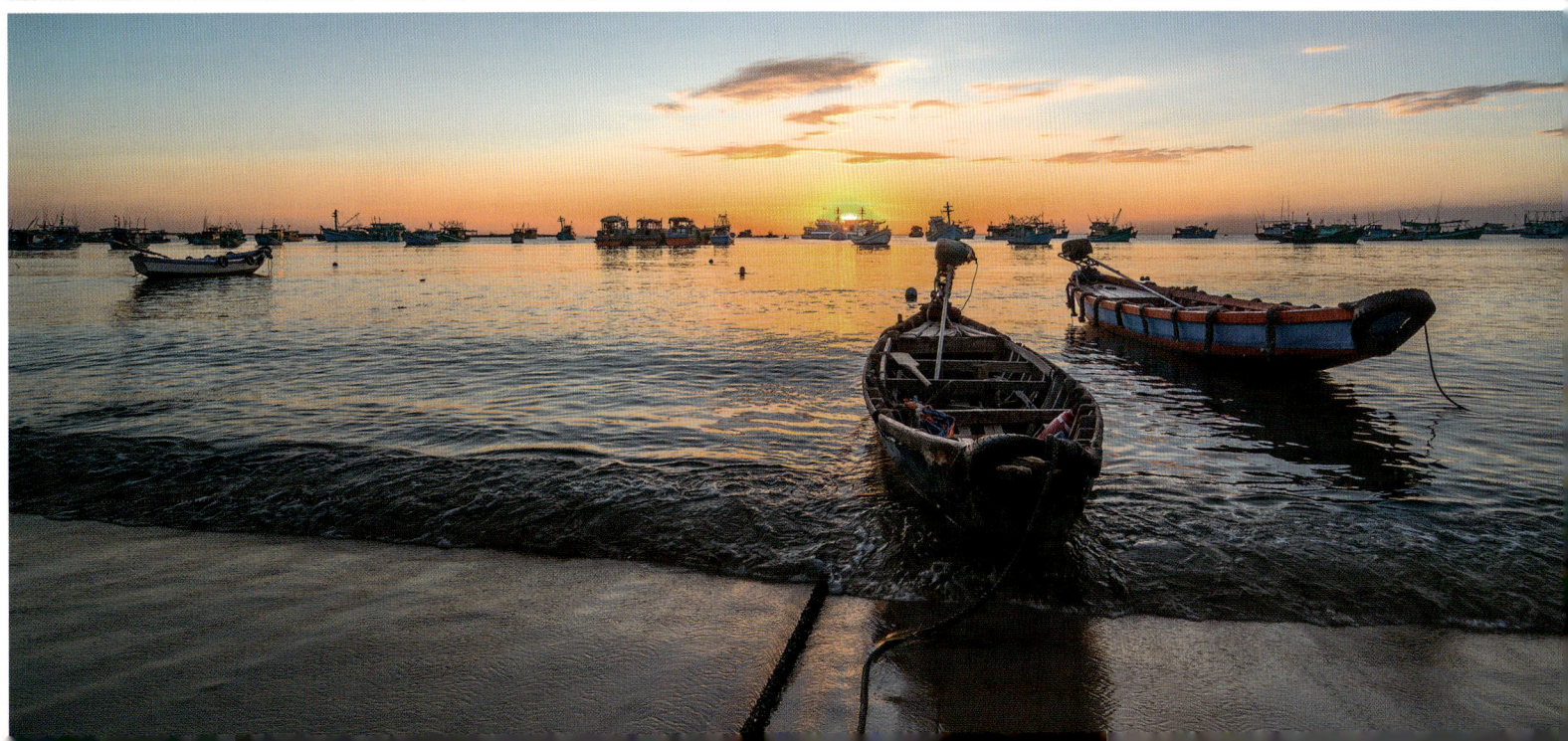

SAO BEACH IN THE SOUTH IS ONE OF THE MOST BEAUTIFUL BEACHES ON THE ISLAND (*BELOW*), WHILE THE PRISTINE BEACHES OF THE OFFSHORE ISLAND OF MAY RUT (*BOTTOM*) ARE PERFECT FOR SNORKELING. SUNSET IS AN EXPERIENCE EACH AND EVERY DAY (*ABOVE RIGHT*). THE LOCAL HATS NOT ONLY ARE PRETTY BUT OFFER GOOD PROTECTION FROM THE SUN (*BELOW RIGHT*).

largest island, Phu Quoc, could well transform itself into the Mallorca of Asia in the medium to long term and attract masses of visitors. There is already an international airport and well-developed transport routes. The number of newcomers keeps increasing. Nobody knows for sure whether there are 70,000 people now spread over Phu Quoc, or twice that number. What does that tell us about the future? Better to arrive today than tomorrow. In addition, get yourself what almost every-one on the island has: a moped. The rental formalities are completed quickly, and you're on your way.

A MODERN BUDDHIST TEMPLE

Far away from the hustle and bustle of Duong Dong—the largest town on the island—and the out-of-place safari park in the northwest, you can catch a breeze as you moped to Thom Beach in the northeast, or to the east coast, where there is another fishing village at Ham Ninh. This is the best place to taste the fresh catch. Or head deep into the southeast, not too far from An Thoi. There a side road leads for a few miles through the greenery to the Ho Quoc Pagoda. Banana trees grow along the roadside. Millipedes as thick as a finger curl up in the grass. A street dog looks bored and has no desire to take on the moped. Soon you are looking across the sea to the right. If you stop, you will hear the concert of the cicadas and the tireless waves. The destination of this detour, a Buddhist temple complex, proves that modern reli-gious architecture can fit harmoniously into the landscape. This visitor attraction doesn't have many years under its belt, but it has charm. Wide outside steps lead up to the central structures. Upstairs, a monk strikes a bell and then turns to something just as important: his cell phone.

BEACHES, TRACES OF HISTORY, AND FISH SAUCE

The most-beautiful island beaches, Sao Beach and Khem Beach, are also in the south; these are palm-fringed bands of sand like those in the travel magazines. When darkness falls, you can see the bright-green lights of the fishing boats along the horizon— a spectacle that seems almost unreal. On the main road through the southern island is Coconut Prison, a former high-security remnant of the Vietnam War. Open to the public, the entrance leads through meter-high rows of barbed wire from which you can see the

A FANTASTIC HOTEL

Luxury in an exclusive location behind Khem Beach in the deep southeast, about a twenty-minute drive from the airport—this is the setting for the Hotel JW Marriott Phu Quoc Emerald Bay. The spacious complex, imaginatively designed by Bill Bensley in the style of a historical campus, is a beacon for lovers of both architecture and design. There is a spa and three large pools, as well as bars and restaurants, bike rentals, and shopping opportunities. Everything has style, down to the last detail. The long, sandy beach spreads out right in front of the door and is kept meticulously clean. There are 244 rooms and a few exclusive villas to choose from.

MORE INFORMATION

The Marriott website provides helpful information about Phu Quoc Emerald Bay: www.marriott.com

watchtowers. Tens of thousands of resistance fighters were imprisoned here starting in 1967 and treated worse than cattle. Sculptures re-create scenes of barbaric torture. This painful piece of history cannot be concealed.

The product made in the Thung Hong factory, near the Coconut Prison, has a different impact on your stomach. It is fish sauce, *nuoc mam*, an important factor in the Phu Quoc economy. The smell coming from huge wooden barrels, in which salted, nongutted anchovies ferment for a year, takes some getting used to.

IN THE REALM OF PEPPER PLANTATIONS

Visitors' taste buds are more likely to encounter a product grown in central locations on the island: pepper, such as that grown on the Natural Farm. "I'm Alice in Pepperland," Alice says. The young woman conducts visitors to the plantations of meter-high towers of plants and tells them all about the pepper harvest between January and March. She also teaches cooking classes, does farm chores, and entertains the dogs. "I like farm life and a quiet place like this one," she says, adding that she first traveled to Phu Quoc as a tourist. To send us off, she serves up pepper tea and laughingly wishes us a "Merry Christmas." The spicy infusion does indeed taste like Christmas. If you like, you can stay in simple rooms on the Natural Farm, away from the main tourist routes.

Don't forget: buy pepper directly from the producer, either at the Natural Farm or elsewhere. In addition to the fish sauce, peppers are the most authentic souvenir from Phu Quoc: highly aromatic, affordable, and easy to transport.

89 HISTORICAL MIX IN WESTERN MALAYSIA—MALACCA

A FOCUS ON FOREIGN INVADERS

First came the Portuguese, then the Dutch, then the British. In Malacca, evidence of each of these colonial epochs has survived. These not only give the historic trading city a special flair but have also made it a UNESCO World Heritage Site.

THE MALACCA RIVER FLOWS THROUGH THE MIDDLE OF THE OLD TOWN (*ABOVE*); **CYCLE RICKSHAW IS THE TRANSPORT OF CHOICE** (*BELOW RIGHT*); **THE STATUE OF THE JESUIT MISSIONARY FRANZ XAVIER WATCHES OVER IT ALL** (*ABOVE RIGHT*).

The legendary Strait of Malacca, between Singapore and Penang, is still used as a sea trade route between the Indian and Pacific oceans. Malacca, also known as Melaka, turned out to be a strategically important trading point. You encounter evidence of its eventful history at every turn, because the city is a concentration of the colonial architecture of various powers.

Malacca experienced its early heyday as an Asian regional port of trade. Then the Portuguese established themselves here at the beginning of the sixteenth century. The much-photographed Porta de Santiago dates back to their colonial rule. It was one of four access gates to the A Famosa fortress, founded

in 1511 by Alfonso de Albuquerque. Cannons are placed here and there, and a weathered relief is emblazoned across the entrance.

A ROLE MODEL FOR TOLERANCE

Saint Paul's Hill looms behind the historic gate. The little hill is planted with bougainvillea and hibiscus and is crowned by the remains of Saint Paul's Catholic Church. You can see the sea from here. On the other side of the hill, the path descends to the heart of Malacca. The Stadthuys, an eye-catcher from the Dutch colonial era, glows an intense red, like some of the surrounding buildings. The house, built in 1645, was the official

280

governor's residence and is the oldest surviving Dutch building in Southeast Asia. Later the British used it as an administrative center. In the neighborhood are the clock tower, a small windmill, and Anglican Christ Church, dating from 1753, in which, strangely enough, a couple of Chinese lanterns dangle.

But what does "strange" mean here? In Malacca, peoples, cultures, and religions are traditionally whirling all around each other, accompanied by mutual acceptance and tolerance in everyday life. In this respect, it is perfectly normal for the Kampung Kling mosque and a Hindu, a Buddhist, and a Chinese temple to exist on the same street. Malacca also offers a colorful culinary mix here, such as Indian Chinese cuisine, which is definitely worth tasting. The Baba & Nyonya Heritage Museum shows how wealthy Chinese once resided here. And of course, this is where Asian and European decor fuses.

ROLLING LANDMARKS—KITSCH AND CRACKLING DECIBELS

No visit to Malacca would be complete without a stroll down busy Jonker Street, which starts just beyond the bridge across the river. You will notice a more chic and polished look to the boutiques, cafés, and pubs. Then again, you walk by a down-to-earth peanut seller, or past an ice cream stand whose owner attracts customers' attention with a tinkling bell. Returning to the river, you can sense that warehouses and goods depots were once located along the banks. If you like, you can take a Melaka River cruise, but the city's real mobile landmarks are the cycle rickshaws. There's something unusual about these trishaws pedaled by both men and women: they are decorated with kitschy plastic flowers, plush toys, and figurines that seem to dance to the loud music, which links history with the pulsating present.

IN THE FOOTSTEPS OF A SAINT

Saint Paul's Hill preserves traces of Jesuit Francis Xavier (1506–52), a saint who frequently visited the former Chapel of Mary. After 1545, it was called Saint Paul's Church. He was a missionary in Asia for many years in the service of his order, whether in India, in Japan, or on the Moluccas. It is said that he wandered tirelessly with a bell in hand, gathering adults and children around him, teaching them to pray, exhorting them to Christian virtues, and baptizing tens of thousands until his arm became tired. Emaciated and ill, he died at the gates of China on Shangchuan Island (Sancian). His body was first taken to Malacca, and nine months later to Goa, India. A brilliantly illuminated monument on Saint Paul's Hill is dedicated to Saint Francis Xavier.

MORE INFORMATION

You can find a lot of interesting information on Malaysia's official website: www.malaysia.travel

90 BALI'S LITTLE SISTER— NUSA LEMBONGAN

WHERE THE GRASS GROWS UNDERWATER

Of the three large islands in the Strait of Badung, Nusa Lembongan is the closest to the famous neighboring island of Bali. White beaches, mangroves, wonderful diving areas, and the touch of days gone by—Lembongan has a lot to offer and is easy to reach from Bali.

ITS NAME IS NOT AN OVERSTATEMENT: DREAM BEACH REALLY IS GORGEOUS (*BELOW*); NUSA CENINGAN ISLAND IS EVEN LESS DEVELOPED THAN LEMBONGAN (*RIGHT*).

In general, Lombok is referred to as Bali's sister island. Yet, the two islands have little in common with each other, and it is hard to compare them. There is an explanation for this: there are only around 25 miles (40 kilometers) between Bali and Lombok, but there is also a deep-sea trench and the so-called Wallace Line. The English naturalist Alfred Russel Wallace, for whom the borderline was named, recognized as early as the nineteenth century that once beyond Bali—and by extension beyond the northern island of Borneo—various forms and species of Asian fauna and flora appear only sporadically. Looked at in this way, we should actually speak of Nusa Lembongan, Nusa Ceningan, and the larger Nusa Penida as Bali's sister islands, since all three also lie west of the Wallace Line.

DISCOVERIES ABOVE WATER AND UNDERWATER

Nusa Lembongan lies about 7.5 miles (12 kilometers) east of Bali and is much more developed for tourism than its two neighbors, Ceningan and Penida. The first resort opened

here in the mid-1990s, and there are now around thirty bungalow complexes on this island of 6,000 inhabitants. Around ten excursion boats call at Lembongan every day from Bali. Each ship has a beach; a resort with a restaurant, bar, and pool; and a pontoon anchored at sea. From there, day guests take advantage of diving and snorkeling or trips in glass-bottomed boats and island-exploration tours. Only in the afternoon, when the catamarans have left the island, does the usual quiet return to its shores.

Most of the overnight guests are divers; after all, the waters around Nusa Lembongan teem with 247 species of coral and 562 species of reef fish. There is a particularly strong current in the channel between the islands. There you can also see large fish such as tuna, barracuda, and nurse shark. Other good places for experienced divers can be found at the northern tip at Mangrove Point, Crystal Bay, Blue Corner Tip, and Manta Point, where manta rays are occasionally seen.

Lembongan is also ideal for surfing, and at low tide you can wade to the southwestern island of Ceningan. At high tide you can cross between islands on the less romantic pedestrian and bicycle suspension bridge. The island has beautiful beaches, such as

Shipwreck Beach and Mushroom Bay. The best are located in the southwest: Sunset Beach, which has earned its name, just as Dream Beach has. You can easily reach all these places on rented scooters, which are available almost everywhere on the island.

A SPECIAL WAY TO CULTIVATE PLANTS

Despite the fact that tourism is firmly established here, 60 percent of the coastal waters off Lembongan are cultivated as seaweed plantations. This is the livelihood for most of the inhabitants of the two villages of Jungut Batu and Lembongan. The descendants of the penal colony of the former Kingdom of Klungkung laid out the plantations at a depth of about 6.5 feet (2 meters) in the bays behind the protective reef, which are consistently warm and calm and are always supplied with fresh water. In a good summer season, a family harvests around a ton of seaweed per month, which brings in several hundred dollars. This cultivation provides for a thousand families and ensures them a largely risk-free income, in contrast to fishing. Japan is the main seaweed buyer. Only a small amount remains in Bali and is used for such things as the preparation of agar-agar, a jellylike dessert, or for seaweed salad.

NUSA CENINGAN

Nusa Ceningan is only a stone's throw from the southwest coast of Lembongan and can be reached across a narrow suspension bridge. For those who fear heights, the island can also be reached on foot at low tide. Small paths lead to a few settlements across the island, which is 1.2 miles (2 kilometers) long and not even 0.6 miles (1 kilometer) wide. You get a particularly beautiful view from Mahana Point, on a 50-foot-high (15 meter) cliff, where the sea roars and daring swimmers plunge into the waves (absolutely not recommended!). Things are quieter at the Blue Lagoon, where dolphins can be seen, and at Ceningan Cliffs, with their view of the large island of Penida. Nusa Ceningan was uninhabited for a long time, but in recent years some bungalow complexes have sprung up there. There is an upscale comfortable hotel at Secret Beach.

MORE INFORMATION

Lembongan can be reached several times a day by boat from Bali. The high season is from June to October and December to January: www.indonesia-tourism.com/bali/nusa-lembongan.html

91 TEARS OF LOVE OR THE WORK OF GIANTS—THE CHOCOLATE HILLS

THE FILIPINO CHOCOLATE HILLS

The name tells the story: this unusual geological formation on the Philippine island of Bohol is made up of almost identical, usually conical hills overgrown with grass. During the dry season, however, the green turns to chocolate brown.

LEFT BEHIND BY GIANTS OR TEARS OF LOVE? THERE ARE SEVERAL LEGENDS ABOUT THE CHOCOLATE HILLS (*ABOVE*). THE PHILIPPINES OFFER A WIDE RANGE OF TROPICAL BEACHES. ONE OF THE MOST BEAUTIFUL IS WHITE BEACH ON BORACAY (*ABOVE RIGHT*). SURFERS FIND HAPPINESS IN MANY PLACES, SUCH AS PANAY ISLAND (*BELOW RIGHT*).

You stand there amazed, silent, overwhelmed. People are too mesmerized even to take photographs. The Chocolate Hills is one of those magical places that transport you to another world for minutes at a time, in absolute peace and quiet. Only a tentative click of a camera brings you back to reality. You begin to notice more photographers, and suddenly there is a staccato of clicks. Now there is no stopping; you are doing it too.

Most people who see the Chocolate Hills for the first time, stretching almost endlessly to the horizon, can barely grasp that such a phenomenon exists and that its uniformity was not created by human hands. At this moment, you try to imagine the amount of work it would take to create some 1,268 hills stretching over more than 31 square miles (50 square kilometers). Building the pyramids, on the other hand, would almost seem like child's play. No other natural formation comes close to the Chocolate Hills.

APRIL IS A CAPRICIOUS MONTH

To see the chocolate side of the hills, you have to arrive in the dry season. This usually comes between December and April. However, rain falls on Bohol from time to time even during the dry season, and the vegetation on the hills gratefully absorbs it. The resilient grasses revive quickly, so there is no guarantee that you will see the Chocolate Hills really brown. However, the best chance of this is in April.

The origin of this strange landscape is not clear. There are several hypotheses, and the simplest and perhaps most conclusive approach goes back to the weathering of the limestone, accompanied by volcanic eruptions and an uplift of the sea floor. Where the science cannot agree, legends also flourish. One says that there were two giants who threw stones at each other. The other claims that tears of love dropped from the sky and raised the hills. The third is perhaps the funniest: A giant saw a beautiful woman in the distance. He wanted to impress her and therefore wanted to lose weight. So he got rid of everything he had eaten. Eventually his excrement covered the entire area.

JUST ONE OF 7,107

The most beautiful view of the excrement—that is, of the hills—is probably from the Carmen observation deck, around 3 miles (5 kilometers) outside the center of the municipality of the same name. Much farther away, you come to Sagbayan Peak, about 12.4 miles (20 kilometers) from Carmen. The advantage there is that on a clear day you can see over the Chocolate Hills to the Pacific and even to Cebu City.

Among the 7,107 islands that make up the Philippines, Bohol is one of the most interesting, and not only because of the Chocolate Hills. There are also many white and fine sand beaches, which range from Anda Beach on the east coast, to Imelda Beach near Damiao, to Santa Fé Beach near the island's capital, Tagbilaran.

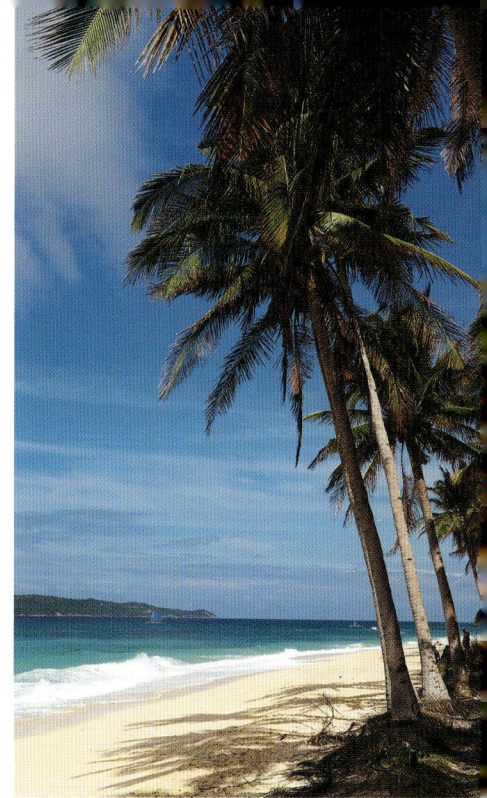

BEACHES AND RICE TERRACES

The Philippines are far off the beaten track. Travel to Manila is typically via Hong Kong, Bangkok, or Singapore, and from there to Tagbilaran or sometimes via Cebu. That's why you should not just plan a trip to Bohol, but a full Philippines tour. In addition to islands such as Boracay—which is said to have one of the most fantastically beautiful beaches in the world at 2.5-miles-long (4 kilometer) White Beach—and Palawan with its postcard-beautiful beaches, there are the rice terraces of Banaue on Luzon, which surpass even the more famous fields of Bali. It is not for nothing that they are called the "stairs to heaven." Be careful about traveling south near Zamboanga: the security situation there has been precarious for years.

MORE INFORMATION

You can get a free visa on arrival; good sun protection and mosquito repellent are necessary. Be careful everywhere!
www.boholtourismph.com

92 FOREST AND HOT SPRINGS— ISE SHIMA

WHERE THE JAPANESE EMPEROR ASKS FOR GOOD FORTUNE

Ise Shima National Park overlooks the Pacific Ocean and a forested, hilly landscape. It contains Jingu, the holiest of all Japanese shrines, as well as the greatest number of hot springs in the country. The bathing culture associated with the *onsen* (Japanese for hot spring) is of great importance in Japan.

THE MEOTO IWA (MARRIED ROCKS) LIE ON THE COAST NEAR THE HOLY ISE SHRINE ON THE SHIMA PENINSULA. THE SHIMENAWA (SACRED BANDS) THAT BIND THEM TOGETHER ARE SOLEMNLY RENEWED EVERY YEAR (*BELOW*). MIKIMOTO STARTED HIS CULTIVATION OF PEARLS IN AGO BAY (*ABOVE RIGHT*), AND VISITORS CAN ADMIRE PRECIOUS EXHIBITS IN THE MUSEUM OF MIKIMOTO PEARL ISLAND (*BELOW RIGHT*).

A young Japanese woman stands on the steps, smiling, and forms a diamond shape with her hands held in front of her stomach. The people standing around giggle, understanding that the woman is copying the "Angela Merkel diamond" (triangle of power). In 2016, German chancellor Angela Merkel stood on these steps to Jingu, or the Great Ise Shrine, the most important in Japan, and held her hands in her trademark gesture of touching fingertips and thumb tips. However, the triangle of power didn't get her inside the shrine. Only the

Japanese emperor is allowed to enter the heart of the 2,000-year-old Jingu Shrine, and only the imperial family can enter the forecourt. Like her other G-7 colleagues, Merkel got only as far as the court before the forecourt. But that is still some 165 feet (50 meters) farther than most mortals are allowed. Legend has it that the closer you get to the shrine, the greater your chances for happiness, and that is what six million annual pilgrims seek. While many do not believe in God, they believe in wisdom and happiness, and these are intertwined with Japan's

WITH THE PEARL DIVERS

The island of Mikimoto in Ise Bay is known as pearl island. This is where women have been pearl-diving for centuries. In the early 1920s, they gave a jewelry dealer named Kokichi Mikimoto an idea: If you could implant a grain of sand in an oyster shell, a pearl would form. Mikimoto was the first to succeed in producing perfectly round cultured pearls. The island was named after Mikimoto, and it is still the source of the most famous cultured pearls in the world today. Dressed in white suits, the women divers show visitors their catch, and in the factory you can learn how pearls are cultivated.

MORE INFORMATION

The nearest airport, Nagoya, is a two-hour drive from the island of Mikimoto.

Hotel Amanemu: www.aman.com

Japanese Tourist Office: www.jnto.go.jp

cultural practices. Under the guidance of a high Shinto priest, Merkel and the other heads of state performed the cleansing ritual before walking together through the forest toward the shrine. This involves putting water on your left hand, putting water on your right hand, and rinsing your mouth.

EVERYTHING EXCEPT LOVE

The shrine is the highlight here, but surfers and swimmers will also find ideal water conditions on Ago-no-matsubara beach. Hikers, on the other hand, wander through the wooded hills and perhaps also to the Asakumayama observation deck, which provides a great view over large parts of the coastal region in the national park. "If you dig deep in Japan, you will always come across a hot spring," an old saying goes. And Ise Shima National Park, where that G-7 meeting took place, also has the greatest number of hot springs in the country. The luxury Amanemu resort has a particularly beautiful onsen, surrounded by dense forests, with a purist Zen design and beautifully re-created Minka farmhouses.

The special quality of onsen water is its mineral composition, which enriches human skin. According to Japanese wisdom, "an onsen can heal everything, except love."

THEY ARE ALL THE SAME

"There have been onsen since about 700 CE," explains Amanemu baths supervisor Chieko Kobay-ashi. "Five hundred years later, even the samurai used the onsen and then switched to meditation." It was only in the seventeenth century that the onsen were opened to the general public. "It was the only place where there was warm water for personal hygiene. Bamboo served as a toothbrush. Natural sponges were used to cleanse the body. Soap was still unknown."

To this day, the Japanese sit on a mini stool in the washroom, scrub themselves as hard as they can, pour gallons of water from a tub over their bodies, and do another meticulous round of cleansing before getting into the onsen. "Everyone is naked. And that means everyone is the same," says Chieko. This is an exception among the otherwise private Japanese.

93 HOT RIVERS AND BOILING FOUNTAINS—THE VALLEY OF GEYSERS

FASCINATING VOLCANIC ACTIVITY ON KAMCHATKA

Volcanism has many faces on the Kamchatka Peninsula, and one of its most beautiful can be seen in the Valley of Geysers. Only 3.7 miles (6 kilometers) long and a few hundred meters wide, it is home to Asia's only geyser field. Here some ninety geysers shoot up to 131 feet (40 meters) in the air.

The Valley of Geysers was discovered thanks to a simple coincidence. When geologist Tatyana Ustinova was on a scientific excursion through the Kronotsky Biosphere Reserve here with two companions in spring 1941, she reached a previously unknown narrow valley crossed by a small river. At first Ustinova could not have known that she had found one of the most spectacular natural wonders in the world. It was only during a rest by the river that she was surprised by the eruption of a geyser that lasted several minutes. The geyser has since been dubbed Pervenets, "the firstborn." The previously unnamed river was called the Geysernaya. It rises at the foot of the active

volcano Kikhpinych to the northeast and winds through the mountain chains of Kamchatka and the Valley of Geysers until it flows into the Shumnaya River, which in turn flows into the Bering Sea.

Ustinova's discovery was initially forgotten, and it was not until 1945 that scientific research of the valley began. Investigations found more than twenty large and many small geysers, hot springs, fumaroles, and mud volcanoes. Nevertheless, the valley remained known only to the scientists. It was not until 1955, some fourteen years after the discovery, that Tatyana Ustinova published a report about her excursion. She did not let go of the

THE BEST WAY TO GET TO MANY PLACES ON KAMCHATKA IS BY BOAT (*ABOVE LEFT*); THERE ARE ALWAYS MORE VIEWS OF THE MANY VOLCANO CONES, SUCH AS HERE FROM THE PARATUNKA RIVER (*BELOW LEFT*). IN THE VALLEY OF GEYSERS YOU WALK ON PLANKS BETWEEN THE STEAMING POOLS (*ABOVE AND BELOW RIGHT*).

Valley of Geysers even in death. When she died in 2009 at the age of ninety-six, her ashes were scattered in the valley.

BOILING GEYSERS AND BUBBLING MUD VOLCANOES

The valley can be reached only by air. From Yelizovo Airport, MI-8 helicopters fly over the Kamchatka Mountains to the Valley of Geysers in just over an hour. There, steep slopes, almost impenetrable undergrowth, but also broad mountain meadows and loose groups of bushes await the visitor, who is repeatedly treated to geysers, bubbling mud volcanoes, and hot springs. Each of the larger geysers has been given a name that refers to its appearance. Troynoy, the "triple one," has three funnels from which it ejects water every two and a half hours. Sakharny Geyser, the "sugary" one, is surrounded by mineral deposits the color of caramelized sugar.

THE ACID LAKE IN THE CRATER OF THE MALY SEMYACHIK STRATOVOLCANO GLOWS BRILLIANT TURQUOISE (*BELOW*). A MOTHER BEAR HAS CAUGHT A FISH FOR HER CUBS (*ABOVE RIGHT*). ON THE EDGES OF A BIG RACE: MUSHER MANDYATOV ROMAN, ON HIS TRADITIONAL DOG SLED, IS WEARING THE NATIONAL DRESS (*BELOW RIGHT*).

The biggest geyser is aptly named Velikan, "the giant." It lies in the middle of the valley on an approximately 5,250-square-foot (1,400 square meter) sinter terrace, and its opening is 9 feet (3 meters) long and 5 feet (1.5 meters) wide. Every four to five hours, there is a huge eruption of water shooting up to 131 feet (40 meters) in the air from the siphon. It lasts for a full two minutes, hissing loudly. The cloud of steam reaches a height of 492 feet (150 meters). You should watch this impressive spectacle from a reasonable distance and with the wind at your back. The water from the geysers and springs, enriched with many minerals, cools down quickly when it comes to the surface. The minerals form beautiful, differently colored sintered terraces on the slopes of the valley and on the rocks surrounding the geysers. The volcanic mud is just as colorful, ranging from almost white to gray and yellow, to infinite shades of brown. At first glance, things seem quieter here than near the geysers. But this can be deceptive. The bubbles of gas, which can be up to a meter in diameter, slowly find their way from the bottom of the funnel, through the liquid mud, and burst on the surface. The mud is boiling hot and occasionally splatters as far as several meters.

FANTASTIC FLOWERS IN RED, WHITE, BLUE, AND YELLOW

Because of the many hot springs and the year-round warm water of the Geysernaya River, the valley has its own microclimate. At the beginning of June, when a large part of the Kronotsky Biosphere Reserve is still covered by a deep blanket of snow, things are already beginning to turn green at the bottom of the valley. The meadows are strewn with thousands of red and white orchids, while bright-blue thread irises bloom in damp hollows and on the banks of the ponds. Over the course of the

HOT BATHS

Some people would like to emulate the bears and take a bath in the warm springs and pools in the Valley of Geysers. It is forbidden in the biosphere reserve, but there are hot springs in many places on Kamchatka. If you are willing to risk taking a short detour on the way back from the Valley of Geysers, you can bathe in springs of water up to 104 degrees Fahrenheit (40 degrees Celsius) in the village of Paratunka, 22 miles (35 kilometers) from Yelizovo Airport. As early as Soviet times, water from the hot springs was diverted into swimming pools. People said that the waters have health-promoting effects. The old pools have long since been replaced by modern wellness facilities that offer massages and other services. Necessary infrastructure, including hotels and restaurants, has meanwhile also become available.

MORE INFORMATION

Efficient hosts for Kamchatka travel: www.kamchatka.org.ru

summer, they will be replaced by orange-yellow sarana lilies, blue monkshood, and nodding thistles. At the higher elevations, low-growing Kamchatka rhododendron transforms the slopes into a sea of blood-red flowers. In the sparse forests of Russian rock birches, herbaceous and perennial plants thrive, while the forests of scrubby alder and pine trees form impenetrable thickets called *stlanik* in Russian.

WARM OASIS FOR BEARS, WOLVERINES, AND MARMOTS

No wonder that the valley is also attractive to animals. After their winter hibernation, many of the Kamchatka brown bears, who otherwise live as loners, gather in spring looking for a partner. After mating, the animals part again, but many remain in the Valley of Geysers all summer. From spring to autumn, food is abundant, and the warm springs invite bathing. The animals are not disturbed by people, because they have learned that they do not pose any danger, even if the rangers are always armed to be on the safe side.

But other animals also feel at home in the Valley of Geysers. Parry's marmot squirrels, a species of ground squirrel, show little fear of humans and are easy to spot. You get to see marmots only if you are lucky, and wolverines, which catch their prey primarily at night, live a particularly secret life.

DISASTER AND A NEW BEGINNING

The Valley of Geysers was almost destroyed in 2007, when, on June 3, after weeks of rain, a huge mudslide broke loose and buried a large part of the region. It dammed up the Geysernaya River, which formed a lake into which many geysers, springs, and sintered terraces disappeared and seemed lost forever. The Velikan was one of the few geysers that wasn't drowned. But nature renewed itself. In 2011, another landslide destroyed the dam, the reservoir ran dry, and the sinter terraces and geysers were exposed once again. In many areas, things look as they did before 2007.

AT DUSK IN THE AUSTRALIAN OUTBACK, THE KATA
TJUTA DOMES, SACRED TO THE ABORIGINAL
AUSTRALIANS, GLOW AN INTENSE RED.

OCEANIA

Red Emptiness, Blue Infinity

94 SELF-SUFFICIENT ISLAND REALM—SAMOA

WHERE THERE IS A FEHMARN ISLAND IN THE SOUTH PACIFIC, NOT JUST THE BALTIC SEA

On Samoa you discover a South Seas world completely different from the posh islands of French Polynesia. Visiting this South Pacific island state is also a way to search for traces of German history, because Samoa was a German colony between 1900 and 1914.

VIEW OVER MOUNTAIN SLOPES, DENSELY OVERGROWN WITH TROPICAL RAINFOREST, TOWARD THE OCEAN ON THE ISLAND OF UPOLU (*BELOW*). ALSO ON UPOLU IS THE FAMOUS TO SUA OCEAN TRENCH, A 98-FOOT-DEEP (30 METER) NATURAL POOL IN A COLLAPSED LAVA BLOWHOLE (*RIGHT*).

The wind brought the first member of the Kruse family to Upolu after a seemingly endless journey on a sailing ship. Upolu is the main island of Samoa, whose 190,000 inhabitants live on the international date line, on the other side of the globe. When sea captain Frederick Kruse entered the port of Apia in 1885, he saw a prosperous little town. German merchants were just beginning to cultivate plantations, develop trading houses, and do business there. The German Godeffroy company grew into the largest trading house in the South Pacific, with forty-five branches, and the Deutsche Handels- und Plantagengesellschaft (German Trading and Plantation Company) is known as the Company in Samoa to this day. The island kingdom has unmistakable German roots. German monuments, colonial buildings such as the National Museum, and the German cemetery bear witness of this time. But the Samoa phone book is the best way to discover people of German origin at the other end of the world. There you'll discover several

Kruses, because in 1885 Captain Kruse decided to stay. He was an orphan who fell in love with a Samoan woman named Luse.

GERMAN ROOTS

Adele Kruse, age fifty-seven, is the great-granddaughter of Frederick Kruse. "Our Vailima beer is brewed according to the German purity law to this day," she says. "For a long time, the master brewers in Apia even came from Weihenstephan," the oldest German brewery. Each day at 7:45 a.m. the police band marches in their blue jackets—on Sundays in white—to the government building, blaring and blowing until the commander raises the flag on the flagpole. This ritual is a relic from the colonial days from 1900 to 1914—only the flag has changed. Even the Samoan currency, the tala, is derived from Germany—from the old taler, because no Samoan could pronounce the name of the mark, the legal currency of the time. And finally, it is thanks to the Kruse family that there is a hotel on Upolu called Insel Fehmarn. The name pays tribute to the home island of the family pioneer Frederick and to sentimentality: "Everyone in our family has a German name," Adele explains.

We feel ourselves to be Samoans, but we are proud to have German roots. My friends say 'Siamagi' to me, 'German,' when I'm sometimes too German for them."

The old colonial power is popular here because the Germans laid the foundation for development. They brought in the telephone and promoted agriculture. It is not just that the coconut palms in the plantations are lined up like tin soldiers; the German also set up land registers and maintained them meticulously. The old copies are written in old-style German script, so that until the twenty-first century, people sometimes needed a German translator for some land transactions. But Samoa also has German-style "Knöllchen" tickets for those who park illegally and are guilty of other traffic violations. One of the first and certainly the most famous transgressor was *Treasure Island* author Robert Louis Stevenson, who once got a ticket for driving too fast.

NO WORD FOR "STEALING"

Samoa is more self-sufficient than almost any other country. On this blessed island, the Fa'a Samoa social system, a complex construct of rights and obligations, humility and respect, ensures stability, while Mother Nature provides a rich harvest—as well as for fantastic beaches, such as those in Vavau and Lalomanu. The Samoan lifestyle is conservative and based on traditional customs, which to outsiders seem to be a remnant of Polynesian culture. In terms of gross domestic product, some of the poorest people in the world live in the Samoan Islands. But observant visitors can see that Samoa's GDP doesn't tell the whole story. Each family is largely self-sufficient, growing enough vegetables, taro—the potato of the South Seas—and fruit. The sea provides fish, and every family has a sow that produces enough offspring for the Sunday table. Hunger is a foreign word in Samoa, and

THE WATER ALONG THE BEACHES IS AN ALMOST UNREAL COLOR OF TURQUOISE (*BELOW*). THESE TWO MEN ARE SPORTING ELABORATE PE'A OR TATAU—HENCE THE TERM "TATTOO"—WHICH ARE CREATED BY PUNCTURING THE SKIN FROM STOMACH TO KNEES IN A PAINFUL PROCEDURE (*ABOVE RIGHT*). AN EARTH OVEN IS ONE WAY OF COOKING FISH (*BELOW RIGHT*).

SUCKLING PIG FROM THE EARTH OVEN

Free-roaming piglets live well in Samoa—until the day they are cooked in the earth oven for a Sunday feast. Every child learns the complicated process of cooking in the *umu*, or earth oven, from an early age, from choosing the right lava stones that will glow with heat without bursting, to cooking times for different ingredients: tender vegetables, crispy plantains, suckling pig. In fact, Samoan cuisine exists only because of the *umu*. Apart from grilled fish, lobster, and chicken, which can be found almost everywhere, the island state's second specialty also comes from the *umu*: palusami, or taro leaves in coconut milk. During celebrations, *umu* dishes are served at resorts.

MORE INFORMATION

A sixty-day visa is provided upon entry. Speaking English is the best way to get by. Hurricane season runs from November to March.

there is no way to translate "steal" into the language. This is why, according to the UN Human Development Index, the country ranks significantly higher on the list than its economic strength would suggest.

As is customary in a barter economy, money is not ultimately necessary unless you want to buy luxury goods. But why do you need a third television set when there are already two in the village—the mayor's and the priest's—and the houses are open for anyone to watch? The same goes for cars in a settlement. They belong to the Matai, as every mayor is called, and the pastor and maybe another person. If complications occur during a birth, the transport becomes an ambulance. If someone needs to haul building materials, the same vehicle does its job as a truck. And for passenger transport there are colorful, reliable buses that connect every village with the capital.

BECKENBAUER EXCITEMENT

The world doesn't need Samoa, and Samoa doesn't need the world, either. Especially not since June 1, 1962, when it became the first Pacific state to achieve independence. Werner J. Schrekenberg, the consul of the Federal Republic of Germany on Samoa, receives three to four letters per month from Germans who want to immigrate to Samoa. Otherwise this man from the Sauerland region of Germany has little to do here in paradise. "Only when Franz Beckenbauer was campaigning in Samoa for votes to make Germany the host of the 2006 Soccer World Cup was there great excitement," he says. The legendary Beckenbauer finally got the South Pacific vote, while Brazil lost its ambassador, a beauty queen: she fell in love with a Samoan named Fred and stayed in Samoa—just like Frederick Kruse did in 1885.

95 KINGDOM OF LONGING— TONGA

THE DREAM OF NOTHING

Tonga is remote, self-sufficient, and beautiful and, above all, is known for its corpulent former king. Meanwhile, his second son has come to power, and the subjects are upset. Sometimes it is nothingness that fascinates tourists, however, and the few foreign visitors are more interested in Tonga's 176 wonderful islands.

THE EUEIKI ISLAND RESORT (*ABOVE*), MOUNU ISLAND, AND THE RESORT ON UOLEVA ISLAND, WITH ITS TRADITIONAL TONGAN HUTS (*BELOW RIGHT*), CREATE AN IMAGE EPITOMIZING THE SOUTH PACIFIC. WATER RUSHES BELOW HA'ATEIHO ROCK BRIDGE ON TONGATAPU ISLAND (*ABOVE RIGHT*).

Any one of them could be the proverbial island on which people imagine themselves stranded. There is a whole lot of nothingness here, as defined by three to ten palm trees surrounded by a smooth, white carpet of sand. The next ring consists of water, ranging from crystal clear to light blue and bright turquoise to deep inky blue. Of course, these jewellike islands are uninhabited, so you don't have to share them with locals.

PICNIC WITH FRIDAY

The much-cherished dream of living like Robinson Crusoe can come true on this beautiful nothing. You can walk around many of them in ten minutes. Their names are Malinoa, Tao, or Nuku, and visitors wishing to imitate Robinson Crusoe can charter a boat for a few dollars and just lie about dreaming, splash around, or snorkel. The skilled and extremely friendly staff at the resort will prepare a picnic basket for you, because

decapitating a coconut isn't that easy to do. This is the photo-ready realm that friends back home expect to see on your Instagram.

A different reality is expressed in a can of Spam—for tourists it is more dog food than delicacy. On Tonga, however, Spam is preferred over lobster and mahi-mahi, over beef steak and leg of lamb. A Tongan thinks in practical terms: it is easier to open a can than to catch a fish. And Spam is more filling. If a member of the royal family is sitting on the podium at an event, it is essential to have a 3-kilo can of Spam on hand as a sign of recognition.

FAMILIAL SHARING

"Fakalahi Meakai" is written on every Tongan coin. It means "a lot to eat," and the coin also depicts sweet potatoes and breadfruit, coconuts and bananas. Tongans are known for their ethic of sharing and cooperation. Often, a few family members work in New Zealand or Australia to support their extended family. Those left behind are largely self-sufficient, growing sweet potatoes and harvesting taro leaves from the family field. But despite this collaborative culture, social upheaval is underway.

THE KING IS DEAD ... LONG LIVE THE KING

It all started back in 2006, when King Tupou IV died. He was known for his corpulence, as well as a string of economic and political mishaps. Government buildings and parts of the capital, Nukualofa, were set on fire shortly after Tupou's death. The time was ripe for the people to have more say and less monarchy. In the course of violent demonstrations, power was wrested from the son—the new king. It must be emphasized that Tongans are generally calm and peaceful people, and they intended to maintain the monarchy, despite all the revolt, but in a different form.

His successor, Tupou V, agreed to political reforms but could not refrain from royal whims. Sometimes the airport was closed so that he could drive his BMW 7 Series on the runway. Tupou V died of cancer in 2012, and his younger brother has been in power since then. Everyone is asking whether the story of the island king will continue. They can't ignore globalization, and their relationships with New Zealand and Australia have taken on an existential character. The people did not complain at the last change of king, because the opposition to parliamentary dictatorship has prevailed. The prime minister and cabinet are appointed by parliament, and no longer by the king.

HUMPBACK WHALES POPULATE THE WATERS OFF THE ISLANDS (*BELOW*); WOODCARVERS TRANSFORM THEM INTO ART (RIGHT).

PROUD ISLANDERS

Tongans are proud people; theirs is the only state in Oceania that has never been colonized by Europeans. During the filming of Somerset Maugham's story *Red*, the director had to play a bar whore in a wig, because Tongan girls refused to take on this bit part. The kitschy images of Tonga and the South Seas painted by writers such as Robert Louis Stevenson and films such as *Mutiny on the Bounty*—whose story was historically documented to have taken place in Tongan waters—are far from the reality. But the mystique of the remote South Seas fulfills our longing for paradise and the Garden of Eden.

ONE ISLAND, ONE RESORT

Fafa Island is the name not only of this small island, which you can walk around in twenty minutes, but also of the only resort there. Opened in 1984, it is by far the best on the island and in the kingdom. The bungalows are comfortably furnished, and the island and islets in the area are fantastic. A ship is ready for excursions, and the restaurant terrace entices you to enjoy sundowner cocktails in Tonga every evening. Parrots hover in the air, flightless birds known as rails whiz around, geckos lurk, looking for mosquitoes, and between July and October whales pass by. www.fafaislandresort.com

MORE INFORMATION

Don't drink the tap water. You can get by with English.

www.thekingdomoftonga.com

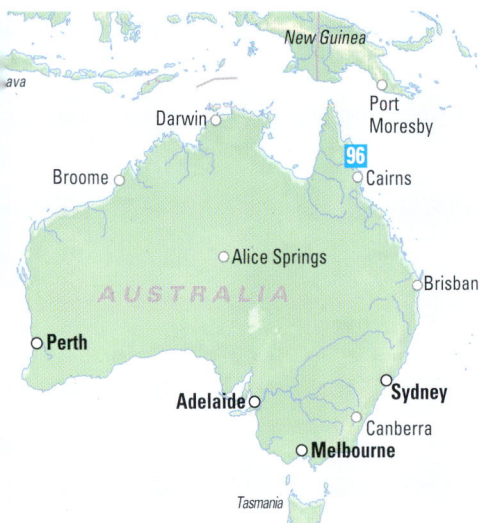

WHERE CAPTAIN COOK WAS STRANDED—CAPE TRIBULATION

TRIBULATION, MY ARSE!

Captain James Cook gave Cape Tribulation its name, because it was here that his ship, the *Endeavor*, ran aground in 1770. UNESCO has designated this beautiful area as the Wet Tropics of Queensland World Heritage Site. Its plant life includes about 3,500 species, making it as rich as the entire flora of Europe.

DENSE RAINFOREST (*BELOW*) AND TROPICAL COASTAL LANDSCAPES (*RIGHT*) COME TOGETHER ON CAPE TRIBULATION.

The golden orb spider is a nasty piece of work. In fact, it is harmless to humans because it isn't poisonous. But this doesn't help the males, who are eaten by their mates, or cassowary birds, ratites that grow up to 6.5 feet (2 meters) tall. If golden orbs feel harassed in any way, they attack—including people. The problem here is their claws, which are as sharp as razor blades.

You might encounter just about anything in the primeval forest on Cape Tribulation: colorful cockatoos, parrots, and parakeets flutter through the air. You can also occasionally see large tree pythons when you look up. Possums scurry and pygmy kangaroos hop by. The evolutionary status of the plants in Daintree National Park, to which the cape belongs, is still that of a hundred million years ago. They include fern palms, which grow to around 65 feet (20 meters) tall, and cycads, which are among the smallest in the world.

FROM ZERO TO 1,400

Within a few miles, as the crow flies, from zero above sea level, this piece of paradisaical nature reaches an elevation of 4,590 feet

(1,400 meters), where a tropical rainforest climate prevails. Until the start of the 1980s, access was by water only. The national park infrastructure is still poor, but you can book tours with rangers and Aboriginal Australians. A night tour in the rainforest is a special experience, because the night temperatures, and especially the moonlight, have a great influence on animal behavior. The most intense experience is on the warmest, wettest, and darkest nights. In fact, it can be rather creepy.

THE CROCODILES' LIVING ROOM

What makes the area extraordinary, in addition to its flora and fauna, is the large number of largely untouched beaches. A cooling dip in the sea is particularly pleasant during the (Australian) winter. In the (Australian) summer, however, the ocean often reaches bathtub temperatures. You can climb up to the cape from Myall Beach. And from below you have the most beautiful view of Cape Tribulation. Coconut Beach beckons from 1.2 miles (2 kilometers) south of the cape. But you should definitely not cross the Myall River where it flows into the ocean there: it is the living room of some mighty

freshwater crocodiles. Afterward, you can camp at the little Noah Beach. Cape Trib Beach, which offers picnic tables and bathrooms, lies north of the cape. The most beautiful beach is probably Emmagen Beach, while Donovan's Beach, 7.5 miles (12 kilometers) north of Cape Tribulation, is extremely difficult to get to.

STEEP, DUSTY TRACKS

The rainforest and the Great Barrier Reef almost collide along the 62 miles (100 kilometers) between Cape Tribulation and Cooktown, a former gold transshipment location. Even for experienced captains like James Cook, this was a high-risk area to navigate.

Today you need a four-wheel-drive vehicle to cross the land. The tracks are steep and dusty at times and lead through knee-high streams. You pass Ngalba-Bulal National Park, along with frightening Rattlesnake Point, and drive through Black Mountain National Park. Black Mountain is a deep-black color; it consists of granite blocks and rubble that look like heaps of coal. It is said that people who climb Black Mountain can mysteriously disappear. And airplane pilots regularly feel turbulence when they fly over it.

FEAR AND LOVE

To be honest, you don't necessarily want to encounter the most dangerous snakes, spiders, or marine creatures alive. On the other hand, they certainly do interest you. So it's off to the Cooktown Botanical Gardens, in that little town that had around 30,000 inhabitants and almost a hundred pubs at the time of the great gold rush. Now, however, there are only a few bars for the town's 1,500 people. But the botanical garden displays specimens, skeletons, and photos of the dangerous species, as well as informational tidbits. Did you know, for example, that green ants can be brewed as an effective cough medicine? That tea tree bark can be used as toilet paper? Or that you can harvest a love potion from the potion tree, which men can use to get any woman they want? "Works every time," says the botanist.

MORE INFORMATION

The park lies 87 miles (140 kilometers), or three hours by car, north of Cairns; avoid the wet season between December and March.

97 BY THE STONE BEEHIVES—THE BUNGLE BUNGLES

BAOBABS AND CROCODILES IN THE LAND OF THE FLYING DOCTORS

Sand, bush, and flies; a gold-rush atmosphere; and farms as large as small European countries: Australia shows its most original side in Kimberley in the Far West. Right in the middle lies the Purnululu National Park, with the fantastic Bungle Bungle mountain range.

Things couldn't get more laid back: "Good morning, John. Go ahead!" That's the short and simple takeoff clearance for the Slingair (now Aviair) flight to the Bungle Bungles. John guns the engines, and the six-seat propeller plane rises from the airfield in Kununurra. Below you can see sand and bush; billions of flies are probably buzzing around down there. Lake Argyle is also spread out in this magnificent natural landscape. There are no fewer than 25,000 freshwater crocodiles cavorting in this huge lake.

LONELY IN KIMBERLEY

A little later, John flies low and circles over the Bungle Bungles. Purnululu National Park, the official name, is one of the four UNESCO World Heritage Sites in the state of Western Australia and is likely among the least-known UNESCO sites. Only 30,000-some visitors lose themselves each year in the remote Kimberley Region, the northernmost part of Western Australia.

"The area of Kimberley extends over around 264,081 square miles (425,000 square kilometers). Thus, this region is 1.2 times the

FROM THE AIR (*ABOVE LEFT*) OR UP CLOSE DURING A HIKE (*ABOVE AND BELOW LEFT*), THE BUNGLE BUNGLE MOUNTAIN RANGE IS FASCINATING WITH ITS UNIQUE ROCK FORMATIONS.

size of Germany," explains John by microphone connected directly to his passengers' headphones. "The population comprises fewer than 40,000 people. Doctors have to fly to their patients because the sick cannot be expected to endure the strains of the overland trip. Well-off farmers even visit their neighbors by small aircraft. Outback cowboys use helicopters to keep their cattle together. And," John continues, never at loss for an anecdote, "men think about sex 730 hours a year, but due to the lack of female company they get it only twenty hours a year." Everyone laughs.

KEEP YOUR MOUTH CLOSED!

Until the 1980s, the area was known only to the Aboriginal Australians. Spectacular aerial shots taken by a film team first aroused public interest. Aviair passengers also take spectacular photos of the 350-million-year-old rock formations created by erosion. "Don't the Bungles look like an infinite

number of beehives lined up in a row?" asks John as he sets the plane down on the red-brown sand runway at the edge of the Bungles.

You just stand there and marvel—a little shaken by the flight. By the way, you won't fare much better if you drive there on the Northern Highway in an all-terrain jeep. Don't let your jaw drop, because the bush flies will discover the moist oral cavity in no time and have a feast. Purnululu means "sandstone" in the language of the Djaru people, who share the area with the Kidja. Verena, the national park ranger from Switzerland, tells her story: "When I was twenty, I came to Australia, carefree, got stuck Down Under, and have been here in the Northwest for some time." She explains that erosion has paved a thousand paths through the striped bedrock and created a labyrinth of ravines and gorge-like incisions, "through which you can sometimes just barely pass."

A NATURAL DELIVERY ROOM

Kimberley means mega-Outback with a Wild West feeling. The dusty Gibb Road runs 414 miles (667 kilometers) across the northwestern Australian plateau, but there are only a dozen farms along this traditional cattle drive route. "An unmistakable sign that you are in Kimberley is the appearance of the bulky endemic Australian baobab trees, which almost look like they are pregnant," says Verena. We are on the way to a very special place in the Bungles, which cover an area of about 15.5 square miles (25 square kilometers) and are surrounded by red-brown earth, rubble, and spinifex. This is how the landscape appears during the dry season. But when dark banks of clouds pile up in the wet season, many farms and settlements lose all contact with the outside world due to flooding. An area the size of half of Germany becomes a lake district with a few islands, the cattle farms.

THE FAMOUS CATHEDRAL GORGE, WHICH HAS BEEN WASHED OUT OF THE ROCK BY EROSION INTO THE FORM OF A NATURAL AMPHITHEATER (*ABOVE RIGHT*), IS AS SPECTACULAR AS THE ENTIRE BUNGLE BUNGLE RANGE (*BELOW*). AROUND 25,000 CROCODILES LIVE IN LAKE ARGYLE (*BELOW*).

SWIMMING WITH CROCODILES

It is hot, very hot. So it's a good day swimming in Lake Argyle. The name means "place of water." The problem: there are crocodiles, as many as 25,000. "No problem," say John, the pilot; Verena, the guide; Jeff, the boatman; a fisherman on the bank; and an Aboriginal girl nearby. "Freshies leave people alone. We're not on their menu," says the angler calmly. Freshies are freshwater crocodiles that grow to be 9 to 13 feet (3 to 4 meters) long. "They couldn't get a good hold on one of us with their long, pointed snouts, so they let us alone." And the Aboriginal girl adds: "If there were only one saltwater crocodile here, no one would go swimming. When I see one of them, I'll really piss my pants."

MORE INFORMATION

The only good time to travel to this region is during the dry season, from May to October; accommodation is available in small resorts, motels, and camps.

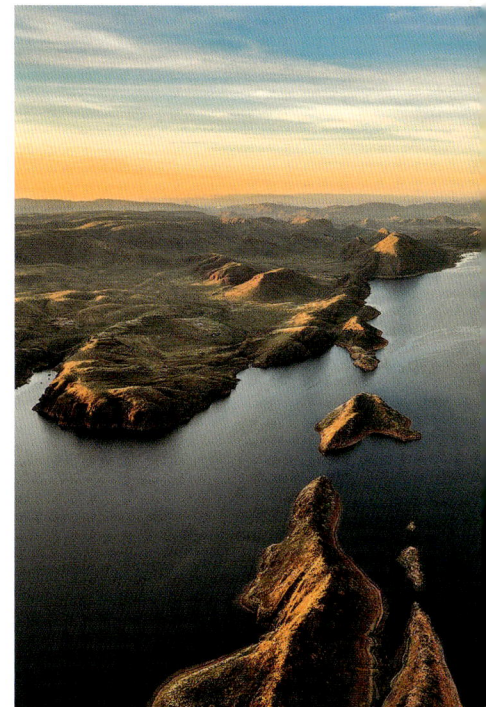

The promised special place has been reached, but you may view it only from above. No white man is allowed in the crevice, because it is a sacred place for the Aboriginal Australians. Mini Palms Gorge is the place of the women who are giving birth. "Pregnant women are brought there with a posse of sisters and other female relatives and looked after until their time comes," says Verena. In fact, the end of the gorge looks like a vagina. "For Aboriginal Australians, such phenomena are always a natural sign," she says.

GOOD ACOUSTICS FOR "WALTZING MATILDA"

About half of the population are Aboriginals, who for the most part still live with their tribes and in a strict hierarchy that is structured according to age and knowledge. Mountains or rivers are considered the boundaries of any living space, and the unwritten code of conduct is passed down from generation to generation through dances and songs. For the Aboriginals, the first white people who appeared in search of the treasures of the legendary Terra Australis Incognita were the souls of the deceased who could also walk again. This turned out to be disastrous misjudgment.

There are several hiking trails to such peculiarities of Mother Earth as the birthing area. Echidna Chasm is a canyon a good 0.6 miles (1 kilometer) long, but in some places only one meter wide. And every national park guide sings "Waltzing Matilda," the unofficial anthem of the Australians, in Cathedral Gorge because of the wonderful acoustics. Others say that the Bungle Bungles owe their Western name to a hearing impairment. "According to legend, a white man asked an Aboriginal for the name of the rock domes. But the latter thought that the man was asking for the name of the grass, which lay on the ground in a strange way. So he replied, a 'bundle' and repeated 'bundle' again for clarity," laughs Verena. "With that, the name Bungle Bungle was born."

98 IN THE REALM OF THE WIND— GUNBARREL HIGHWAY

SPINIFEX AND DESERT OAKS

In the Outback you experience the feeling of vastness, freedom, and loneliness and can fulfill your dream of adventure. The dust-dry red Gunbarrel Highway, for example, takes you from the center of the continent to Western Australia—an experience you'll never forget.

From the tourist settlement of Yulara—which visitors from all over the world use as a starting point for trips to fascinating Uluru and the impressive Kata Tjuta mountain range—the journey suddenly takes you into a desertlike steppe landscape. As you drive past Lasseter's Cave, named after gold prospector Harold Lasseter (1880–1931), your off-road trip begins. For hundreds of miles, you will see nothing but sun, sand, and stones as well as spinifex grass in every imaginable shade of color—white and yellow, green and bluish.

OFF INTO THE WEST
Suddenly the rusted corrugated iron huts in the village of Kaltukatjara (Docker River),

founded in 1968, appear; then you cross the Northern Territory border into Western Australia. There are a half-dozen scientists working in the meteorological station in Giles, far removed from civilization, and from their wives and children, for six months. The Warburton mission station there was named after the explorer Peter Warburton, the first European to cross the Great Sand Desert.

FROM THE STEPTOE TURNOFF TO THE GUNBARREL HIGHWAY
The drive continues to the Steptoe turnoff, and from here along the miserable Heather Highway. It is named after Heather Hewitt, daughter of the then superintendent of

THE DREADED CROSSWISE GROOVES OF DESERT TRAILS ARE APTLY CALLED "CORRU-GATED IRON TRACKS" (*ABOVE*). THE DOME-LIKE SUMMITS OF THE KATA TJUTA TOWER 1,791 FEET (546 METERS) ABOVE THE BUSHLAND (*BELOW RIGHT*). CLUMPS OF SPINIFEX GRASS, LOOKING LIKE HEDGEHOGS IN SHADES OF WHITE, YELLOW, GREEN, AND BLUE, ARE CONSTANT COMPANIONS WHEN BUSH CAMPING IN THE AUSTRALIAN OUTBACK (*ABOVE RIGHT*).

Warburton. At Len Beadell's Tree and Plaque the road finally merges into Gunbarrel Highway. This leads in a wide arc across a huge area of dunes and is one of the tracks that Leonard (Len) Beadell (1923–1995), the last great explorer of Australia, took across the West.

Barren tree stumps protrude abjectly from the dry, deep-red sandy soil. Our special Australian map says, "caution—heavy sand" and "abandoned." In fact, the highway is getting worse and worse, and parts of it turn out to be a treacherous track full of washboard-like crosswise grooves that make the vehicle's suspension system groan loudly.

BUSH CAMPING AT MOUNT BEADELL

Mount Beadell, named after the aforementioned road builder Len Beadell, is far from any human settlement. The little red mountain, stretched out against the evening sky, offers the perfect setting for bush camping, complete with a crackling campfire and grilled steak. The next section of the route is full of spinifex—gray-green bushes of prickly grass. Mount Everard turns out to be little more than a nose of rock, but from there you have a magnificent view over the Gibson Desert. At Everard Junction, the trip continues to the Geraldton Historical Society Bore, a well dug years ago. "It may save a life," reads

the signboard. "Use it, respect it & leave it here." A small hand pump produces drinking water from the depths.

On the following track, behind Carnegie Homestead, we are tortured by the "corrugated iron"—the dreaded crosswise grooves. At the edge of the track are a few desert oaks, and the spinifex steppe extends into the distance. Many metal signs reference Len Beadell. The next day we reach Wiluna, the first settlement we've seen in days. Here the adventurous journey across the Gibson Desert comes to a happy end.

THE KATA TJUTA

It is a good idea to take a side trip from Alice Springs to the Kata Tjuta range. This group of thirty-six reddish-ocher mountains is 32 miles (51 kilometers) west of the village of Yulara. In 1872, Australian researcher William Ernest Powell Giles christened them Mount Ferdinand in honor of his sponsor, Baron Ferdinand von Müller—who decided, however, that they should be named Mount Olga after Queen Olga of the historic German kingdom of Württemberg. Since 1993, the striking rocky peaks have been officially called Kata Tjuta, which in the Anangu language appropriately means "many heads." The highest peak, Lotherio, is 3,517 feet (1,072 meters) high and rises 1,791 feet (546 meters) from the bushland. The most famous hiking trail to Kata Tjuta leads through the Valley of the Winds, which is closed on very hot days.

MORE INFORMATION

For information on Aboriginal sites: www.daa.wa.gov.au

Central Australia Tourism site: www.discovercentralaustralia.com

99

WILD WEST IN THE OUTBACK— COOBER PEDY

AT THE WHITE MAN'S HOT HOLE IN THE EARTH

Coober Pedy, the opal capital of the world, has 1,700 inhabitants and is the largest treasure trove of opals on our planet. Otherwise, the small town in the middle of the Outback offers a police station, bank, post office, and comfortable underground caves.

THE KANTU BREAKAWAYS ARE A HILLY LANDSCAPE NEAR COOBER PEDY (*BELOW*). OPALS ARE NOT ONLY MINED HERE BUT ALSO SOLD (*ABOVE RIGHT*). THE SO-CALLED DUGOUTS MAKE THE MOST COMFORTABLE PLACES TO LIVE UNDERGROUND (*BELOW RIGHT*).

Out into the endless Australian Outback: The last section of the Stuart Highway, which connects Adelaide in the south with Darwin in the north, is also called the Explorer Highway. Out here, where the heat is flickering and the road trains—monster trucks with several trailers linked together and up to 165 feet (50 meters) long—rule the highway, the opal-mining town of Coober Pedy breaks up the monotony of never-never land. The place is as dusty as the surrounding desert, but also as surreal as a science fiction film. It is as puzzling as its inhabitants, who seem to

drink more beer than water. There is a beer barrel lying on a grave in the cemetery with the inscription "Have a drink on me!"

HOT SAUSAGES FOR THE POLICE

We receive a great reception in this backwater: a thud at three o'clock in the morning. Car doors slam, angry voices can be heard, but there is nothing to be seen, apart from a police vehicle that has seen better days. What happened? A resident of Coober Pedy, it says in the newspaper next day, was stopped by the police for driving too fast on the way home from Adelaide. The traffic ticket enraged

IN THE UNDERGROUND HOTEL

For an overnight stay in Coober Pedy, try the Desert Cave Hotel, which opened in 1988—the first and best underground hotel in the mining town. Twenty of the fifty rooms are dugouts: The walls are made of unplastered bare stone; not a single ray of light penetrates from the outside; the air smells slightly musty—and it is pleasantly cool, which is certainly important when the temperature is 104 degrees Fahrenheit (40 degrees Celsius) aboveground. There is even room service to get an underground dugout dinner Fred Flintstone style. The rest of the rooms are similar to those everywhere: TV, telephone, minibar, hairdryer, and other amenities. Some guests say they've never slept as well as they did here. www.desertcave.com.au

MORE INFORMATION

The town is 528 miles (850 kilometers), or a nine-hour drive, northwest of Adelaide. Bring good sunscreen and fly repellent! www.cooberpedy.sa.gov.au

the miner, and when he saw the police car parked in Coober Pedy at night, he stuck two sticks of dynamite in the exhaust pipes and blew the car up. "Hot sausages" is what the opal miners call the dynamite sticks used to blast holes in the stone and earth.

You can actually buy these sticks of dynamite in the supermarket, like sausages. However, you have to show a dynamite license. Coober Pedy, in Australia's Wild West, was founded after the rare, rainbow-colored minerals were discovered in 1911. Today the Coober Pedy opal field produces around 90 percent of the world's opals. Every day, people of all nationalities come to dig in this lunar landscape. The name Coober Pedy translates from the Aboriginal language as "the white man's hole in the earth." Most of life happens underground, and not just in the mines. Many local residences are dugouts blasted into the rocks and furnished like normal homes, with living rooms and

bedrooms, kitchens and bathrooms. That's because living underground is the only way to escape the heat. You can visit some of these dwellings, such as Crocodile Harry's place, the model for the Crocodile Dundee films. Even the churches have gone underground. And the golf course is typically brown. Lush green has no chance here.

SALT AND PEPPER FOR EVERYONE

A visit to Coober Pedy isn't complete without going underground, where machines eat their way into the soft rock and spit it upward. This moved earth creates the innumerable conical mounds found in this strange place, as if giant moles have dug their mounds here. If you don't want to go underground, stop by the Salt 'n' Pepper, a few miles outside Coober Pedy. Here, the land breaks off abruptly, exposing the colorful layers of rock. As the sun sets, they begin to sparkle.

100

TASMANIA'S HEAVENLY PENINSULA—FREYCINET

A BAY LIKE A WINE GLASS

Wonderful bays, the Hazards mountain range, and Wineglass Bay: you could actually reduce Tasmania to the Freycinet Peninsula and its oldest national park. In any case, these approximately 93 square miles (150 square kilometers) are considered the most beautiful on the island—which itself is the "last stop" before Antarctica.

A HIKE THROUGH FREYCINET NATIONAL PARK PROVIDES VIEWS OF FANTASTIC COASTAL LANDSCAPES (*BELOW*); THE SEA IN SLEEPY BAY IS ANYTHING BUT SLEEPY (*RIGHT*).

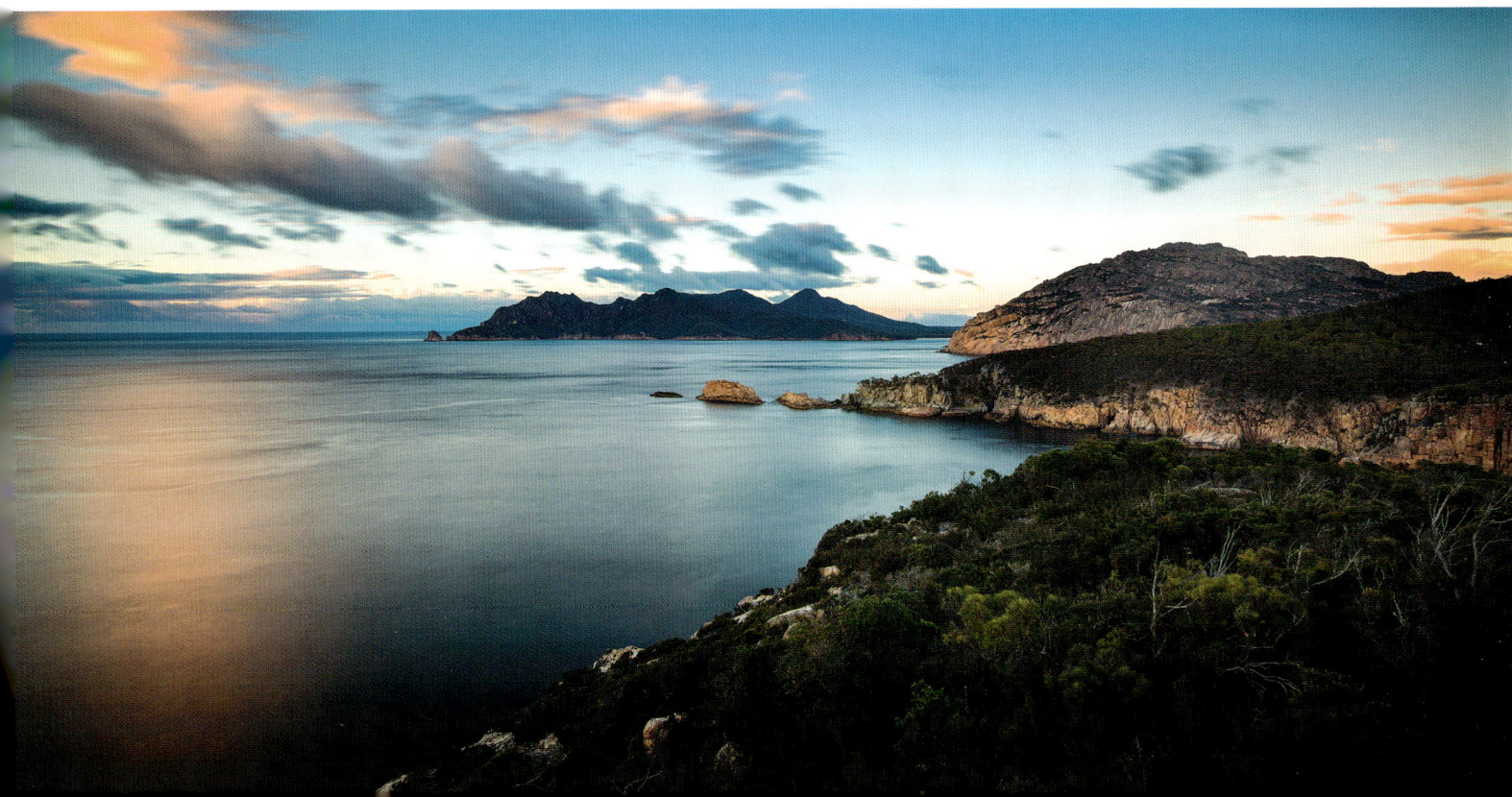

Anyone who sees a picture of this place says: I have to go there. Now, right away! It looks as if an artist had painted the perfect bay and maybe had paradise in mind when he did it. From the small natural platform on Mount Graham, you can see it lying to your right: the wonderful Wineglass Bay.

It is curved in a goblet shape like a bulbous red wine glass. The only difference being that it has dark-blue Pacific water sloshing around inside, and this water keeps getting ever lighter toward the edge of the bay—up to an unreal-looking shimmer of turquoise—to finally be delimited by a white fringe of sand as a rich contrast to the green vegetation. On the left gleams the fringe of Hazard Beach, which is a little narrower. It runs along Promise Bay on the side of the peninsula facing the Tasmanian mainland. And although both bays differ somewhat from each other, the whole thing looks like a complete work of art, each reflecting the other side and rounding off along several miles. The trail to the platform is garnished by oversized boulders of round and rugged

shapes and the occasional hopping wallaby, the smaller relatives of the kangaroo.

THE HOLIDAY STATE IN BLUE ON WHITE

Many travelers to Australia simply forget about Tasmania when planning their trips. This may also be due to the weather, which is like that of central Europe. And actually, there are dense rain clouds hanging over Tasmania, the smallest Australian state after Canberra, as we approach for landing. The self-proclaimed Holiday State—that's what the car license plates say in blue on white—sometimes doesn't make things that easy for vacationers. Even in high summer, there is no guarantee of good weather. You always have to be prepared for rain, and the temperatures are moderate. The dry Outback heat of more than 85 or even 100 degrees Fahrenheit (30 or 40 degrees Celsius) is unknown on this island. The weather remains changeable even in high summer, and temperatures rarely exceed 77 degrees Fahrenheit (25 degrees Celsius). This is the last stop before Antarctica, as the Tasmanians joke when tourists complain about the weather . . .

Whatever the mood of the weather gods, this is a worthwhile travel

destination—especially because of Freycinet National Park, which often proves the predictions of allegedly bad Tasmanian weather to be wrong. Here on the east coast of Australia's largest island, visitors can often experience the blue miracle of the park. The climate is like that of the French Riviera, accompanied by many hours of sunshine.

ALL BLACK—THE TASMANIAN DEVIL

Coles Bay, a small town north of the park, is the gateway to Freycinet National Park, perhaps the most beautiful 93 square miles (150 square kilometers) on Tasmania. The peninsula curves like a finger into the Pacific Ocean and protects the main island from the frequently swirling Tasman Sea. In between lies Great Oyster Bay, one of the best fishing areas. The park itself is very varied with rugged cliffs, dense forests, long beaches, and boggy areas. When it comes to food, wombats, wallabies, and possums are not shy of people. In the evenings they come begging at the rustic wooden lodges and look forward to being fed rolls, potatoes, or carrots.

These cute animals also show up for breakfast. It is only at lunchtime that they won't find a soul in the forest resort. Because in the morning, people lace up their hiking boots. The tourists set out to visit the animals in their natural surroundings. If you're lucky, you'll even meet a cheeky little black Tasmanian devil. Today, apart from in a few zoos, the largest representative of carnivorous marsupials can be found only in Tasmania. It had already died out on the Australian mainland in the fourteenth century. Since the little devil with black fur was also being hunted in Tasmania and was threatened with extinction, the Tasmanian devil was made a protected species in 1941.

WHITE MUCOUS

The national park was founded in 1916 and, along with Mount Field National Park, is the oldest in Tasmania. Hikers have a choice among trails ranging from 3 to 18.6 miles

A HIKER ENJOYS THE VIEW FROM MOUNT AMOS TO WINEGLASS BAY (*BELOW*). FROM THE BAY, THE VIEW RUNS ACROSS THE WHITE SAND TO THE STRIKING ROCK MOUNTAIN (*ABOVE RIGHT*). WALLABIES ARE OFTEN SEEN IN THE NATIONAL PARK (*BELOW RIGHT*).

FRIENDLY BEACHES

A few miles north of Freycinet National Park, the Friendly Beaches invite you to take a swim in the South Pacific. Located in the middle of a dune landscape, the white sandy beaches are among the most beautiful in Australia. However, don't expect South Seas bathtub temperatures: usually your big toe will already signal to you that the water temperatures leave a lot to be desired, even in high summer. A dirt road, about 6.2 miles (10 kilometers) after the turnoff for the Tasman Highway toward Coles Bay, leads east to the beaches. You can surf or fish, go for a walk, or sunbathe. Often enough, you don't meet a soul. Things can be wildly romantic when you stay in the bush camp overnight.

MORE INFORMATION

www.parks.tas.gov.au

(5–30 kilometers) long, depending on their level of fitness and desires. The highlight of every trip is Wineglass Bay, which can be seen at its most beautiful under a cloudless sky.

The Freycinet Peninsula is probably the best argument against the cliché that Tasmania actually merely looks like Scotland or parts of New Zealand. Only one prejudice is really confirmed: in Tasmania, the environment is still in fine shape. The air is clear and fresh, so the starry sky is unbelievably bright, and if you wipe your nose, you will notice something. Here, your mucous is white. Which proves that the almost 500,000 Tasmanians and their guests have been breathing the purest air in the world.

Tasmania was first discovered by a white man in 1642. It is only some British history books that mention James Cook as its discoverer. It was the Dutchman Abel Tasman who named the island Van Diemen's Land, before his own family name became the island's name more than two hundred years later. It isn't necessary to see the simple

marble memorial plaque, the Tasman Monument commemorating his first landing, shortly after the village of Dunalley. Only the location of the small harbor is worth making a detour in good weather.

RED LEVEL ALERT?

No such thing! In 1642, Abel Tasman sailed along the east coast of Tasmania and discovered the Freycinet Peninsula for Europeans. It was later named after the French navigator Louis de Freycinet, who arrived 160 years after Tasman did. Whaling, tin, and coal mining provided for the first settlers. Since then, Tasmania has apparently been floating on the edge of world events in the paradisaical Pacific. Terror alarms and bomb threats are unknown in Tassie Land, nor are there any environmental problems or traffic chaos. And you should always remember: Australia doesn't simply end at Melbourne. Tasmania hangs off the state of Victoria like a tail, separated from the mainland only by the 155-mile-wide (250 kilometer) Bass Strait.

THE CORDILLERA DEL PAINE MOUNTAINS ARE
THE HEART OF TORRES DEL PAINE NATIONAL
PARK IN SOUTHERN CHILEAN PATAGONIA.

INDEX

TEXT & PHOTO CREDITS

TEXT APPROVAL

J Jörg Berghoff: 5–8, 11–13, 15, 17, 32; Margit Brinke and Peter Kränzle: chapters 42–48; Andreas Drouve: chapters 19, 52, 53, 55, 56, 61, 62, 64, 66, 68, 70, 88, 89; Jochen Müssig: introduction and chapters 9, 10, 14, 16, 18, 20, 24, 33, 34, 36–38, 41, 49–51, 54, 57–60, 65, 71, 73, 74, 76, 77, 81, 82, 85, 86, 90–92, 94–97, 99, 100; Michael Rinn: chapters 29, 40, 69, 75; Bernd Schiller: chapter 87; Lothar Schmidt: chapters 28, 30, 31; Hans-Joachim Spitzenberger: chapters 1–4, 72, 93; Herbert Taschler: chapters 25–27; Klio Verigou: chapters 21–23; Rainer Waterkamp: chapters 35, 39, 63, 67, 78–80, 83, 84, 98

PHOTO CREDITS

Front cover: Tidal channels through coral reefs, Aldabra (age fotostock); *back cover*: above (*from left to right*): Kato Lagadi Beach in Cephalonia (Gelner Tivador-shutterstock), toucan in the Belize rainforest (Michael Boyny-Lookphotos), Naoussa on Paros (Bill Anastasiou-shutterstock); *below*: monks in Bagan (nuttavut sammongkol-shutterstock

P. 1 Na Pali coast on Kauai, Hawaii (Maridav-shutterstock)
P. 2–3: Bandon beach, Oregon coast (Elena_Suvorova–shutterstock)

J Jörg Berghoff: pp. 29, 31b, 34–37, 45, 54–55a, 61a, 111; Andreas Drouve: pp. 67a, 167, 169b, 170, 171a, 200, 202–203, 206, 208, 224–225b, 276, 279b, 281a; Michael Rinn: pp. 94b (*right*), 95, 132, 134–135, 217b (*right*), 218–219a; Lothar Schmidt: p. 103a; Rainer Waterkamp: pp. 120–121, 130–131, 198–199, 210–213a, 244–249, 251, 253, 262–267, 308–309; Margit Brinke: pp. 141a, 148–149, 151, 155b; Jochen Müssig: p. 235b; Lookphotos: pp. 12–13 (robertharding), 14 (SagaPhoto), 16 (ClickAlps), 17 (Denis Feiner), 19a (robertharding), 20 (Rainer Mirau), 21 (ClickAlps), 23 (Rainer Mirau), 24 (age fotostock), 27 (Jan Greune), 28 (Holger Leue), 30–31a (Denis Feiner), 38–39a (age fotostock), 39b (Spaces Images), 40a (Franz Marc Frei), 40b (*left*) (Spaces Images), 41 (Franz Marc Frei), 43a (Tina und Horst Herzig), 43b (TerraVista), 46 (age fotostock), 47a (Thomas Stankiewicz), 49b (TPX), 50–51 (age fotostock), 52 (Franz Marc Frei), 53 (robertharding), 56 (Photononstop), 57a (Saga Photo), 57b (Hemis), 58 (age fotostock), 59a (Brown Cannon), 59b (*left*) (Hemis), 59b (*right*) (age fotostock), 60 (Brown Cannon), 61b (age fotostock), 62a (Florian Werner), 62b (*left*) (Thomas Stankiewicz), 62b (*right*) (Andreas Strauß), 63–64 (Andreas Strauß), 65a (Rainer Mirau), 65b (Andreas Strauß), 69 (Ingolf Pompe), 70 (Franz Marc Frei), 72a (robertharding), 72b (*left*) (Hemis), 77b (Franz Marc Frei), 78 (Juergen Richter), 79b (*right*) (Kay Maeritz), 81 (Juergen Richter), 82 (Rainer Martini), 83b (age fotostock), 87 (Konrad Wothe), 89a (Kreder Katja), 91 (Rainer Mirau), 92–93 (age fotostock), 94a–b (*left*) (Juergen Richter), 96 (Tobias Richter), 97a (Arthur F. Selbach), 97b (age fotostock), 98–99 (David Köster), 100–102 (age fotostock), 104a–b (*right*) (age fotostock), 104b (*left*) (Arthur F. Selbach), 105 (Aurora Photos), 106 (Arthur F. Selbach), 107 (Kay Maeritz), 108 (Engel & Gielen), 109a (age fotostock), 110 (Hauke Dressler), 112–113 (Minden Pictures), 114–115 (Engel & Gielen), 116–118 (age fotostock), 119a (Franz Marc Frei), 119b (age fotostock), 122–123a (Minden Pictures), 123b (*left*)–b (*right*) (robertharding), 127b (age fotostock), 128–129b (Minden Pictures), 133 (Travel Collection), 138–139 (Photononstop), 143a (age fotostock), 143b (TerraVista), 147 (age fotostock), 150 (Brown Cannon), 152 (Rainer Martini), 153a (robertharding), 153b (Brigitte Merz), 154 (Minden Pictures), 156 (Franz Marc Frei), 157a (age fotostock), 157b (Christian Heeb), 159a (age fotostock), 159b (Franz Marc Frei), 160 (Design Pics), 161a (Minden Pictures), 161b (age fotostock), 162–163 (Brown Cannon), 164 (Konrad Wothe), 165a (Konrad Wothe), 165b (robertharding), 166 (Konrad Wothe), 171b (Juergen Richter), 172b (*left*) (age fotostock), 173 (Thomas Stankiewicz), 174 (Hemis), 175 (Minden Pictures), 176 (Thomas Stankiewicz), 178–179 (age fotostock), 180a (Bernhard Limberger), 181 (David Köster), 182 (age fotostock), 183a (N. Eisele–Hein), 183b (Holger Leue), 184 (age fotostock), 185a (Hauke Dressler), 185b (Holger Leue), 188 (Minden Pictures), 190b (*left*)–b (*right*), 191 (age fotostock), 192 (Ingrid Firmhofer), 193b (Holger Leue), 201 (robertharding), 204–205 (robertharding), 209a (age fotostock), 213b (age fotostock), 216 (Michael Boyny), 217a (David Köster), 217b (*left*) (age fotostock), 219b (age fotostock), 226 (age fotostock), 227a (Photononstop), 227b (Konrad Wothe), 228–229 (Minden Pictures), 230 (Design Pics), 232–233 (Per-Andre Hoffmann), 234 (age fotostock), 235a (Design Pics), 236 (age fotostock), 237 (ClickAlps), 238–239a (Hermann Erber), 239b (Günther Bayerl), 240 (SagaPhoto), 241a (age fotostock), 242 (age fotostock), 250a (Spaces Images), 252 (age fotostock), 254 (Florian Stern), 255 (Hauke Dressler), 256 (Florian Stern), 257b (Konrad Wothe), 258 (Travel Collection), 259b (*left*) (age fotostock), 259b (*right*) (robertharding), 260–261 (robertharding), 269b (Holger Leue), 270 (Frank Waldecker), 271–272 (Thomas Stankiewicz), 273a (Frank Waldecker), 273b (Design Pics), 275a (age fotostock), 275b (Hemis), 277a (age fotostock), 280 (Don Fuchs), 281b (Hemis), 285a (age fotostock), 285b (Per-Andre Hoffmann), 286 (robertharding), 287b (age fotostock), 289–290 (Page Chichester), 294 (Günther Bayerl), 297a (Design Pics), 297b (Holger Leue), 298 (Design Pics), 299a (robertharding), 299b (*left*) (Design Pics), 300 (Minden Pictures), 301 (Design Pics), 304a (age fotostock), 304b (Katharina Jaeger), 305 (The Travel Library), 311b (Don Fuchs), 314–315a (Günther Bayerl), 316–317 (age fotostock); Shutterstock: p. 10 (Von EhayDy), 11 (nuttavut sammongkol), 15 (Smelov), 18 (Alizada Studios), 19b (Ingrid Maasik), S 22 (Jakob Schulz), 25 (Pete Lambert), 26 (np), 32 (strelka), 33a (Urmas Haljaste), 33b (Sharkshock), 40b (*right*) (Natalia Fedori), 42 (Tono Balaguer), 44 (rphstock), 47b (nevio), 48 (Daniel TravelPixer), 49a (diane vose), 55b (Allard One), 66 (Slobodan Kunevski), 67b (Andrej Antic), 68 (Xenia Chowaniec), 71 (jordeangjelovik), 72b (*right*) (Maekfoto), 73 (Gelner Tivadar), 74 (Pitk), 75 (Bill Anastasiou), 76–77a (leoks), 79a (Roman Evgenev), 79b (*left*) (Rontav), 80 (Marcin Krzyzak), 83a (Oleg Znamenskiy), 84 (Martin M303), 85 (Mauxphoto'Arts), 86 (Tony Coke), 88 (Emiliano Pane), 89b (Eugenio Marongiu), 90 (Michael Thaler), 103b (Roctrip), 109b (*left*) (Karol Kozlowski), 109b (*right*) (Victor Suarez Naranjo), 124–125 (Janos Rautonen), 126 (Stefano Ember), 127a (Dan Costa), 129a (Radek Borovka), 136 (Simon Venables), 137a (AfricaWildlife), 137b (Gerry van der Walt), 140 (Andreas Juergensmeier), 141b (Alexander Sviridov), 142 (Bonnie Fink) 144 (aceshot1), 145 (Gleb Tarro), 146 (cdrin), 155a (Sharon Day), 158 (Vadim Petrakov), 168 (Pete Niesen), 169a (Travel With Passion), 172a (FRiMAGES), 172b (*right*) (Kevin Wells Photography), 177a (P. Harrison), 177b (Gianfranco Vivi), 180b (mbrand85), 186 (Rene Holtslag), 187a (Anton_Ivanov), 187b (R.A.R. de Bruijn Holding BV), 189 (Rene Holtslag), 190a (Inspired by Maps), 193a (Barna Tanko), 194–195a (Fotos593), 195b (JaimePorElMundo), 196 (Inspired by Maps), 197a (Matyas Rehak), 197b (reisegraf.ch), 207 (Rafal Cichawa), 209b (Matyas Rehak), 214 (Aleksandra H. Kossowska), 215a (Denis Kabanov), 215b (RPBaiao), 220–221 (Skreidzeleu), 222 (Milosz Maslanka), 223 (Hugo Brizard), 225a (Dudarev Mikhai), 231a (cleanfotos), 231b (Mohamed Selim), 241b (Mandeep Singhs), 243 (Ashraf Hamdan), 249a (Oksana. perkins), 249b (Rafal Chichawa), 250b (Neale Cousland), 257a (Aleksei Kornev), 259a (Kai_19), 268 (MAGNIFIER), 269a (TAMVISUT), 274 (Khoroshunova Olga), 277b (nopealter), 278a (gg-foto), 278b (meogia), 279a (DeltaOFF), 282 (asiatravel), 283 (Tublu_Subham), 284 (rasti sedlak), 287a (yoko_ken_chan), 288a (sinker), 288b (*left*) (petropavlovsk), 288b (*right*) (ehaydy), 291a (Guiseppe_D'Amico), 291b (Alexander Piragis), 292–293 (mdmworks), 295 (mvaligursky), 296 (mvaligursky), 299b (*right*) (Nina Janesikova), 302 (Danny Allison), 303 (Darren Tierney), 306 (greetingtheworld), 307a (David Cowles), 307b (healthylaura), 310 (rloesche) 311a (fridolin), 312b (pelooyen), 313 (Rob D—Stock Photos), 315b (Visual Collective).

Other Schiffer Books on Related Subjects:

Secret Cities of Europe, Henning Aubel, ISBN 978-0-7643-6289-7

Lost Places: Images of Bygone America, Heribert Niehues,
ISBN 978-0-7643-6394-8

Type set in TheSerifB/Stone Sans II

ISBN: 978-0-7643-6367-2

Printed in India

FRONT COVER: TIDAL CHANNELS THROUGH CORAL REEFS, ALDABRA (AGE FOTOSTOCK). BACK COVER: *ABOVE. LEFT TO RIGHT*: KATO LAGADI BEACH IN KEFALONIA (GELNER TIVADOR-SHUTTERSTOCK), TOUCAN IN THE BELIZE RAINFOREST (MICHAEL BOYNY-LOOKPHOTOS), NAOUSSA ON PAROS (BILL ANASTASIOU-SHUTTERSTOCK); *BELOW*: MONKS IN BAGAN (NUTTAVUT SAMMONGKOL-SHUTTERSTOCK)

Layout: graphitecture book & edition
Translated from the German by Simulingua, Inc.

Originally published as *Secret Places: 100 unbekannte Traumreseziele weltweit*
© 2020, 2019 Bruckmann Verlag GmbH, München, Germany

Published by Schiffer Publishing, Ltd.
4880 Lower Valley Road
Atglen, PA 19310
Phone: (610) 593-1777; Fax: (610) 593-2002
Email: Info@schifferbooks.com
Web: www.schifferbooks.com

For our complete selection of fine books on this and related subjects, please visit our website at www.schifferbooks.com. You may also write for a free catalog.

Schiffer Publishing's titles are available at special discounts for bulk purchases for sales promotions or premiums. Special editions, including personalized covers, corporate imprints, and excerpts, can be created in large quantities for special needs. For more information, contact the publisher.